THE ANCIENT TOWN
OF YARMOUTH

The Ancient Town of Yarmouth

by

C. W. R. WINTER

PRINTED AND PUBLISHED BY
THE ISLE OF WIGHT COUNTY PRESS
NEWPORT - ISLE OF WIGHT - PO30 1ST

ISBN 0 9501779 7 0

Contents

Illustrations

ILLUSTRATIONS

Between pages 188 and 189

Acknowledgements

The Author wishes to acknowledge his indebtedness to the following individual and written sources of information. Without them this book would not have been possible.

A new, correct, and much improved history of the Isle of Wight. J. Albin, 1795.

R. H. Adams, Esq.

The late Charles Andrews, Esq.

The Brailsford Scrapbook. M. Mallett, Esq.

A. B. Cooke, Esq.

The Dashwood Scrapbook. Mrs. D. Foster.

H. W. Doe, Esq.

R. Doe, Esq.

Early Solent Steamers. Captain F. T. O'Brien. 1973.

H. W. Farmar, Esq., M.V.O.

Miss Gillian Fryer.

A Guide to the Isle of Wight. Rev. Edmund Venables. 1860.

The late Harry Guy, Esq.

S. Herapath, Esq.

History of the Isle of Wight. Sir Richard Worsley. 1781.

Architectural Antiquities of the Isle of Wight. Percy Goddard Stone. 1891.

The History and Topography of the Isle of Wight. W. H. Davenport Adams. 1864.

The Isle of Wight County Record Office, Newport.

Letters Archeological and Historical relating to the Isle of Wight. Rev. E. Boucher James. 1896.

N. Noyes Lewis, Esq.

Man of War. Richard Ollard. 1969.

The Mills of the Isle of Wight. J. Kenneth Major.

Mrs. Ena Morton.

H. Morse Payne, Esq., Lincoln, Mass., U.S.A.

Miss K. Payne.

The Rector and Churchwardens of Yarmouth.

Mrs. Blanche Smith.

Tour of the Isle of Wight. J. Hassell. 1790.

The Victoria County History of Hampshire and the Isle of Wight.

The Headmistress and Managers of Yarmouth School.

Yarmouth, Isle of Wight. A. G. Cole. 1948.

Yarmouth Pier and Harbour Commissioners.

The Yarmouth Society.

Yarmouth Town Trust.

From a plan of Yarmouth, dated 1824

CHAPTER I

Some Yarmouth Dates

Ethelred (979 – 1016)

991 First mention of ERMUD, where lived two Saxons, Aluric and Wislac.

William I (1066 – 1087)

1085 Aluric and Wislac's holding mentioned in Domesday Book.

Stephen (1135 – 1154)

c.1135 First Charter granted by Baldwin de Redvers, Lord of the Island.

John (1199 – 1216)

1200 The town is reputed to have two churches, one at the east end, and one in the market place.

1206 The town visited by King John.

1214 Another visit from King John.

Henry III (1216 – 1272)

1260 Chaplain appointed to say daily Mass in church of St. John the Baptist.

Edward I (1272 – 1307)

1272 A market place stood on the site now occupied by the Town Hall.

1295 Yarmouth sent a representative to Parliament for the first time.

1305 The town contained 50 houses.

Edward III (1327 – 1377)

1334 Second Charter, granted by Edward III.

Richard II (1377 – 1399)

1377 Town burned by the French. Church of Blessed St. John the Baptist destroyed, and Church of St. James much damaged.

1385 Third Charter, granted by Richard II.

Henry VI (1422 — 1461)

1439 Fourth Charter, granted by Henry VI.
Men of Yarmouth formed their own Borough.

1440 The right to elect a Mayor granted.

Edward IV (1461 – 1483)

1466 Fifth Charter, granted by Edward IV.

Henry VIII (1509 – 1547)

1543 Town again reputed to be burned by the French, and churches destroyed (one at east end, one on site of Castle).

1543 Church of St. John Baptist re-built.

1545 Castle building begun as part of scheme to defend Island against future attacks.

1547 Castle operational.

Elizabeth I (1558 – 1603)

1559 Survey of Yarmouth carried out. Number of houses in the town, 26.

1560 Sixth Charter, granted by Elizabeth I.
Another survey carried out.

1584 Representation in Parliament increased to two.

1597 "House" built on top of Castle.

James I (1603 – 1625)

1609 Seventh Charter, called the Great Charter, granted by James I. Market day changed from Monday to Wednesday.

1610 Castle strengthened by the addition of buttresses.

1614 Work begun on building St. James's Church on the present site.

Charles I (1625 – 1649)

1625 An inventory of the town's defences shewed that the Butts were in decay, and there were few or no bows and arrows in the town.

1626 St. James's Church finished and consecrated.

1628 Scheme put forward to make Freshwater and Totland an island by letting the sea in at Freshwater Gate.

1635 Church of St. John Baptist beginning to fall down. People of the town petitioned for it to be demolished.

1647 Charles I visited Yarmouth.

1648 Charles I passed through Yarmouth as a prisoner from Newport to Hurst Castle.

Commonwealth (1649 – 1660)

1650 Population approximately 400.

Charles II (1660 – 1685)

1660 Charles II presented a silver-gilt Mace to the Town in recognition of the people's loyalty to his father.

1662 The Governor of the Island cut a passage round the eastern side of the town, thus making Yarmouth an island.

1664 The Mill embankment built.
A drawbridge thrown across the moat at the eastern entrance to the town.

1668 Sir Robert Holmes made life Governor of the Isle of Wight.

1671, 1675, 1677 Charles II visited Yarmouth and stayed with Sir Robert Holmes.

1679 St. James's Church presented with a bell by Sir Richard Mason.

1679 Nicholas Paris of Warwick made the Church clock.

James II (1685 – 1688)

1692 Sir Robert Holmes died.

Anne (1702 – 1714)

1706 Ferry to Norton established.

1711 Captain David Urry bought the house in the High Street known as the Refuge, and re-built it. (Now known as the Towers).

George I (1714 – 1727)

1725 Population falling, now said to be 300.

George II (1727 – 1760)

1735 Mention of four Alms Houses in Eremue Lane, three of

which are still standing.
It is believed at this time there were six inns in the town.
1752 Foundation of the Thomas Lord Holmes Charity in memory of his son.

George III (1760 – 1820)
1763 The Town Hall re-built by Thomas Lord Holmes.
Originally known as the Guildhall.
The town now had four Gates – the Inner and Outer Town Gates, The Sea Gate (on the Quay) and the Hither Gate (St. James's Street).
1764 The Governor of the Island, Thomas Lord Holmes, died, and his house became the George Inn.
1766 Population now 240 in 59 houses.
1770 Two houses on the Common washed away by the sea.
1778 As the market was declining in popularity, market day was changed from Wednesday to Friday.
1784 Town Chest, containing many town records, lost or stolen.
1793 Yarmouth Mill built by William Porter of Newport.
1795 Population 333 in 63 houses.
1799 George Morland, the artist, stayed at the George, and painted a portrait of the landlord, Mr. Plumbley, which was for many years used as the Inn sign.
1809 The Mount, the largest house in Yarmouth, built by Rev. George Burrard, and used as the Rectory.
1810 Sir James Clark, famous physician, pronounced the climate in Yarmouth to be greatly beneficial to health.

George IV (1820 – 1830)
1825 The Townspeople protested against the closing of Love's Lane, and won the ensuing Court case.
1830 The first steamship, the S.S. Glasgow, commanded by a Yarmouth man, Captain R. Dore, came into the harbour, starting a regular service between Yarmouth and Lymington.

William IV (1830 – 1837)
1831 Church tower raised 30 feet by D. A. Alexander, in memory of his son.
1832 The Reform Act was passed, depriving Yarmouth of the right to send two members to Parliament.
1836 Several local people accused of smuggling. A Court of

Enquiry was held at the George Hotel and all the accused were found Not Guilty.

1837 The Corporation held an enquiry into Common Rights. It was held that a Commoner could "turn out" an animal, provided it was tethered by a chain no longer than 12 yards.

Victoria (1837 – 1901)

1841 The Census gave population as 567 in 114 houses.

1843 Breakwater across the Harbour started.

1847 Breakwater completed at a cost of £1,200.

1851 Alum Bay sand business came to an abrupt end.

1852 At this time there were four Public Wells in Yarmouth – in the Square, South Street, Baskets Lane, and Mill Road.

1855 Yarmouth Church of England Primary School built, at a cost of £1,100.

The Yarmouth-Lymington Ferry service was taken over by the Railway Company.

1858 The bridge across the River Yar was begun. Opened to traffic in 1860 as a toll bridge.

1861 Yarmouth became the headquarters of the Bible Christian Fellowship Church.

1862 Coastguard Cottages built.

1863 The Ancient Court Leet was suspended by the Mayor and Corporation "until further notice".

1864 The crane on the Quay was presented to the town by Admiral Henry Ommanney Love.

1871 Population 806 in 182 houses.

1873 Extensive alterations carried out in the Church.

1875 Admiral Sir Erasmus Ommanney took up residence at the Towers.

Work on building the Pier started.

The Castle Garrison was withdrawn.

1876 The Pier was opened by the Mayor, 19th July.

Municipal Corporations Commission set up to enquire into the management of a number of towns, including Yarmouth.

1878 Solent Yacht Club formed, with headquarters at the George Hotel.

1880 Municipal Corporations Commissions declared that Yarmouth was a "Rotten Borough".

1881 Solent Steam Packet Co. started running ferries in conjunction with the train timetables.

1883 Municipal Corporations Act passed.
Mayor and Burgesses petitioned the Queen for a new Charter, but this was rejected by the Privy Council.

1889 The Freshwater, Yarmouth and Newport Railway was opened in July.

1891 Yarmouth lost its Borough status.
The Yarmouth Town Trust was formed to manage town property, the Harbour, the Quay, and the Pier.

1893 On Bonfire Night, 6th November, Jesse Loch Warder was accidentally burned to death.

1894 Old Houses in Bank Street were demolished, and Pier Square formed.

1897 The George Hotel stables were pulled down and new wing built. The name was changed to the Pier Hotel, but this did not prove popular and it was changed back to The George in about 1929.
During the Diamond Jubilee Celebrations in August there was dancing in the Square, which was lit by electricity for the first time.

1900 Electric light was installed in the Church.

Edward VII (1901 – 1910)

1901 Population now 948.

1903 The Town Trust sued the Freshwater Gas Co. for mooring fees, but lost the case.

1907 Yarmouth's coal trade came to an end.

1908 In April, in a storm, a collision occurred off Black Rock between H.M.S. Gladiator and S.S. St. Paul, 30 lives being lost.

George V (1910 – 1936)

1925 The first Yarmouth lifeboat was commissioned.

1928 Some old buildings on the Quay were demolished to make way for a new slipway.

1931 The Yarmouth Pier and Harbour Commissioners were set up to manage the Harbour and Pier.

1934 The Isle of Wight County Council acquired the Yar Bridge and freed it of tolls.

George VI (1936 – 1952)

1938 The new slipway was built and an improved ferry service inaugurated.

1948 Population now given as 850 in 200 houses.
1949 Two local boys, the Smith brothers, sailed the Atlantic in the small boat the Nova Espero.

Elizabeth II (1952 –)
1953 The Freshwater, Yarmouth and Newport Railway closed.
1965 H.M. The Queen visited Yarmouth when installing her uncle, Lord Louis Mountbatten, as Governor of the Island.
1966 The Mount demolished to make way for a new road.
1977 Yarmouth's new high speed lifeboat entered service. Population now 1055.

CHAPTER II

Early History

Almost exactly one hundred years ago, in 1880, the Municipal Corporations Commission found that Yarmouth was a "Rotten Borough", and deprived it of its municipal status. Two hundred years ago, in 1784, the Borough was recovering from the loss of its Town Chest containing all its records and documents. Three hundred years ago, in 1679, the parish Church of St. James was presented with its single bell, and its clock. Four hundred years ago, in 1584, Yarmouth's representation in Parliament was increased from one member to two. Six hundred years ago, in 1379, the town was still reeling from the devastating blow of having been burned down by the French. Eight hundred years ago, in 1179, Yarmouth was a bustling and thriving town, and the most important port in the Isle of Wight. And nearly one thousand years ago, in 991, we have the first recorded mention of ERMUD, where lived two Saxons, Aluric and Wislac.

One thousand years is a long, long time, and for a town to have a thousand years of history, though it may not be unique, is at least rare and exciting.

It is not surprising that very little information has survived from those far off days, but we know about Aluric and Wislac because of the Danegeld, a tax levied by the King Ethelred – nicknamed the Unready – for the purpose of buying off the Danes who had covetous eyes on England. Later on, after the Norman Conquest, another survey which came to be known as the Domesday Book was instituted, and the holding of Aluric and Wislac is again mentioned.

The name Ermud would appear to mean "the muddy estuary", and over the next few hundred years many variations on the name occur, practically all without the initial "Y". Examples are – Eremue, Eremuth, Erumouth, and Ermowth. Not until the end of the 13th century do we find the name spelt "Yarmouth" or "Yaremuthe", the Isle of Wight dialect being responsible for the letter "Y" being prefixed. Thereafter, and up to the end of the 17th century alternative spellings occur, the Great Charter itself in 1609 using the words "Eremuth alias Yarmouth". Phonetic spellings are not really surprising when it is considered that few people could read and write, and that many records were written from dictation.

Tradition has it that Yarmouth was granted its first Charter as a town in the year 1135 by Baldwin de Redvers, Earl of Devon, and Lord of the Island, but the Charter itself has been lost and we only know of its existence through the record of four witnesses between 1166 and 1179, and the confirmation of its terms in the Second Charter granted by Edward III in 1334.

Earl Baldwin granted in his Charter all the liberties and customs belonging to free burgesses, and freedom from tolls throughout all his lands in fairs and markets. These privileges were accorded not only to the burgesses themselves, but also to their heirs and successors "to enjoy as freely as they and their predecessors". This meant that the men of Yarmouth ceased to be serfs and became free citizens, one of the most important privileges thus acquired being security of tenure. Yarmouth was the first town in the Island to be so honoured, and as a result became the most important town and port.

Yarmouth began to look up, and in 1206 a Royal visit to the town is recorded. King John arrived on 28th May, together with the Earl of Salisbury and a number of Courtiers, and stayed until 1st June, when they all left for La Rochelle with an invasion fleet that had been assembling in Portsmouth.

About this time too another interesting and intriguing incident is recorded. William de Vernon, who was Lord of the Island from 1184 – 1216 gave to a William Mackerel "the land and house that Guy the Clerk held for making a hospital in honour of God and St. Mary the Virgin and All Saints, for the soul of King Henry son of Earl Geoffrey and for the soul of Earl Baldwin and Richard his brother (nephews of William de Vernon) and for the soul of William Mackerel and his ancestors". The document from which the above quotation is taken refers to the hospital as "the hospital of Eremue".

William de Vernon's grant was confirmed by Baldwin, Archbishop of Canterbury (1185 – 90) and by Godfrey, Bishop of Winchester (1189 – 1204). William Mackerel apparently gave the hospital together with its endowments to the Knights of Soloman's Temple, and this gift was later confirmed by Ralph his brother and successor, and by William de Vernon. Ralph stipulated that the endowment was to be held of him and his successors, and that if he should ever want to become a Knight of the Temple he was to be received into that religious order by that agreement.

There is no further reference to "the hospital of Eremue", and its endowments subsequently passed to the Knights Templars. But it is strange that until comparatively recent times there was a house in the High Street known as The Refuge (now the Towers), and the little lane which runs down to the sea beside it was called Refuge Lane or Friars Lane. The present house was built in 1711, and in the 500 years preceding that date, which included two devastating French raids, who can say how many buildings existed on this site and were subsequently destroyed or demolished. But it is an intriguing thought that perhaps the name of The Refuge had survived all those years, and that this is the site of William Mackerel's Hospital of Eremue.

Alternatively, the name of Friar's Lane might lead us to connect this with Quarr Abbey, who are known to have had property in the town in the 13th century. Just before 1249 Walter Lovel had granted the Abbey a house in the town, and this survived until sometime before the Dissolution. In the 15th century the Abbey was paying rents of 12d and 3d on two houses, the larger of these being let on a life-lease to Nichola, the widow of William Inglelonde.

In 1214 King John stayed in Yarmouth again, from February 3rd to 9th, and many years later there is a reference to the King's House, which may refer to the house in which he stayed. On this occasion he was on his way to Poitou in an attempt, along with the Count of Flanders, the Count of Boulogne, and the Emperor of Germany to subjugate France, which was to be divided up between them. If this had succeeded John would have received all the territory beyond the Loire, but in fact it failed dismally.

From 1273 – 1293 Isabella de Fortibus, Countess of Albemarle, Countess of Devon (born Isabella de Redvers), was Lady of the Island. She died on 11th November 1293 and on her death-bed the Bishop of Durham, on behalf of the King (Edward I), bought the Island from her for 600 Marks (£4,000). There is a tradition that says she lived and died in Freshwater and that the foundations of her palace were found many years ago in Middleton.

The King may subsequently have had a conscience about this rather dubious transaction, as in 1295 he called a Parliament and invited representatives from the West Wight, including one from Yarmouth. After this Yarmouth was entitled to send a member to each Parliament until 1584 when the number of representatives was increased from one to two.

Another reason for inviting representatives from the Island may have been the ever present threat of trouble from the French, the Isle of Wight being a logical and attractive bridge head to an invading force. For very many years Yarmouth lived under the constant threat of invasion and this caused great anxiety and unrest amongst the inhabitants and inhibited the growth of the town.

Each port in the Island had a Warden, or Baliff, whose job was to stop inhabitants from leaving and to control exporting by means of licences and in 1340 several regulations were issued with the object of tightening up security. One of these was that there should in future be only three official ports in the Island, namely La Riche (Ryde), Shamblord (Cowes) and Yarmouth.

These regulations did little to help Yarmouth for in 1377 a combined French and Castillian fleet attacked the town and virtually rased it to the ground, destroying the Church of St. John the Baptist and seriously damaging the Church of St. James. This attack followed hard on the heels of an outbreak of the Black Death in the town, and to the few inhabitants who escaped it must have seemed that the end of the world had come.

The Bailiff, who was appointed by the Lord of the Island, was in effect the town manager. Between 1378 and 1385 the town was farmed by the Baliff at a rent of 40/-, paid at Easter and Michaelmas in equal portions, but from Easter 1380 to Christmas no rent was paid for the town, because it had been burned by the French and neither the Baliff nor the townspeople had any goods on which the rent could be distrained.

In an attempt to put Yarmouth back on to its feet Richard II granted the town a further Charter in 1385, but the climb back to prosperity was long and arduous and it can be argued that Yarmouth never fully and completely recovered.

The fourth Charter followed in 1439 from King Henry VI and as a result of this the men of the town got together and officially formed themselves into a borough. Application was made for the right to elect a Mayor and this was granted in 1440. This was really the beginning of the Borough of Yarmouth in the form which lasted until 1891.

Another Charter, the fifth, was granted by Edward IV in 1466 and gradually the town was re-built and was able to forget the dreadful events of August 1377. And then in 1543 tradition has it that a fleet of 200 French ships visited the Solent and the ordeal of Yarmouth was lived all over again. Both Churches were destroyed and the town itself was left in ruins. There is a legend that the French decamped with some of the Church bells, but this story and indeed the story of the raid itself, is open to question. Some authorities claim that the raid took place in 1524 and at least one maintains that the date was 1545 and that the French never actually reached Yarmouth.

A study of the struggle for power in Europe in 1524 will probably serve to settle the argument as far as this date is concerned. In 1523 a secret treaty was made between the Emperor Charles V, Henry VIII of England, and the renegade Duke of Bourbon, Constable of France, who had been wronged in a lawsuit with the king of France, Francis I. The treaty was aimed at Francis, who was pursuing his own little war in Italy, and the plan was for the Emperor and the King of England to invade France simultaneously, one from the south and the other from the north, while Bourbon himself was to excite a rebellion in the heart of the kingdom.

In the event the plan miscarried, mainly because Francis got wind of it, and put off his expedition into Italy until the following spring, but early in 1524 he entered Italy and met an army commanded by Bourbon, who won a decisive victory and chased him back into France. Bourbon followed him into the south of France, but Francis was able to re-group his forces and once again assumed the initiative. In pursuit of Bourbon he re-entered Italy and spent the last few months of the year there.

The purpose of this little story is to demonstrate that in 1524 Francis I had far too many problems in the southern half of his kingdom to even think of invading the Isle of Wight.

In 1543 the situation was quite different, though there is still no positive proof. Invasions and counter invasions were being planned by Francis I and Henry VIII, and an English force did cross over into the Low Countries where it suffered considerable loss in a clash with the French army. Henry was not present on this occasion as he was too busy courting his sixth wife, but he did find time to declare war on France. But there is no definite proof of a raid in 1543. Worsley says the raid took place in the 35th year of Henry VIII's reign, i.e. in 1544, and Albin repeats this. A raid on the Isle of Wight in 1545 is well documented, but the raiders met with stout resistance, and did not stay long.

So the date of the raid is somewhat doubtful. But it at least seems likely that there was one about this time, and this is supported by the fact that in 1545 it was decided to build a Castle in Yarmouth to keep out unwanted visitors.

The date of the building of the Castle has been fairly well established as being in 1545 or 1546, on account of its design. Prior to this date all Henry VIII's castles had been designed to have low, round bastions to carry the guns, but in 1545 these were being superseded by the new pointed, or "arrow-head" bastion – and Yarmouth Castle has one of these arrow-head bastions. What is more, it is thought that Yarmouth was the first Castle to be so designed. Another interesting point is that much of the stone used in building the Castle came from the dissolved monasteries of Quarr and Beaulieu.

The economy of Yarmouth at this time hit a new low. Many Island families moved to the mainland to obtain a little more security from harassment, and the whole Solent area laboured under a severe economic depression. Yarmouth managed to survive, but Newtown, which had been sacked and burned in 1377, foundered never to recover.

In 1559 the Government carried out a survey in Yarmouth which listed every property with its owner and tenants, and a note of whether it was occupied or not. The Government were particularly sensitive to empty properties because of the fear of invasion and the need to keep up manpower.

The 1559 survey shows that there were 26 houses in the town, which probably means that the population was not more than 100 souls. Many of the names listed survived in Yarmouth for between two and three hundred years, but only one has survived to the present day, that of Wavill (now spelt Wavell).

The presence of the Castle obviously brought badly needed security of the town, for the population began to rise dramatically. A hundred years later, in 1650, there were said to be 400 people living in Yarmouth.

In 1560 Queen Elizabeth I granted a Charter to the town – the sixth – the terms of which basically confirmed previous privileges and rights. In 1584 she called a Parliament, and invited two representatives from Yarmouth. In 1601 the town was invited to send two members to another Parliament, but an indication of how "rotten" the Borough had become, even at this early date, is given by a letter from the Governor of the Island, Lord Hunsdon, to the Mayor and Burgesses saying quite bluntly that he would appoint the members. (See page 48).

In 1607 the Mayor and Burgesses approached the Cinque Port of Hastings applying to become a "Limb" of that Port, but this was turned down, the ancient privileges accorded the Cinque Ports being jealously guarded.

And so we come to the Great Charter of James I, the seventh and last granted to the town. Dated September 18th, 1609 it reiterates all the rights and privileges enumerated in previous Charters, and some of these are worth mentioning.

Firstly, Yarmouth is declared to be a Free Borough, a "Body Politic" and Corporate by the name of the Mayor and Burgesses of Yarmouth in the Isle of Wight, with power to purchase property and goods, etc, and to "give, grant, let and assign" the same. To have a Common Seal. There shall be twelve Chief Burgesses to be the Common Council of the Borough, and one of these shall be chosen Mayor. They shall have power to make Laws, Statutes and Orders for the government of the Borough. They shall elect "a good honest discreet Man and expert in the Laws of England" to be Common Clerk of the Borough and Steward of the Courts. They shall also elect an Officer to be known as "Sergeant of ye Mace" to serve in the Court. Both of these appointments to continue during the pleasure of the Mayor and Burgesses.

All fines, forfeitures, and profits of the Court to be the property of the Mayor and Burgesses, also a grant of strays and the goods of felons within the limits of the Borough. A market is granted to the town to be kept every Wednesday, and an annual fair on St. James's Day (July 25th), the eve before and the day after, with all profits and emoluments belonging to such Markets and Fairs.

The Charter itself runs to 1,000 words and is couched in 17th century legal phraseology which to our ears is now rather quaint. But the sentiment and meaning remains the same, as the following extract from the preamble will illustrate:

> " . . . We therefore willing yt from henceforth for ever . . . for ye keeping of Our Peace and for ye Rule and government of ye same burrough and our people theire inhabiting and of others resorting theire and that ye same burrough might be and remaine att all times for ever hereafter a burrough of peace and quietness to ye dread and terror of ye wicked and to rewarde and maintaine ye good and yt Our Peace and other deeds of Justice and good government may be there the better keept and donne att ye humble petition and request of ye Nowe Mayor and Burgesses of ye s'd Burrough".

The Great Charter marked a significant step in the development of the town, and under it Yarmouth continued to grow. The presence of the Castle deterred any further attentions from the French, so that peaceful expansion was possible, and had it not been for the cupidity and greed of some of its Mayors and Chief Burgesses it might have continued to flourish and develop. In which case, of course, it might not have become the sleepy, charming little town it is to-day, "a burrough of peace and quietness".

CHAPTER III

The Middle Period

17th and 18th Centuries

The 17th Century dawned bright and fair for Yarmouth. The building of the Castle had put an end to the depredations of the French, Yarmouth was now a garrison town and relatively prosperous, and a period of peaceful expansion seemed not only possible, but highly likely, The Great Charter of 1609 set the seal on this, and the economic barometer seemed to be set fair.

The present parish Church of St. James bears the date 1614, this being the date at which building began. It is just possible that there was a church on this site before that date, and if so then this was the date of the re-build. It was completed in 1626 and consecrated by the Bishop of Salisbury on 11th March in that year. The consecration, not only of the Church, but also of the Churchyard, suggests that this must have been the first Church on this site.

The first Rector was Richard Faulkner who was appointed in 1621 and stayed until 1651 when he was supplanted by Thomas Bowerman. Towards the end of his term of office he was getting a bit old and feeble, as the following report shows.

> "The returne for the parishe of Yarmouth in the Isle of Wight concerning the survey to be made for preachinge ministers and mayntenance for them, etc. There is a small Parsonage here only belonginge to this Towne. The said Parsonage is not worth above twenty marks per annum, one yeare with another, at utmost. There is one, Master Richard Faulkener, a feeble old man who was only a Reader here for neare thirtie yeares till he was putt out by order sixe or seaven yeares since for his debility and insufficiency and hath and doth receive the profittes of our Parsonage for his livelyhood, having noe other meanes to mayntain him. Wee have noe preaching minister here at all,

neither have had a long tyme albeit there are aboute foure hundred soules in our Towne and all the howses compact neere together, and noe other Church within a myle of us, and that a very small one twoe, and if the tide be up it is about twoe miles thither. We have onely one Church in our Towne which is large enough and well fitted for all our congregation, onely wee want a godlie preaching minister which is rare, and the Towne's humble desire may be speedily obtayned for the glory of God and the comfort of our poore soules".

Two interesting points arise out of the above survey, the first concerning the "feeble old man" Richard Faulkener, who was perhaps only a lay Reader and who gave up even in this capacity in about 1644. The new Rector, Thomas Bowerman, or Bowreman, who was appointed in 1651 as a result of the above report, wrote in the parish registers in 1654 the following:

"I doe hereby Signifie that in pursuance of an Act of Parliament and by a Certificate from the Inhabitants of the Towne of Yarmouth of their free choice and Election of Richard Faulkner to bee their Register I have approved and sworne the said Richard Faulkner accordingly the 9th Day of May 1654, Given under my hand at Brook the day and yeare above written.

Tho: Bowreman".

"Whereas the above named Richard Faulkner since he was sworn Register as above sayd was for some apparent misdemeanor put out of the sayd Office, and that now the Inhabitants of Yarmouth have of their free choice and Election chosen Thomas Saunders for their Register, according to the Act above specified as by a Certificate under the hand of the sayd Inhabitants appeares, I have therefore approved and sworn the sayd Thomas Saunders accordingly. Given under my hand this eighth day of November 1654.

Tho: Bowreman".

There is no clue as to what sort of misdemeanor he committed, but three years later, on 25th February, 1657/58, he got married, so he could not have been too old or too feeble. He married Elizabeth Chambers, and a search of the Registers for her produces another marriage, between Andrew Chambers and Elizabeth Cooke in 1648.

So she could possibly have been a widow, though there is no record of the death of Andrew Chambers in the Register.

Elizabeth Cooke was born in 1621, so that if she was the one who married Richard Faulkner in 1658 she would have been 37 years old at the time. Her parents were Elias and Dorothy Cooke who were married in 1617, and her mother Dorothy was the daughter of a John Wavell who had a house on the south side of the High Street. In 1616 John Wavell gave his house to his daughter Dorothy, and in 1628 it was conveyed to her husband Elias Cooke.

In the same year (1628) the next door house to the west was taken by Richard Faulkner, the minister, and so he would have had every opportunity of getting to know the Cookes and their daughter Elizabeth. On the east, part of Elias Cooke's house was let in 1628 to a Richard Cotton, and it is an interesting link with these old and forgotten days that there are still Wavells and Cottons living in Yarmouth to-day. The very first entry in the Parish Registers, which begin on 4th August 1614, is the christening of a Robert Cotton, son of Robert and Elionor Cotten. There are also Cookes still in Yarmouth, though they have not lived here through all the intervening years.

The other interesting point arising out of this old survey is the mention of the nearest church being above a mile away, "and if the tide be up it is above two miles thither". In those times of course the mill embankment had not been built, and the tides flowed freely in and out of what is now Thorley Marsh. In fact the area from the present mill embankment right up to the Thorley Road was known as the Draft Haven, and quite large ships would anchor there. Only a few years ago a large wooden anchor was dug up on the marsh.

One can assume that the Church to which the writer refers is Freshwater Church, though the Causeway is well over a mile from Yarmouth. But it might have been possible to ford the mouth of the Draft Haven at low water, and yet have to walk round it when the tide was in, thus doubling the distance covered.

Another theory is that there was once a small Fishermans Church or Chapel just the other side of the Draft Haven and near the river, though there is no trace of this now.

Prosperity took a long time to come back to Yarmouth following the French raids, although the population increased at an extraordinary rate in the first half of the 17th century. In 1625 a levy was imposed on all inhabitants for the repair of the Quay, which was in a bad state, and at the same time a defence survey produced the rather alarming news that the Butts were in decay, and there were few, or no, bows and arrows in the town.

In 1628 defence from attack was very much in everyone's mind as a scheme was put forward for turning both the West Wight and Yarmouth into islands. The West Wight plan was to cut the narrow neck of land at Freshwater Gate and let the sea flow through into the River Yar. The island thus created would then provide a refuge in the event of an invasion, and would be comparatively easy to defend. This plan was vigorously opposed by the Mayor and Burgesses of Yarmouth on the score that it would reduce the flow of the current in the river, which they claimed was only just sufficient to keep the harbour clear from silting up as it was.

The Yarmouth plan was similar, i.e. to cut the narrow strip of land east of the Common and let the sea flow straight through from the Solent to the Draft Haven, thus turning Yarmouth into an island.

Sir John Oglander, in his Memoirs, records the above and says that the purpose of the two places of retreat was as follows:

> "Freshwater for owre Cattel, and ye mayne bodie of our companies; and Yarmouth for ye better sort of people".

The Yarmouth plan was in fact carried out, though not until 1662, and for two years Yarmouth was without contact with the rest of the Island, except by boat. But in 1664 a drawbridge was thrown across the moat, thus ending what must have been a hideous inconvenience.

Also in 1664 the Mill embankment is reputed to have been built, thus effectively destroying the Draft Haven – which had probably been gradually silting up for very many years anyway. This Mill embankment has been attributed to Sir Robert Holmes, but in 1664 he was on the high seas waging his brilliant action against the Dutch off the Guinea Coast, so he cannot be held responsible for this. (See page 60).

Prior to this, in 1630, an interesting event took place when a fleet of ten ships called at Yarmouth on their way to the New World, and stayed for a week before starting on their long and hazardous voyage across the Atlantic. This "armada" of ships was under the leadership of John Winthrop, who subsequently became Governor of New England, and it carried nearly 1,000 pilgrim emigrants and crew, and 200 head of cattle. One of the ships in this fleet was the Mayflower, which only 10 years before had carried the first of the pilgrim fathers.

Charles I visited Yarmouth in 1647, having arrived at Carisbrooke on Sunday 14th November seeking safety in the Isle of Wight. During the following week he came to Yarmouth and was entertained to a banquet given by Alice, wife of Captain John Urry of Thorley, the town paying for the entertainment of his retinue. A portion of the town account covering this visit has survived:

"Mo' pd. the Kinges footemen when his Magesty Came into Towne.	002	00	00
Mo' pd. unto his Magestyes padman.	001	00	00
Mo' fo' part of the Charge of Entertayning of the Gentelmen that Came w'th the King to town.	000	10	00

A padman was a groom who rode after his master.

Charles I came to Yarmouth again almost a year later, but in much less happy circumstances. He had been imprisioned for some time by the Parliament, first in Carisbrooke Castle, and then in Newport, and towards the end of 1648 the Army took over responsibility for his safe keeping. On the last day of November 1648 they decided for security reasons to move him to Hurst Castle. Early the following morning he was conducted to Worsley's Tower on the Norton bank of the river, near Yarmouth, where a boat was waiting.

> "Meanwhile the coach conveyed the Royal person, guarded by two troops of horse, went westward toward Worsley's Tower, in Freshwater Isle, a little beyond Yarmouth Haven. In the vicinity the Monarch and his attendants res ted about an hour, and then the vessel, with a favourable wind, crossed the narrow sea in three hours, and landed at Hurst Castle".

The time taken for this short voyage of about one mile suggests that though the wind was fair it was either very light, or it must have been a spring tide, which runs hard through Hurst Narrows.

In 1660 Charles II presented to Yarmouth a silver-gilt hand mace, in recognition of the town's loyalty to his father. It is not remembered now what this particular act of loyalty was, but possibly it was connected with an escape plan when Charles I was imprisoned in Carisbrooke Castle. One such plan was engineered by a Captain Burleigh, the son of the Captain of Yarmouth Castle.

Sir Robert Holmes, who received his knighthood from Charles II in 1666, had a love-hate relationship with his monarch. There was an occasion in 1665 when the King visited the Island but refused to see Holmes, who had omitted to patch up a quarrel he had had with the Duke of York, the King's brother (who subsequently became James II). But there were three occasions when the King did actually come and stay with Holmes in Yarmouth. (See page 65). Worsley refers to one of these in the following terms:

> "Sir Robert Holmes appears to have been in great favour at Court; the King making an excursion, in the summer of 1671, paid the Governor a visit at Yarmouth, where he had built a handsome house, on lands granted by the Crown. Yarmouth was at that time a garrisoned town, strongly fortified, having a draw-bridge at the East entrance. The King landed at Gurnard Bay, in the parish of Northwood, and passed through the forest of Parkhurst, to the Park, now the Park-farm, belonging to the Governors of the Island, by a road made by Sir Robert, some traces of which still remain. The forest is said to have then been so full of wood, that squirrels leaped from one tree to another. This timber has long since been cleared, and nothing but underwood remains".

The Rev. Edmund Venables, writing in 1860, also records this visit, but dismisses it perfunctorily in a few lines:

> "In July 1671 Holmes enjoyed the honour, such as it was, of entertaining his royal master, accompanied by the Duke of York and Prince Rupert – who had landed at Gurnard Bay, and for whose convenience he had caused a road to be constructed through Parkhurst Forest – at his recently erected mansion. Charles paid him a second visit in 1675".

Sir Robert Holmes died in 1692, and with his passing, and the end of the 17th century, much of the romance and adventure of the age seems to have left Yarmouth. The reigns of William and Mary, Anne, and the first few Georges have a quite different atmosphere, and the town enters a new and more pedestrian phase of its life.

By the middle of the 18th century the population had dropped from the 400 reported in 1560, to 240, living in 59 houses, though 50 years later it had picked up to over 300, and in fact it has steadily increased ever since.

In 1735 there were said to be six inns in the town. These were the Bugle, the King's Head, the Wheatsheaf, the Bull's Head, the Whyte Lion, and the New Inn. The latter was in the High Street, and is now an antique shop, Marlborough House. Both the Bull's Head and the Whyte Lion were in St. James's Street, one of them in what is now Port House, and the other on the opposite side of the street on the site now occupied by the Yarmouth Institute.

The George did not become an inn until 1764, and later on there was another one in Bank Street known as the Dolphin. This was pulled down in 1894 along with several other old buildings in creating Pier Square. In passing, the word "Bugle" does not necessaily signify the musical instrument.

It could also be derived from the Latin "Buculus" meaning a young ox. Apparently the Bugle Hotel in Newport was originally known as the Bull, and the old inn sign was an ox.

Also in the middle of the 18th century there were four gates into the town. These were the Sea Gate, which was on the Quay somewhere between the end of Quay Street and Bridge Road, the Inner Town Gate or East Gate, near the top of the High Street, the Outer Town Gate, near the drawbridge, and the Hither Gate, which was at the end of St. James's Street. On many old documents the Hither Gate is shown as the Lithergate, the explanation being the use of the French definite article, which was quite common, in calling it Le Hithergate. Inevitably this was soon pronounced Lithergate.

A number of other place names, and street names, have also been changed during the passage of the centuries, and some have been completely lost. We know where Adder Lane was (near the old Churchyard) since this survived until comparatively recently and Snakes Lane, but where were Saddlers Lane, Goldsmith Street and the Bowling Alley? In 1365 there was a Middilstret, which presumably became the High Street, and in 1605 a St. John's Lane, which must have been up by the old Churchyard. There is still a little lane running alongside the old Churchyard from the High Street to Tennyson Road – perhaps this is St. John's Lane.

In an old map of Yarmouth, date 1793, the street plan is most intriguing, in that South Street is shown to be as wide as the Square, and at the northern end, near its junction with the High Street, there is an isolated building in the middle of the road. Could this be the "Stone Cross" which is mentioned in several old documents? By the year 1600 Stone Cross had become Crosse Stone, and later Crostone, and even Crestone.

This old map also shows the Mill, but whether this is the new mill, which was built in 1793, or the old one it is impossible to say. There is reputed to have been a tide mill here since the middle of the 17th century, and perhaps it was built at the same time as the embankment in 1664.

The present building was erected by a Newport man, William Porter, who was a most interesting character. In his early years he was "a hawker of penny pies about the streets", but though uneducated he was a man of ideas and possessed of tremendous drive. He managed to buy the old house he lived in, and successfully re-built it. Encouraged by this he launched out as a builder, and built a mill on the east side of the Medina River. Though the official name of this was the East Medina Mill, it became known to all as the Botany Bay Mill, because of a joke.

At this time it was the practice to deport undesirable convicts to Botany Bay in Australia, and the ships that transported them used to lie off the Mother Bank. Prisoners were taken down the river from Newport in small boats, and William Porter's labourers used to travel to their work in the same way. Wags on the Quayside would ask them if they were going to Botany Bay, and the nickname stuck to the Mill they were building.

Porter next built seven elegant town houses at the bottom of Newport High Street, and these became known as Porter's Row. Following this he built another Mill on the west of the Medina, which again received a nickname – Port Jackson Mill. And lastly, in 1793 he built Yarmouth Mill.

His next project was to have been a crescent of houses in Cowes, but alas this was never built. William Porter could apparently neither read nor write and kept no accounts. All his building operations were done on credit, the necessary finance being supplied by a Newport Bank. Suddenly the Bank took fright at the extent of the empire he was building, and withdrew their support, and overnight Porter was ruined. Albin says of his failure:

> "the event shewed that he had not abounded in prudence and economy. His deficiency in the first was manifest, in building the three mills on life tenures, without making provision for a renewal; and in the latter that he kept a phaeton and pair, with a post chaise and single horse chaise, which involved him in unnecessary expenses, before he had realised the permanent means".

It is said of William Porter that he was a staunch Methodist, and that he died in 1794 in poverty in the prime of life.

Yarmouth Mill is situated where the Thorley Brook enters the River Yar, and has been out of use for many years. In the 19th century a steam engine was installed to drive the machinery, and it is odd that there is now no visible trace on the outside of the Mill that there ever was a water wheel. The building of the Railway in 1888, which crosses the mill pond, is thought to have been responsible for its silting up.

George Morland the artist was a frequent visitor to Yarmouth towards the end of the 18th century, and for a time lived at The George where he was friendly with the landlord, a Mr. Plumbly. A. G. Cole, in his book on Yarmouth, tells the story of how Morland was arrested as a spy for making sketches of the Castle, and was marched off to Newport, whence Plumbly followed and obtained his release. The road to Newport was in those days little better than a cart track, and a contemporary writer on Yarmouth said:

> "Yarmouth's distance from Newport is ten miles; but the road for pleasurable travelling is the worst in the island. There are not less than fifty-two gates to be passed between the two places, which greatly adds to the irksomeness of it".
>
> The same writer expressed surprise at Yarmouth itself:
>
> "When we entered the town we were not a little disappointed, but it was an agreeable disappointment. From its appearance at a distance, we expected to have seen a contemptible place; but on the contrary, we found the buildings in general neat and clean, though rather low. They were mostly of stone, or white-washed. If Yarmouth was paved, it would be littel inferior to Newport in neatness".

Our old friend Albin finishes his account of his visit to the town by recommending both the George and the Bugle to travellers who wish to stay the night.

> "We are also informed from the pen of another ingenious gentleman of the island that the chief supports of two good inns are from the ships that occasionally anchor in the road, and passengers to and from Lymington; and that strangers who visit the western part of the island, and find it inconvenient to return to Newport for the night, may here be very commodiously accommodated. It is essentially necessary that our readers, some of which are doubtless unaware of this description should be acquainted with such an important and agreeable fact".

This was written nearly 200 years ago, and it is nice to be able to report that the two hostelries – together with others in the town – are still dispensing comfortable and efficient hospitality to travellers.

CHAPTER IV

The Church

The origin of the church in Yarmouth is – as they say – lost in the mists of antiquity. The excellent little guide to the Parish and Church of Yarmouth, which can be bought in the present church, says that the earliest reference to a church in Yarmouth is when Baldwin de Redvers, Lord of the Island, who presented the town with its first Charter, granted the tithes which belonged to Sir Alfred de Bockley to the Priory of Christchurch, but retained "the Advousen of the church of Eremue".

There is a record which says that even before the year 1200 there were two churches here. The site of one of these, dedicated to St. John the Baptist, is fairly well authenticated, this being at the east end of the town at the top of the High Street, where the old churchyard still is. Charles Andrews, who lived most of his life in Yarmouth and remembered the early days of the 19th century said:

> "Going into the churchyard by the late Mr. Little's house you will see the foundation on the left hand. Mr. Stephens' grave was in the enclosure of the church, there was an old tomb not far from the Communion end of the church who died in his Mayoralty. I don't know his name. There was some glass and windows dug up at the right hand in digging a grave, I don't know what became of it. None of the inhabitants was buried there for many years, only soldiers and sailors and strangers. It was called Upper Litten, a name never heard now".

Charles Andrews was very old when he wrote that in 1878, but many of his statements can be corroborated. The Mr. Little he mentions was the Rev. Robert Little who was Rector of Yarmouth from 1841 to 1853, and lived in Myrtle Cottage right at the top of the High Street. Robert Little succeeded the Rev. Sir George Burrard as Rector after having been Curate for many years.

The word "Litten", meaning a graveyard, occurs again in the Corporation Minute Book for 1870 when a complaint was lodged about the state of Snakes Lane, which ran along the west side of the "Lytton". It is also still in use in Newport in the street known as Church Litten.

The church of St. John the Baptist is mentioned again in 1260 when a Chaplain was appointed to celebrate Mass daily from Michaelmas for the soul of Alexander Duele or Dwele who was buried in the church.

J. Albin in his History of the Isle of Wight published in 1795 says:

> "The church originally stood at the east end of the town, and in the time of Bishop Woodlock it was returned into the registry of Winton in 1305, by the dean of the Island, that it paid or received a pension of 13/4d to or from the church of Shalfleet; but though the expression of the return is in this and some other instances ambiguous, we are disposed to conclude that it paid the pension".

This church of the Blessed St. John the Baptist, along with much of the town, seems to have been completely destroyed by the French in their raid of August 1377.

The second church, dedicated to St. James the Apostle and Martyr, which was contemporaneous with the one mentioned above, was said to have been in the Market Place, but at this distance in time it is almost impossible to say where the Market Place was in the 12th century. In 1272 there is a record that there was a Market Place where the Town Hall now stands, but there is no mention of a church on this site.

There are however,, several mentions of a church having at one time existed on part of the site now occupied by the Castle, and it is possible that in those early days the market place was near there.

Albin claims that the second church was built

> " . . . at the west end of the town, in the place where the Castle now stands; but also this was demolished by the French in the 35th year of Henry VIII . . . The king, in consequence of this mischief, caused a castle to be erected immediately on the spot; and the old wall of the church forms a part of it, as may be seen on the east side of the fortress".

Our old friend Charles Andrews confirms this, claiming to have seen traces of the wall, and of the adjoining graveyard.

> " . . . and there was a church or chapel somewhere abreast the Castle. I have seen some of the granite columns broken up and built in. Mr. Stephens pulled part of a wall down

and found them built in the graveyard. The graveyard was where Mr. Blake's coal yard was. We disturbed some of the remains in putting in a post".

That was written in 1873 or 1874 and Charles Andrews repeated the story again in another letter written in 1878.

"There was a church or chapel where Mr. Blake had once a coal yard and old Harry Dore's house stood. It was pulled down and the (builders of the castle?) worked it to the Castle wall. I gave Mr. Blackburn (the Rector) a piece or two of some Pembroke marble columns taken out of the wall when altered. There is a burying ground, as I saw the bones taken up at digging a post hole".

Mr. Blake's coal yard was plot No. 3 on the Tithe Map, measuring 5 perches, and situated immediately behind a barn which is now the George Hotel Garage, and alongside the alleyway that leads to the Castle entrance.

In the second French raid which took place in the 35th year of Henry VIII's reign (1543) both churches were again extensively damaged, and the decision was taken to build a Castle for the defence of the town. The design of the castle with its arrowhead bastion is radically different from earlier castles erected by Henry VIII, and enables its date to be fairly confidently placed at 1546.

But before that date, in 1543, the church of St. John the Baptist was re-built, and for the next 70 years was used for public worship. Due to the unstable nature of the ground on which it was built however, trouble was experienced, and a new site was looked for in the centre of the town.

In 1614 work began on the present church, and this was completed in 1626. A full account of the consecration of the building by the Bishop of Salisbury on March 11th, 1626 was written by Sir John Oglander of Nunwell, who was present. This account has been preserved in Sir John's memoirs, and was reprinted by the late Harry Guy in his "Historical Notes on Yarmouth and the Neighbourhood" which he wrote in 1911.

An interesting sideline in this account is that the Mayor at the time was William Hide of Berkshire "Whoe kept an Inne, and there gave ye Bischop and all an entertaynment at a ordinarye". The Inn mentioned is probably the Bugle, but it could have been one of the other five that existed in the town at this time. William Hide died in 1648 and is buried in the centre aisle of the church, the inscription on his tombstone reading "Here lyeth the body of William Hide

Gent an Alderman of this towne who deseesed the 21 of May 1648".

There is a tradition in Yarmouth that when the French burned the town in 1543 they stole the church bells and took them back to France. Cole says they were hung in the church of S.S. Peter and Paul in Boulogne, another report says they went to Cherbourg. Still another report claims they were subsequently located in some village on the west side of the Cherbourg peninsula.

But there is another possible theory as to the fate of these bells and the birth of the tradition that they were stolen. As it was fire that destroyed the Yarmouth churches, the most natural explanation of their fate is that they perished in the flames, and the story that they were taken by the French could have been a later addition, based on the following incident. In 1553 an inventory was taken throughout the Island of all church goods, including bells, and under Yarmouth, having listed the chalice and vestments, the following item occurs:

> "One of there belles was takine out of the styple by the p'ishe in an'o iiij E.vj (1551) to be solde, and the soldiers of the Castell supposing hit sholde be conveyed over the seas arrested it and so it remayneth upon their chardge".

It would seem that at this date (1551) there was more than one bell in the steeple, suggesting that perhaps they were not destroyed in the fire. Also, the bell that was "arrested" by the Castle may not have been the only one that the Parish took down and sold, and what better excuse can you have than blaming the French for it?

In 1635 the re-built church of St. John the Baptist, which had been having trouble with its foundations, was getting into a dangerous state, and following a petition by the parishoners it was demolished. This left Yarmouth with one church only, and this one has survived to the present day and is in good shape and actively used.

There is one bell in the tower inscribed "The Gyft of Sir Richard Mason, Knight. 1679". This bell was cast by a well-known Whitechapel bell-founder, James Bartlett, and in spite of its being 300 years old it still delivers its message loud and clear.

The church clock is also 300 years old, having been installed in 1679, and bears the inscription "Nicholas Paris in Warwick. 1679". Originally there was only one clock face, to the north overlooking the Square, but in November 1900 a west face was presented to the church by Captain Scott-Rogers, R.N. who was a great benefactor to the church and for many years a churchwarden. The clock is wound regularly every Tuesday evening by Mr. John Awty of

Freshwater, and it is worthy of note that in spite of its advanced age it keeps meticulous time, losing half a minute per fortnight in the summer, and one minute per week in the winter when (like old men) its joints are that little bit stiffer.

It is also worthy of note that John Awty, and his father and grandfather before him, have been winding this clock week in and week out for over 50 years, and this must be something of a record. He regards the winding of the clock more in the nature of a service to the church and community than a profitable part of his business, and there is little doubt that over the years the profitability of the contract in money terms cannot possibly have kept pace with the increased cost of coming over from Freshwater each week.

There are compensations, however, and Mr. Awty admits that he finds Yarmouth church especially peaceful and relaxing. There are some churches, when he is alone in them in the dark and quiet of winter evenings, that he finds – and I use his own word – "shadowy", but Yarmouth breathes peace, and after winding the clock he usually spends a few minutes in meditation before unlocking the door and letting himself out.

Over the centuries various sums of money have been left to found "Charities", mainly to help the poor of the town. Perhaps the best known of these is the Holmes Charity, set up by Thomas Lord Holmes in 1752 to commemorate the death of his small son Henry. Lord Holmes left a sum sufficient to provide an annual bounty of £30, which after paying for the upkeep of the Holmes Chapel was to be distributed equally between the Rector, the deserving Poor, and to establish any worthy apprentices.

Every year since 1752, on 11th June, these sums have been disbursed at a simple little ceremony in the church. When it was instituted £30 was a lot of money, but now of course it is considerably reduced in value, and compared with the cornucopia of the Welfare State it is almost worthless. This is perhaps the reason why it is proposed to redeem the Charity with a lump sum, and abolish it. Purely in material terms this is perhaps logical, but it seems to have been forgotten that this tradition, and others like it, are part of our heritage. Once gone they can never be replaced, but we shall have lost something of priceless value.

Many alterations were carried out to the fabric of the building during the 19th century, and considerable sums of money were spent in renovations and modernisation. Not all the alterations received universal acclaim. In 1831 the Tower was raised a matter of

30 feet, mainly in order to provide a distinguishing sea-mark, to the design, and by the generosity of D. A. Alexander in memory of his third son, Henry.

Mr. Alexander was the designer of several well-known buildings, including *inter alia*, Dartmoor Prison, Maidstone County Gaol, certain warehouses and buildings in the London Docks, and several lighthouses. It may be that it was this background which caused his style of architecture to be frowned on in certain quarters, the Rev. Edmund Venables saying of Yarmouth church tower, "There is a square tower at the west end, which has recently received an addition to its height, with but small increase to its beauty". Another cleric, the Rev. J. Charles Cox, said " . . . the modern tower of 1831, raised considerably after an utterly unsuitable and repellant fashion" Possibly the tower did look better before it was altered, but Yarmouth has learned to live with it, and in this case familiarity has bred affection.

While the tower was being re-built other alterations were carried out, also to the design of Mr. Alexander. The gallery was built, affording – as was said at the time – room for 150 poor people, the chancel and Holmes chapel were renovated, and when it was finished 11 months later the church was said to be the most decent and warm in the Island.

There was also a debt of about £400, and a public subscription list was opened to cover this. Inside the church door there is still a large painted board containing the names of those subscribing, it being a Victorian custom to publish such names *"pour encourager les autres"*. The list is headed by H.R.H. the Duchess of Kent, and contains several other noble names including the Bishop of Winchester, the Dean of Ely, and the Governor of the Isle of Wight. The Rev. George Burrard (Rector), the Rev. Robert Little (Curate), and the Rev. Samuel Wilberforce (Vicar of Brighstone who subsequently became famous in another place), are also on the list.

In 1873 further repairs were carried out. The organ was moved from the body of the church up into the chancel, the pews were "modernised" so that they all faced the same way, a new vestry and covered entrance to the gallery were provided and paid for by the Misses Leigh, and the Mayor, James Blake, and his family installed a new Reredos in memory of his wife. A new pulpit, lectern and font were also provided.

Another £400 had to be found to defray this cost, and this time a printed Balance Sheet was published shewing who had contributed, and how the money had been spent. There were one or two strange items amongst the payments, as for example – "Hire of Sails – 2/6", and "Poole Pottery Co – £2. 9s. 6d".

Several new names appear in the subscription list, thus recording the inexorable march of time. The Rev. Sir George Burrard is dead, and the subscription comes from Emma, Lady Burrard. Several Rectors have come and gone, the current one the Rev. C. T. Fisher, and his predecessor, the Rev. J. D. Ostrehan, both figuring in the list. One of the principal contributors is the Rev. R. L. Dashwood.

Yarmouth church contains a number of pleasant, though undistinguished, stained glass windows. The most pleasing of these is the large east window which was erected in 1867 by the Rector, the Rev. J. Blackburn, in memory of his youngest son who died of consumption at the age of 24. The subject of this window is Our Lord blessing a number of little children, and some of the colours used are very satisfying. Particularly worth noting is the kingfisher blue smock worn by one little boy in the centre of the group, and also the sparing but clever use of the colour pink in the lining of robes, and for the shoes of one child on the right of the picture.

Another window near the font is interesting in that it was erected in 1928 to the memory of the Rev. Robert Lewes Dashwood and Edith Theresa his wife under the will of Sarah Anne Newman, their faithful servant. Proof indeed, if proof were needed, of the sterling qualities of Mr. Dashwood, and of the love and affection which he and his wife inspired.

In the summer months Yarmouth church attracts large numbers of visitors, and many of these comment on how friendly and comforting they find the atmosphere in this old building. This atmosphere is of course the concentrated distillate of the prayers of thousands upon thousands of people who have worshipped here through the ages. It is an atmosphere of peace which in this troubled and discordant age has a tremendously therapeutic value, and which is there for the asking, free gratis and for nothing. All you have to do is to come in, sit down, and let it flow over you, allowing it to cleanse you, soothe you and rejuvenate you.

If more people understood this the church would seldom be empty.

CHAPTER V

Proceedings of the Corporation of Yarmouth

1710 — 1785

The only claim to fame or notoriety of Lieutenant Charles Cunningham Crooke of his Majesty's Cutter "Expedition" is that on the 18th October, 1784 he inadvertently purloined a large box containing the Yarmouth Court Leet Records, Corporation Minute Books, and other papers, and took them aboard his ship, from whence they never returned.

Thus many years of records were lost to the Town, adding more confusion to an already confusing situation caused by two major invasions – in 1377 and 1543 – when the town was largely destroyed, as well as by the normal ravages of time. So it is not surprising that prior to 1785 records are somewhat scant.

Two years later, on 20th December, 1787, a member of the Corporation, Jervoise Clarke Jervoise, presented to the town a fair copy of the Corporation Proceedings for the years 1710 – 1785, this containing much of the information lost by Lieut. Crooke. Where this copy came from is something of a mystery, and it is curious that Jervoise Clarke Jervoise is reputed to have been in touch with Lieut. Crooke with a view to getting back the lost records. Whether he succeeded or not we shall probably never know.

The book he presented to the Corporation is an extraordinary volume, written in exquisitely neat handwriting, with no mistakes or erasions. It records meetings of the Mayor and Burgesses, i.e. the Corporation, who on average at this time met about three times per annum. But it records little else. In very few entries is there any reference to any business connected with the upkeep or welfare of Yarmouth, in fact practically all entries are concerned only to record the election of Free or Chief Burgesses, the election and the swearing in of the Mayor for the ensuing year, and occasionally the resignation of Burgesses.

In the book there are several entries recording the election of Members of Parliament – appointment would be a better word – and several long entries recording squabbles and arguments over the legality of elections of various people. It could be said that the Book records 75 years of fiddling while Rome is burning. Some of the squabbles are interesting in that they demonstrate the clash of rival factions in the Corporation, as also the introduction as Burgesses of very many people who did not reside in Yarmouth and had no connection with the town.

A few typical entries will illustrate these points:

5th October, 1710

Assembled

Jno Combes Esq., May'r
David Urry Snr. Gent
Wm. Urry. Gent
Henry Holmes Esq
Wm. Hooke. Gent
Anthony Morgan Esq
Robert Holmes, Gent
Wm. Bowreman Esq
Jo'n Leigh Esq
David Urry Jnr. Gent
Sir Tristram Dillington. Bart

At this Assembly Sir Gilbert Dolben Baron't was unanimously admitted and sworn a free Burgess of this Borough as appears and is entered on a Two Shillings Stampt piece of Parchm't hereunto annexed according to the Act of Parliam't in that case made out and provided. Alsoe att this Assembly Henry Holmes Esq and the a'd (aforesaid) Sir Gilbert Dolben p'suant to a precept from the High Sheriffe for electing two new Members to serve in Parlyam't were duely elected and returned to serve for this Burrough.

In other words Dolben was brought in solely to be "elected" M.P. for the Borough. And the election was carried out by eleven Burgesses, which number included one of the candidates.

9th October 1710

Assembled

Jo'n Combes Esq. Mayo'r
Col. David Urry
Col. Henry Holmes
Mr. Wm. Hooke
Col. Wm. Bowreman
Capt. David Urry

Mr. Rob't Holmes

Mr. Lancelot Coleman, Mr. Wm. Holmes, Wm. Dore, Mr. James Goodman, and Wm. Prickett admitted and sworne free Burgesses of this Burrough and are entered on the two Shillings Stamps hereunto annexed according to the Act of Parlyam't.

Alsoe Mr. David Urry of Afton as appeares on his entry on a stampt piece of Parchm't according to the Act of Parlyam't hereunto also annexed.

Alsoe att this Assembly it is agreed and resolved upon by the Mayor and Majority of the Cheife Burgesses p'sent that the following Gentlemen were not legally chosen free Burgesses (that is to say) Mr. James Salter, Mr. Edward Eversley, Mr. William Jolliffe, Mr. Jo'n Grimes Jun'r, Mr. Benjamin Newland, Mr. John Gilbert Clarke, Capt Alexander Cosby, Mr. Walter Urry, Mr. John Urry, Mr. Thomas Urry, Mr. Thomas Morgan, Mr. James Dore, and Tho: Serle for the reasons following first that by ye Charter the Mayor and greater p'te of the chiefe Burgesses should be p'sent but att ye choosing the above mentioned Gentlemen as appears by theire entry there was only the Mayo'r and three Cheife Burgesses p'sent at one time and the Mayo'r and two Chieife Burgesses att another time and the rest of the Cheife Burgesses not Summoned but instead of that an opportunity taken when they could not be there.

Alsoe it is agreed upon and resolved by the Mayo'r and Majority of the Cheife Burgesses now p'sent that Capt John Wood, Mr. Rob't Shukler, Mr. Rori Morrison, Mr. Benjamin Miller, Mr. John Beere, Mr. Rob't Martell, Lieut. Jonathan Warr, and Mr. John Birkett Clarke who were lately elected and sworne free Burgesses of this Borough as appears by theire Entryes on Stamps in the old Booke According to the Act of Parlyam't be att this Assembly confirmed in the same and they are allowed of Accordingly.

The majority of these names here quoted are not of Yarmouth people. The "old Booke" has disappeared – or was it one of those lost by Lieut. Cunningham Crooke? – but it is apparent that there is a history of trouble with regard to elections, and this may be the reason why these Proceedings have such an emphasis on this subject. It is interesting to note that the date is 1710 and it was not until 1891, i.e. 180 years later that the Borough was agreed to be "Rotten", and abolished.

By this time (1891) the situation had changed and the Corporation were in fact doing some very good work on behalf of the Town. I hope to be able to demonstrate that Yarmouth was slightly unlucky to lose its Borough status in 1891.

In 1711 however there were already signs that all was not completely well, and that there were dissensions within this tight little coterie, although it was another four years before the struggle for power came to a head. The Minutes of the next few meetings tell their own story, and indicate that trouble is brewing.

21st September 1711.

Assembled – Jo'n Combes Esq. Mayor
David Urry of Easton. Gent
Henry Holmes Esq
Wm. Hooke. Gent
Rob't Holmes. Gent
Wm. Bowreman

Henry Holmes was elected Mayor for the next year at this meeting, and there was apparently no other business.

24th September 1711.

Three days later the same six Burgesss were assembled.
Att this Assembly Henry Holmes Esq the Mayor elect was duly Sworne into the office of Mayor of this Burrough for the Yeare ensueing when he alsoe tooke all the other Oaths by Law required and afterwards tooke his place in the Guildhall accordingly.

6th October 1711.

Assembled – Henry Holmes Esq. Mayor
David Urry of Easton. Gent
Wm. Hooke. Gent
Rob't Holmes. Gent
John Combes. Gent
Wm. Bowreman. Esq

Ms. that a Hall being ordered by the Mayor on this day and Timothy Heath the Serg't att Mace to this Corporation being ordered to sumon all the other Cheife Burgesses of this Corporation to attend the Hall. Butt they being all out of

Sumons except Mr. David Urry of this Burrough the Serg't warned the a'd Mr. David Urry to attend the Hall this Day notwithstanding w'ch he refused to attend this Hall in contempt of Mr. Mayor's order.

6th October 1711.

Alsoe att this Assembly William Stephens of Barton. Esq was duly elected and sworne one of the cheife Burgesses of this Corporation in the Roome of Capt. Wm. Urry dec'd late one of the cheife Burgesess of this Corporation as appeares on the stampt piece of Parchm't annex't according to the Act of Parlyam't in that case made and provided.

Alsoe att this Assembly Mr. John Crosby of the City of Bristol Merchant was duly admitted and sworne a Free Burgess of this Burrough and is entered according to the Act of Parlyam't on a Stampt piece of Parchm't hereunto annex't.

21st September 1712.

An assembly with the Mayor and six Burgesses present elected John Combes as Mayor for the next year.

22nd September 1712.

Assembled – Henry Holmes Esq. Mayor
Col. David Urry of Easton
Mr. Wm. Hooke
Mr. Rob't Holmes
Mr. John Combes
Col. Wm. Bowreman
Col. Wm. Stephens

Whereas it appeares att this Hall that Wm. Leigh one of the cheife Burgesses of this Burrough was sumoned to attend yesterday att the eleccon of a new Mayor for ye Yeare ensueing and the said Mr. Wm. Leigh having been sumoned the last Yeare on the like Occasion and having each time absented himself without assigning any cause for neglecting his Duty (Coppeys of the said Several Summons being kept in the Town box) it is now agreed on by the Mayor and the above six Burgesses p'sent that the said Mr. Wm.

Leigh be further sumoned to attend at a Hall now appointed to be here holden on this day sevenight att tenn of the clock in the forenoon.

Whereas Sir Tristram Dillington another of ye cheife Burgesses of this Burrough was also Summon'd to attend yesterday on the occasion afores'd he returned for answer that he believed he could not be there neither did he attend according to the said Sumons the other cheife Burgesses who were absent were out of the reach of being sumon'd (except Col. Leigh who upon his being sumon'd made excuse and said . . . his Business called him another way soe that he could not well attend the Hall.

Att this Assembly Mr. John Combes the Mayor elect was duely sworne into the s'd office of Mayor of the Burrough for the ensueing Yeare when he took all the other Oaths by Law required.

There is no record of a "Hall" being held seven days later as specified above, and one wonders if the summons to Wm. Leigh was merely to prove later that every attempt had been made to get him to attend. It would seem by the other excuses offered that these meetings were already regarded as somewhat farcical and not worth attending. But as the struggle for control of the Corporation developed attendances improved, and for a time were reasonably good.

At a meeting on 27th August, 1713 only the Mayor (John Combes) and three other Burgesses (Henry Holmes, William Hooke, and William Stephens) were present, but they proceeded to elect two Members of Parliament to represent Yarmouth. Those elected were Henry Holmes and Sir Gilbert Dolben (of Finedon, Northampton).

At the next meeting, on 21st September, 1713, nine Burgesses were present, including three members of the opposition – Anthony Morgan, David Urry of Yarmouth, and Sir Tristram Dillington.

Robert Holmes was elected Mayor for the following year, and the Hon. John Richmond Webb, Captain and Governor of the Isle of Wight was elected and sworn a free Burgess.

At the annual meeting in the next year, on 21st September, 1714, the following were present. Robert Holmes, Mayor, David Urry of Easton. Gent, David Urry of Yarmouth. Gent, Wm. Leigh Clarke, Henry Holmes Esq, Wm. Hooke, John Combes, Wm. Bowreman, John Leigh, Sir Tristram Dillington, Wm. Stephens, and Anthony Morgan.

John Combes was elected the next Mayor and a new free Burgess was sworn in, another Henry Holmes, the son of Robert the Mayor.

In the above list of Burgesses appears William Leigh Clarke, and it seems probable that this should really read "William Leigh – Clerk", as in future lists the word "Clarke" changes its spelling and then is dropped altogether. Could this in fact be the William Leigh that all the fuss was about in 1712?

Further new Burgesses were on the way, and at the meeting in September 1714 the following were elected – John Scott Clarke, Nicholas Glegg, Edward Kebblewhite, David Worsley, Milborne Bloome, Stephen Shotter, William Coleman, and Henry Woodford. Few of these names sound like Yarmouth people, and one wonders how much the "foreigners" paid for the privilege of becoming a Burgess.

At the next meeting the struggle for power suddenly came out into the open and we see the first serious challenge to the supremacy of the Holmes family.

21st September 1715.

Assembled – Mr. John Combes, Mayor
Henry Holmes Esq
Wm. Hooke. Gent
Anthony Morgan Esq
Rob't Holmes. Gent
Wm. Bowreman Esq
David Urry. Gent
John Leigh Esq
Mr. Wm. Leigh. Clerke
Sir Tristram Dillington – objected against
Wm. Stephens Esq

At this Assembly John Leigh Esq, Wm. Hooke. Gent, Wm. Leigh. Clerke, David Urry. Gent, and Sir Tristram Dillington offered to sett up and vote Anthony Morgan Esq to be Mayor of this Burrough for the yeare ensueing. But Mr. Combes the Mayor together with Mr. Henry Holmes, Mr. Rob't Holmes, Mr. Wm. Bowreman and Mr. Wm. Stephens cheife Burgesses of this Burrough objected against Sir Tristram Dillington being legally chosen a cheife Burgess of this Burrough (the majority of the Corporation not being p'sent in the Hall at the time of his Admittance) after wh'ch Mr. Combes the Mayor, Mr. Henry Holmes, Mr.

Rob't Holmes, and Mr. Wm. Bowreman (all the other cheife Burgesses (except Mr. Stephens) having left the Hall) chose the said William Stephens Esq one of the cheife Burgesses of this Burrough to serve the Office of Mayor of the same for the Yeare ensueing.

There was obviously a row at this meeting, causing Anthony Morgan and his supporters to walk out. But five days later they were back again.

26th September 1715.

Assembled – Mr. John Combes Mayor
Henry Holmes Esq
Wm Hooke Gent
Anthony Morgan Esq
Rob't Holmes Gent
Wm Bowreman Esq
David Urry Gent
John Leigh Esq
Wm Leigh Clerke
Sir Tristram Dillington – objected ag'st
Wm Stephens Esq

Att this Assembly Anthony Morgan Esq one of the cheife Burgesses of this Burrough demanded and offered himself to be sworne Mayor of this Burrough for the Yeare ensueing. But Mr. John Combes the Mayor declared that Wm Stephens Esq was duly elected Mayor and the s'd Wm Stephens was accordingly sworne Mayor of the s'd Burrough for the Yeare ensueing after having taken the Oaths by Law required.

It would seem that Combes was quite wrong in pushing the election of Stephens as Mayor when there were only four chief Burgesses present. A by-law of 1670 specified the quorum to be five, and though this law was subsequently repealed it was in force at the time. However, it does not look as though Stephens enjoyed the position of Mayor for very long for within a few months Morgan was back again with the law on his side, and won the day.

14th January 1716.

Assembled – John Combes Mayor
Mr. William Hooke
Capt David Urry

At this Assembly Anthony Morgan Esq was sworn Mayor for the remaining part of the Year pursuant to a "peramtory Mandamus" out of his Ma'ties Court of Kings Bench and took all the Oaths appointed by Law for that purpose.

At the next meeting, on 30th January, 1716, the first one under the new Mayor Anthony Morgan, and not attended by any of those who had opposed him, Sir Tristram Dillington said he had been elected a chief Burgess in 1708 but there had been a dispute about the legality of his election. Consequently he would like to take the oath of office again, so that there should be no argument in future, and this was accordingly done.

Also at this meeting Thomas Morgan was elected a chief Burgess in the place of Col. David Urry, deceased. Also on the same date the following were made free Burgesses. Capt. Benjamin Newland, Mr. Edward Eversley, Capt. William Jolliffe, Mr. John Grimes, Mr. Walter Urry, Mr. Maurice Morgan, Mr. Wm. Hooke Jnr, and Mr. John Urry. Some of these were the men declared illegally elected on 9th October, 1710. In other words Morgan and Dillington and their friends were now completely in control of the Corporation.

21st September, 1716. Thomas Morgan was elected Mayor for 1717.

1st October, 1716. More elections of free Burgesses took place, presumably to strengthen still further the Morgan faction – Thomas Ridge, Esq., Henry Stamford, Esq., Mr. John White, Mr. John Kind, Mr. Thos. Terrell, Mr. Richard Taylor, Mr. Charles Morgan, Mr. Robert Morgan, Mr. Robert Terrell, Mr. James Salter, Mr. Robert Eyre, Mr. Peter Baker, Mr. John Bull, Mr. Richard Temple, Mr. Edward Stockman, Mr. John Mingham (the Common Clerk and Steward) and Mr. Thomas Urry.

How many of these were Yarmouth men?

21st September, 1717. Sir Tristram Dillington was elected Mayor.

21st September, 1718. Anthony Morgan was elected Mayor.

21st September, 1719. William Hooke was elected Mayor.

21st September, 1720. Capt. David Urry was elected Mayor.

10th February, 1721. William Plummer Esq. was elected M.P. in place of Sir Theodore Jansen who had been expelled from the House of Commons.

21st September, 1721. Thomas Morgan was elected Mayor.

26th October, 1721. Capt. Maurice Morgan was elected a chief Burgess. Also more free Burgesses were elected – Mr. John Blake, Mr. Thomas Loader, Mr. Thomas Grimes, Mr. Newland Reynolds,

Mr. Samuel Mitchell, Mr. John Read, Mr. James Blake, Capt. James Farrell, Capt. Morgan Calhan, Mr. George Oglander. Also Robert Henley, Esq., Henry Knowles, Esq., George Trenchard, Esq. and Mr. Anthony Morgan.

This is the first time that the name Blake occurs in the Yarmouth records, a name that was to feature very prominently in the Town's history in the years to come.

24th March, 1721. Edward Worsley, Esq. elected a chief Burgess. Maurice Morgan elected Mayor.

21st September, 1723. Edward Worsley was elected Mayor.

21st September, 1724. Thomas Morgan was elected Mayor.

10th April, 1725. Maurice Morgan was elected M.P. in place of Thomas Stanwix, deceased.

And so it went on, each taking it in turn to be Mayor. William Hooke in 1726, Maurice Morgan in 1727 and 1728, David Urry 1729, Thomas Morgan 1730, Maurice Morgan 1731. In 1732 a Court of Common Council was held to consider the case of William Stephens who had not attended a Court since 1715. He was solemnly "disburgessed".

21st September, 1732. The Holmes faction at last hit back, but it does not seem to have been a very powerful blow.

> **Burg' de Yarmouth.**
> We the underwritten do hereby protest against all Elections of any Chief Burgesse or Chiefe Burgesses of this Corporation made since the 21 of September 1731 contrary to the Charter granted to the said Borough for the Government thereof – and alsoe against all other illegal proceedings in the said Burrough whatsover and do demand that this be entered in the Town Book used for the like purposes dat. Sept. 21st 1732.
>
> Hen. Holmes
> Wm. Hooke
> Jo. Leigh
> Wm. Leigh

This was their reply to the meeting on 3rd June, 1732 when William Stephens was disburgessed and a Maurice Bocland was elected a free Burgess – "and immediately after the sayd Maurice Bocland was sworn such free Burgess he the sayd Maurice Bocland and also Charles Morgan Gent, Robert Morgan, Esq., and Anthony Morgan Gent" were made chief Burgesses. At this meeting only the

Mayor and three others were present, so that the elections were certainly not legal.

The reply to this was a Court of Common Council held on 1st January, 1733 which confirmed the elections made on 3rd June, 1732. The Burgesses present on this occasion were Thomas Morgan Mayor, Will Bowreman, David Urry, Maurice Morgan, Charles Morgan, Robert Morgan, Maurice Bocland and Anthony Morgan.

For several years that followed David Urry and Thomas Morgan shared the Mayoralty between them, until in 1741 the old feud seems to have lost its fire and a meeting decided that many of the elections in the past had in fact been illegal, and a large number of Burgesses – both free and chief – were discharged. Thomas Morgan was Mayor at the time but John and William Leigh came back into the picture, as did Col. Henry Holmes – the latter being chosen Mayor for 1742, Barnabas Leigh 1743, Henry Holmes 1744, Thomas Holmes 1745, Henry Holmes 1746, Maurice Bocland 1747, Henry Holmes 1748, John Leigh 1749, Maurice Bocland 1750, Thomas Holmes 1751, Henry Holmes 1752, Charles Holmes 1753, John Leigh 1754.

This struggle could well be called the Holmes-Morgan Feud as it seems that these were the two principal families involved – in one sense somewhat similar to the Montagues and Capulets. It is odd too that in the Church there are two Chapels, on the South side the Holmes Chapel, and on the North side the Lady Chapel, the only monument in which is to Elizabeth Morgan, daughter of Anthony Morgan.

In 1754 the Mayor (John Leigh) and Burgesses were required to elect two of their number to serve in Parliament, and I quote in full the record of the Meeting since this rigmarole was a standard form and was repeated word for word – with only the names changed – at similar meetings over a period of many years.

Borough of Yarmouth.

At a Meeting of the Mayor and Burgesses of the Borough aforesaid the 19th day of April 1754 by Virtue of a Precept from Sir Thomas Heathcote Baronet Sheriff of the County of Southampton bearing date the 10th day of this Instant April directed to the said Mayor for the electing two Burgesses to serve in Parliament for the said Borough in his Majesty's Parliament Ordained to be holden at Westminster on the 31st day of May next (Proclamation being first made)

John Leigh Esq Mayor of the said Borough took and subscribed the following Oath pursuant to the Act of Parliament in that Case made and provided.
I John Leigh do solemnly swear that I have not directly nor indirectly received any Sum or Sums of Money Office place or Employment Gratuity or reward or any Bond Bill or Note or any Promise or Gratuity whatsoever either by myself or any other Person to my Use or benefit or advantage for making any return at the present Election of Members to serve in Parliament And that I will return such Person or Persons as shall to the best of my Judgement appear to me to have the Majority of legal Votes.

In the presence of	John Leigh Mayor
James Blake	
Chas Holmes	

The Mayor and Burgesses of the Borough aforesaid being assembled and met in the Town Hall of the said Borough pursuant to the direction of the said Precept which together with the late Act of Parliament Intitled "an Act for the preventing Bribery and Corruption in the Election of Members to serve in Parliament" was publickly read and the Mayor of the said Borough having openly and publickly taken and subscribed the s'd Oath The s'd Mayor and Burgesses of the said Borough then and there assembled as aforesaid unanimously elected Thomas Holmes Esq and Henry Holmes Esq two of the Burgesses of this Borough to serve as Burgesses for the said Borough in the ensuing Parliament

John Leigh Mayor	Edward Clarke
Henry Holmes	Jos Squire
James Blake	David Doudney
Thos Holmes	Tim'y Heath
Chas Holmes	Rob't Clarke
Rob't Warner	John Woodford
James Heath	Thos Woodford
Wm. Hooke	John Harris
Thos Grimes	Wm. Mearman
John Read	Ephraim Smith
Geo. Oglander	Hen. Devenish
Jno Morgan	John Plumley

Thos Bowreman	John Eames
Jno Dowdney	Thos Troughear
	Benj. Leigh

From this and other meetings being held at this time it certainly looks as though the wheel had turned full circle, and that the Holmes family had re-established their supremacy. Henry Holmes was elected Mayor for 1755, Thomas Holmes 1756, John Leigh 1757, Thomas Holmes 1758, Benjamin Leigh 1759, John Leigh 1760, Thomas Grimes 1761, Thomas Lord Holmes 1762, Benjamin Leigh 1763, Thomas Lord Holmes 1764.

Sometime between April 7th and September 21st, 1760 Thomas Holmes, Esq. became Thomas Lord Holmes, and Col. Henry Holmes became Lieut. General Holmes, but there is no reference in these Proceedings to either of these promotions. Nor is there any reference to the fact that Thomas Lord Holmes rebuilt the Town Hall in 1762 or 1763 in the Mayoralty of Benjamin Leigh – as witness the plaque on the Town Hall announcing this.

Irregularities in elections still continued, as for example in 1762 when Thomas Lord Holmes was Mayor and at an Assembly Benjamin Leigh was chosen as the man to succeed him. At this Assembly there were only the two of them present, as also at a further meeting a week later to swear him in.

Matters came to a head again in 1769 when there were two rival candidates for Mayor – John Leigh and Benjamin Leigh. On this occasion there were objections and counter objections to the legality of election of various Burgesses in the past, and wrangling went on for some time. In September 1770 the Common Council repealed the old By-Law of 1670 specifying the Mayor plus five Chief Burgesses to constitute a legal quorum at elections, and substituted for this the Mayor and a majority of the Chief Burgesses existing at the time.

Records of the Proceedings of the Corporation became longer and more involved, but very seldom did they record any practical business done on behalf of the Town, confining themselves almost exclusively to the election of Burgesses, Mayors and Members of Parliament.

In connection with the latter it is interesting to note that a Mr. Jervoise Clarke of Hanover Square, London, who was a chief Burgess, was elected to represent Yarmouth in Parliament in October 1774 and continued to do so until 1780. He was a regular attender at Corporation meetings, his name being given as Jervoise Clarke,

Esq. up until September 1777 when it suddenly changes to Jervoise Clarke Jervoise, Esq. No explanation is given. This is the man who subsequently was the contact with Lieut. Crooke.

An innovation at the Assembly held on 21st September, 1781 was the granting of a Lease to John Urry of Brambles Orchard "containing by Estimation One place of ground bounded with the highway on the East with the Town field on the South and on the West and North with the lands belonging to the said John Urry". The highway mentioned is now Basketts Lane, and the Town field stretched southwards from, and included, what is now Tennyson Road. John Urry lived at the Refuge, now known as the Towers, and the Lands referred to comprised practically all the then fields bounded by Tennyson Road, South Street, the High Street and Basketts Lane.

Another Lease was granted to Capt. John Moore of a small piece of land called Roaches situated on the north side of the High Street. This lease was for 21 years at 5/- per annum.

Also a Lease was granted to Joseph Squire of three Places of Land lying at the East side of the Town Field, and of four other Places of Land called the Long Ground bounded on the West with the Town field, on the East with the land of Mrs. Jane Urry, on the North with the Highway, and on the south with the Road called the Mayors Butt. This lease was for 21 years at £3 per annum.

In September 1784 Stephen Squire was elected Sergeant-at-Mace in place of his father Stephen Squire who had died, and a year later it was his duty to serve the Demand in Writing on Lieut. Charles Cunningham Crooke for the return of the Box of Papers taken away by him from the George Inn after dinner one October evening in 1784. The official account of this incident, and the steps taken to recover the Corporation's property, is given in the Corporation Proceedings, as follow:

> Whereas at his Majesty's Court Leet held for this Borough on the eighteenth day of October 1784 the Box containing the Papers Writings and Records of this Corporation was taken from the Guildhall to the George Inn in this Town by the Town Clerk for the purpose of Receiving the Presentments of the Jury and Lieutenant Charles Cunningham Crooke commanding his Majesty's Cutter the Expedition then lying in Yarmouth Road having dined with the Corporation the Box was in the evening of the same day taken by Mistake with other Baggage on board the said Cutter, and Mr. Crooke having thus obtained Possession

of it converted it to his own use and demand being made thereof pursuant to the Resolution made at said Assembly held the 21st day of September 1785 and he neglecting or refusing to give up the same an Action of Trover was commenced against him but previous to the Proceeding in such Action a Bill of Discovery was by advice of Counsel filed in the Court of Chancery against said Crooke to which Def't put in an insufficient Answer. An amended Bill was therefore filed and Defendants further Answer obtained in which he admitted such facts as were thought sufficient to proceed with safely in the suit at Law. Declaration was then filed and the Damages laid at Ten Thousand Pounds. To this Declaration Defendant did not plead but suffered Judgement to go against him by Default. A Writ of Enquiry was in Consequence executed at the George Inn in Winchester on Thursday the 19th day of July last before the Sheriff who impannelled a very respectable Jury under an Order of one of the Judges obtained for that purpose. And the Jury after hearing the Case very ably stated by Joseph Jekyll Esq and Nathaniel Bond Esq who were of Counsel for the Corporation and having heard both Defendant's Answer fully read and the other Evidence produced upon the Occasion assessed Damages at Five Hundred Pounds.

The above is dated September 1787 and it is virtually the last entry in the book donated to the Corporation by Jervoise Clarke Jervoise. In the 75 years of meetings which it records, only on rare occasions have the Corporation thought fit to discuss any business connected with the welfare of Yarmouth, so intent were they in preserving their own position and keeping out undesirables. In this they were successful, but at the expense of the Town, and their behaviour led ultimately and inevitably to the loss of their municipal powers.

CHAPTER VI

The Rotten Borough

Until the advent of the Reform Bill of 1832 parliamentary representation in England was far from being democratic. The generally accepted system employed was for the County Sheriff to receive a writ instructing him to obtain representatives from such boroughs as he thought fit. The Sheriff would then pass on these instructions to the Mayor and Burgesses of each Borough requiring them to send two representatives to Parliament on a certain date.

This was not a popular command, since it involved the Borough or the representatives in expense, and also it was felt – with some justification – that the effort of attending was hardly worth the trouble. Most of the business to be transacted had already been decided upon beforehand, the assembly merely being arequired to put their rubber stamp on the proceedings. Also, representatives from country districts were likely to feel completely out of their element in the sophisticated quasi-legal atmosphere of Westminster.

Many Boroughs therefore petitioned for exemption from the obligation. In 1329 Sir Robert Lisle of Newport, who petitioned for exemption, was excused attendance at parliaments and juries for his whole lifetime. It was also quite usual for Sheriffs to return the writ saying "There are no citizens or burgesses of . . . able to attend this parliament; they are neither used nor ought to be required to come on account of their Poverty".

Under such a system it was natural that representation was haphazard and inefficient. It was also natural that it fell into the hands of men whose only qualification was that they had the time and the money necessary to take them to London, and keep them there during the life of the Parliament.

Writing of the Parliament summoned by Elizabeth I in 1584 (in which Yarmouth's representation was increased from one to two) Albin says:

"In 1585 almost all the boroughs that obtained this revised

or newly conferred privilege of representation, were either in the hands of the Crown, or in those of men of influence and power dependent on the Court. Gentlemen of family and fortune, who were able to bear their own expenses in attending the parliament, were now also for the most part elected everywhere".

In a previous chapter the Parliament of 1601 is mentioned. Two representatives from Yarmouth were called for, and the Mayor and Burgesses received the following letter from Lord Hunsdon, Lord Chamberlain to Queen Elizabeth, and Governor of the Isle of Wight:

"To my verie loving Freindes the Maior and Burgesses of Yarmouth.

After my verie hastie commendations. – Whereas her Majestie is purposed, for certaine urgent and greate Affayres of her Kingdome and Commonwealth to summon a Parliament, for the better service whereof you are to send twoe Burgesses to that Assemblie, theire to attende untill that Court shall be dissolved; these shall be to desire you, that inasmuch as I was the Means and Procurer of the Libertie for your Corporation, you will, with all the Convenience you may, assemble yourselfs together, and, with your united Consent, send up unto me (as heretofore you have done) your Wrytt, with a Blank, wherein I may insert the Names of such Persons as I shall think fittest to discharge that Dewtie for your Behoofe, whom I shall take Care shall likewise free you of whatsoever shall be dewe by you for the Place, which I desire may be don with all expedicion after your Receipt of the Wrytt. Whereto not doubting you will have all dewe Regard, I bidd you very heartily farewell.

From my Howse in Blackfryers, the 20th of September 1601.

Your verie loving Freinde
G. HUNSDON"

Lord Hunsdon was previously Sir George Carey, who gave his name to Carey's Sconce, the fortification he erected on the Norton side of the River Yar. In the letter quoted above the Mayor and Burgesses must have derived great comfort from his assurance that representation in this Parliament was not going to cost them anything.

Another Governor of the Island, Lord Cutts, later incensed the Islanders by the high-handed and arbitrary way in which he execrcised his authority, and caused a number of the "gentlemen of the Island" to send a strongly worded petition to the House of Commons. This resulted in an agreement being signed between the Governor and the leaders of the gentlemen, detailing:

> "a reall, sincere, mutuall, and lasting Friendship between the Governour and Gentlemen of the said Isle . . . That all Quarrels, Lawsuits, Animositys, and the like, relating to Corporations and Elections, that have at any Time hapen'd between them, their Dependants and Servants, shall, ipso facto, cease, and be absolutely forgotten, as if they had never been".

Apparently this friendship did not last very long as in 1717 the House of Commons was being asked to adjudicate on the vexed question of choosing candidates in Yarmouth. This was at a time when a struggle for power was going on in the Borough of Yarmouth between the Holmes family and the Morgan family. (See page 42). An argument had been raging over the legality of the election of certain Burgesses, and in the end the House of Commons pronounced judgement on the bye-law in question:

> **"11th April 1717.** That the bye-law made 21 Sept. 1670 by the Mayor and 5 Chief burgesses of Yarmouth, being the major part of the chief burgesses then existing, for electing free burgesses by the Mayor and 5 chief burgesses, was a good bye-law".

As a result of this dictum Sir Theodore Jansson Bart, and Anthony Morgan, Esq. were declared by the House of Commons to be duly elected members of Parliament, in the room of Sir Robert Raymond and Henry Holmes Esq.

Again in 1769, the House of Commons was asked to decide on the legality of certain elections, and came up with the following resolutions:

> "That Thomas Grimes Esq being elected a chief burgess during the pretended mayoralty of John Leigh Esq whom the house resolved was not legally elected a chief burgess of the said borough, and was therefore incapable of being elected mayor of the said borough on 21 September 1765.
> That the Rev Dr. Walker and the Rev Mr. John Oglander, being elected chief burgesses during the pretended mayoralty

of the said Thomas Grimes, were not legal chief burgesses of the said borough.

That the election of the 25 free burgesses, objected to by the counsel for the petitioners, elected during the present mayoralty of the said Thomas Grimes Esq at an assembly, in which the said Dr. Walker and Mr. Oglander attended, and voted as two of the five chief burgesses in the election of the said twenty five burgesses, was illegal and void".

In this year (1769) the House of Commons again rejected the two appointed members of Parliament (Jervoise Clark Jervoise and William Stroude) in favour of two from the opposite faction (the Hon. George Lane Parker and Thomas Dummer).

Yarmouth was well on its way to becoming a really rotten borough, and 20 years later the situation was possibly even worse. Two reports were issued, the first one of which said:

"The only resident burgess of this town is a barber and slop seller".

The second report went even further:

"The town is without a single resident burgess, but that one gentleman, Mr. Devenish, thus dignified, retiring from business, intends to relieve so grievous a reflection. After obtaining a very large fortune from fifty years well-conducted agriculture in the fields of Thorley, he seeks his repose of life in this healthy town; – and by his munificent disposition, to diffuse blessings on the neighbourhood".

The gentleman here mentioned was Henry Devenish of Thorley who married Mary Shotter the younger on 26th January, 1737 at St. Swithun's Church, Thorley. He was Mayor of Newtown in 1773 and died in December 1796, being buried in Thorley under the description of Henry Devenish of Yarmouth. One of his daughters married (by licence) Benjamin Leigh of Thorley, in January 1772.

Albin is very forthright in his opinions about the situation.

Writing in 1795 he says:

"Yarmouth contains about 50 houses, cottages included. The right of election is in the capital and free burgesses. The capital burgesses are chosen from the free burgesses which are unlimited by the constitution of the borough, but at present there are only nine.

Mr. Holmes and Mr. Jervois Clarke Jervois have each their

friends and dependants as burgesses, and by mutual compact have agreed that each shall nominate one of the two members. The capital burgesses are equally divided between the two parties.

These free burgesses are of old standing, and will not be made capital. Formerly there were many (the number being unlimited) but in the year 1756, after a dispute between Mr. Holmes and Mr. Jervois, and the Leigh family of North Court in the island (of which Mr. Jervois's lady was a part) a compromise took place, by which it was stipulated that a great number of free burgesses, then newly made, should be disfranchised, which was accordingly done; that each party should thenceforth name one Member; and to keep the interests even, whenever a capital burgess should die, the side to which he belonged should immediately nominate another person to be a free burgess, and then made capital, as the charter prescribes".

Albin's final comment is also very much to the point:

"It is plain that the four members of Newport and Yarmouth are returned by only two persons; three by Mr. Holmes, with the minister's assistance, and one by Mr. Jervois. The members for Newtown are chosen at present by four persons; in all six members by six electors only; and this small body may be further diminished by an union of interests in the borough of Newtown, between the Worsley family and Mr. Holmes; in which case four men would return six persons to represent them in parliament. If this unadorned recital does not impress on the mind the fullest conviction of the absolute necessity of some reform in the representation, it is surely fair to conclude that the utmost power of reason and eloquence would be exerted in vain".

From the above it would seem that Mr. Holmes had also acquired the right to nominate the two Newport members of parliament as well, which is an indication of the immense power wielded by this influential Yarmouth family. In 1760 plain "Mr" Holmes became Thomas Lord Holmes, this being the first peerage achieved by the family.

It was another 40 years before the Reform Act took the necessary steps to correct some of the abuses of which Albin wrote, but when it did become law its provisions were revolutionary. Sixty boroughs, not having a population of 2,000, were to be totally disfranchised, and 46 boroughs, having a population of not more than 4,000. and returning two members each, were to be deprived of one. Sir Archibald Alison, a political commentator, said:

> "No words can convey an adequate idea of the astonishment which the announcement of this project of Reform created in the House of Commons and the Country. Nothing approaching to it had ever been witnessed before, or has been since. Men's minds were prepared for a change, perhaps a very considerable one, especially in the enfranchising of new cities and towns which were unrepresented; but it never entered into the imagination of any human being out of the Cabinet that so sweeping and entire a change would be proposed, especially by the King's Ministers".

Once the House had recovered from its surprise the Bill had a comparatively easy passage through the first reading, which was passed without a division. The Vote on the second reading however, produced a majority of only one, and the Government felt that on such a major and controversial issue this was insufficient to enable them to proceed, and so they decided to go to the Country.

The new Parliament met in June 1831; and this time the second reading of the Bill was passed with a majority of 136. The third reading had a majority of 109, but it was then thrown out by the Lords. By this time the country was in a ferment of excitement, and the failure of the Bill resulted in civil disturbances and rioting in various places.

The Government persevered however, and ultimately sent the Bill to the Lords for the second time. The debates here were long and acrimonious, and it was only finally passed after a threat had been made that if necessary a sufficient number of new peers would be created to swamp the Opposition. Feeling ran very high in the country, and for a time there was a distinct threat of Civil War. The King (William IV), though he gave his Royal Assent to the Bill, is said to have been so hurt by the coercion to which he had been subjected, and by the insults heaped upon himself, the queen, and all belonging to him, that nothing could persuade him to go to the House and give his Assent in person.

The Bill became law, but it was nearly another 60 years before the axe finally fell on Yarmouth. In the meantime other incidents occurred which served to emphasise that all was not well with the Borough of Yarmouth.

In 1859 complaints were received that the Mayor and Corporation were guilty of selling, or even giving away, town lands and property to private individuals. In March 1876 a public attack on Yarmouth was made in the House of Commons by Sir Charles Dilke (See page 134), and shortly afterwards a Commission of Enquiry, known as the Municipal Corporations Commission was set up. The results of this Enquiry were published in 1880, when it was found that the charges made were true in substance, as a result of which Yarmouth was declared to be one of the "Rotten Boroughs".

While these momentous events were taking place, the Mayor and Corporation of Yarmouth were solemnly discussing the inadequacy of the town drains, and the illegal tethering of goats on the Common! (See page 137).

CHAPTER VII

Sir Robert Holmes

In Yarmouth little is now remembered of Sir Robert Holmes, the town's most celebrated "Overner", apart from his statue in the Church, and the brief and slightly inaccurate inscription underneath it. The inaccuracies may exist in the original Latin, or in the translation, but the inscription ascribes to him virtues that he possibly did not possess, and omits to mention many characteristics which were an essential part of the personality of this remarkable man.

On the other hand Sir Robert Holmes has been described by a modern historian as "swaggering, roystering and corrupt, and exactly the kind of courtier – officer whose indiscipline was to be the curse of the Restoration Navy . . . a man who though dashingly courageous, was hopelessly irresponsible!" This appellation is almost equally as inaccurate as the other and was probably based on the writings of Holmes' contemporaries such as Pepys and Sir William Coventry, men who themselves were far from being angels, and with whom Holmes did not see eye to eye.

What was the truth then about this man whose career reads like the script of an Errol Flynn film, who amassed a large fortune, and who retired and spent the last twenty five years of his life in Yarmouth as Governor of the Isle of Wight?

Robert Holmes' grandfather was an English gentleman and an officer in Queen Elizabeth's Irish wars, who settled in Mallow, County Cork, becoming Provost of that town in 1612. His children included a son, Henry, who in his turn had four sons, the third of which was born in 1622 and named Robert after his grandfather. Young Robert's early years are a mystery, though he obviously received a good education, and he first attracted attention as a young and dashing officer in the Royalist Army during the Civil War. In the battle of Roundway Down he rescued his commanding officer, Captain Richard Atkyns, from a tight corner, and in his report of the battle this officer gives us a clue to Holmes' character when he writes "In the nick of time came up Mr. Holmes to my assistance (who never failed me in times of danger) . . ."

Robert Holmes' career in the Royalist Army came to an end with the surrender of Oxford in 1646. The dashing commander of the Royalist Cavalry, Prince Rupert, was given permission to go overseas, and he and his followers, including the twenty four year old Robert, went to France where they became involved in the tail end of the 30 years war, and fought against Spain. Robert left England with the rank of Major; several war wounds which already were beginning to affect his health; and having formed an abiding friendship with Prince Rupert which lasted for the rest of his life.

In 1648 part of the English Fleet revolted and sailed for Holland, Rupert and his entourage joining up with them in July. Ultimately Rupert was made Commander in Chief, and carried on a guerilla warfare against the Parliamentary Forces from his base in Holland. And so young Robert Holmes became a sailor.

In 1649 Rupert's Fleet of twelve ships had for one reason or another dwindled to seven and it was decided to seek a new base in Kinsale, the objects of the move being firstly to keep the remnants of the Fleet together, and secondly to make money in order to meet the necessities of the Exiled Court. In October of this year another move was made, this time to Portugal, Kinsale having proved unsuitable.

Exactly a year later political pressure from England forced them to move on again, and the Fleet, now reduced to six ships, sailed for the Mediterranean. During all this time their only revenue came from the ships they piratically captured on the high seas, and during all this time too their own ships were steadily growing older and leakier. After many ups and downs in the Mediterranean a Fleet of five ships set sail in the summer of 1651 for the West Indies, arriving in the Azores in July. Their troubles continued, Rupert's own ship being sunk in a storm with the loss of 350 men, and another ship wrecked. In December, 1651 they sailed for the Canaries, and after a short stay put into a natural harbour on the African coast for careening and repairs in preparation for the Atlantic crossing. Holmes was twenty nine years old and Rupert thirty two.

Before leaving Africa Rupert decided to investigate the fabulous Gold Coast and after many adventures – in one of which Holmes was captured by natives and very nearly lost his life – they sailed for the West Indies in May 1652, Holmes in Command of the "John", a small coastwise trading vessel, recently captured. The crossing was achieved without incident, the fleet anchoring off St. Lucia on May 29th. Much work needed to be done on the ships, none of which was really seaworthy any longer. Four only were retained, the others being stripped of any serviceable gear, then burned.

In August the little Fleet of four vessels was back at sea, but in September disaster overcame them in the shape of a hurricane which sank three of their company with the loss of their crews, including Rupert's younger brother Maurice. It became obvious that the expedition was nearing the end of its natural life, and consequently after one final cruise, in which they were lucky enough to capture several ships, they set sail for Europe, arriving off the mouth of the Loire in March 1653. Rupert immediately left for Paris, leaving Holmes in charge to wind up the expedition.

Robert Holmes then disappears from the records until the Restoration in 1660. It is possible, however, that he travelled in Europe with Prince Rupert and may even have seen service in Germany and Austria, for Rupert was certainly living in Vienna when Charles II came back to England.

With the restoration of the monarchy a new career opened up for Robert Holmes. In May 1660 he was appointed to command the Medway Guardship "Bramble". Several promotions came his way in quick succession and in the autumn he was appointed Captain of the "Henrietta", and leader of a squadron bound for West Africa. This was obviously a big step forward and his appointment may have been influenced by Prince Rupert who had returned from Vienna. At the same time he was appointed Captain and Commander of Sandown Castle – his first connection with the Isle of Wight – as a reward for previous service.

The object of the West African trip was primarily to acquire gold – plus a little trading and slave traffic. A Company was formed, known as the Royal African Company, and many individual members went with the expedition. Holmes was a natural choice as leader since he knew the Gold Coast from his visit there in 1652, and his experience as a rebel commander under Prince Rupert was also likely to be useful because there would almost certainly be trouble with the Dutch, whose traders were already well established on the coast. In the event his piratical activities towards the Dutch, both on the high seas, and on land – where he arbitrarily confiscated their Trading Posts – led to violent complaints from the Dutch, and ultimately to war between the two countries.

The mouth of the Gambia river is protected by an island, hitherto known as Dog Island, and Holmes' first action on arriving was to re-christen it Charles Island and to commence building a fort. He was at pains to fraternise with the natives, and accepted an invitation to visit the local king who resided about ten miles inland. Some idea of the difficulties involved and the conditions under which they were operating is given by Holmes himself in the following extract from his journal:

> "Wednesday, March 13th. This day I went ashore with Captain Stokes (of the "Amity") and divers others to see the watering place at Combo and to visit the King of that place with 2 boats of armed men along with us for our Guard in case the Blacks should prove false to us. The King living ten miles up in the country we walked up thither where I was very civilly received by that King after their manner.
>
> It was a very hot day, no breath of wind stirring. The King accommodated me with the only horse that was there to be had, but being young and strong and Captain Stokes old, fat and burly, I let him ride and I walked, which was one of the hardest tasks that I ever undertook, the sun shining so very hot, and all our way upon dry sand it was so very hot that our Chirurgeon's mate (whom I took along with me for fear of any accident) not able to walk and keep us company fell down dead upon the way, and so did a greyhound I had with me; nay one Mr. Fowler, a Factor, walking along with me carrying a gun upon his shoulder the excessive heat of the sun fired it off upon his shoulder, which I would not have believed if I had not taken the gun in my hand and felt the heat of it and found the cock stand at the half bent.
>
> When I went ashore I gave orders to all the officers of the ships that they should fire no guns, except they saw some ships coming into the river; then to fire several guns to give me notice that I might make the more haste on board. After my tedious hot march in the morning I was not sat above one quarter of an hour by his Majesty who had sent for some palm wine for me and my company to drink, but the guns began to fire on board the ships, which when I heard I scarce took leave of his Majesty but flung out of his doors and marched towards my boats as hard as I could go, leaving my horse with Captain Stokes. It was in the very heat of the day that I began to march with five or six and twenty men with me. The rest came with Captain

Stokes who could not endure the heat but put himself in the wood under the shadow of the trees till the cool of the evening. And my Cockswaine fell down 2 or 3 times, but the poor fellow having a great kindness for me did endeavour to get to the boats as soon as I did. All the rest of my company left upon the ground gasping for breath, when I got to the boats I ordered my pinnace to row me on board, and the rest of the boats to stay for those that were left behind.

I got on board early that afternoon. Presently at my arrival on board I called the officers of the ship to know the reason of the firing of the guns. They told me they could not tell; that they were fired on board Captain Stokes's ship. I ordered the Gunner of that ship to be sent for. When come on board I asked him whether he had not orders from his Captain not to fire any guns unless they saw a Fleet of Ships coming into the river. (He answered) that his Captain has said nothing and the occasion of his firing was that they has struck 10 or 11 of their guns at Gravesend which they hoysed up and mounted yesterday and seated them this day. Now I did heartily repent me of letting Stokes have the horse for I was so angry with him that I would have been well contented to have seen him hanged. I was 3 or 4 days so dazed in my head that I thought I should never have recovered".

The above account, besides reciting the details of the incident, tells us much about the character of the writer. To march ten miles inland in the heat of the day in those latitudes shows a considerable degree of toughness, and to turn round almost immediately and march back demonstrates courage and resolution of a high order. It also confirms the adage about mad dogs and Englishmen. But tough and determined though he was, Holmes was humane and compassionate enough to surrender his horse to an older man.

Financially this first expedition of the Royal Company to Africa was a failure. On his return to England in July 1661 the books showed an income of £1,567 against expenses of over £4,000. On paper Holmes appears to have fared equally badly as he was deprived of his pay for exceeding the complement authorised for the voyage, but as from then onwards he openly lived a fashionable life of some extravagence it can be inferred that he had managed in some way to protect his own interests. Pepys found Holmes' life style somewhat alarming, and his diary entry for 22nd December, 1661 throws further light onto Holmes' character.

> "My wife and I go to Church and there in the pew, with the rest of the Company, was Captain Holmes, in his gold laced suit, at which I was troubled because of the old business which he attempted upon my wife".

Pepys does not record what "the old business' was, but one can guess. Another outcome of the voyage was the vigorous protest received from the Dutch Government about Holmes' high handed action in taking over Dutch Trading Posts, and their retaliation against English ships along the West African Coast. A further debit was the high rate of mortality among the voyagers, one ship alone losing thirty eight men.

On the credit side of the balance was the undisputed fact that Holmes had proved himself to be a most capable commander, equal to every emergency, able to inspire his officers and men, and to handle not only the members of the Royal Company, but the Dutch and the Africans as well. Should another voyage ever be contemplated he was the obvious choice to lead it, and at this point in his career the glass would seem to have been at "set fair".

But Holmes found it impossible to keep out of trouble. In November 1661 he was made Captain of the "Royal Charles", the flagship that had carried Charles II to England from exile, and was now to fetch Catherine of Braganza from Lisbon, but this appointment was shortlived. In taking his ship down the Thames he met the "Drake" a 66 gun ship bringing the Swedish Ambassador to England, and failed to make him strike his sails, as courtesy demanded. For this he was summarily dismissed his ship by Charles II, who also threatened him with further punishment.

Six months later this incident had obviously been forgotten as he was appointed to another ship, and was awarded £800 – a large sum in those days – out of the balance left over after paying off Cromwell's army. Meanwhile he continued to live in luxurious style in his lodgings in Trinity House.

His new ship "Reserve", brought him no luck either, since it was the direct cause of a furious quarrel with Samuel Pepys. This was over the appointment by Pepys of one of his friends, Richard Cooper, as navigator and pilot of the ship, an appointment which Holmes found quite unacceptable, as he claimed Cooper was a drunkard and incompetent. The quarrel nearly led to a duel, the prospect of which frightened Pepys considerably, and left him with a wary dislike for Holmes, which almost certainly later on was the reason for Holmes not achieving the high Flag rank in the Navy to which he felt he was entitled.

While Captain of the "Reserve" an intriguing incident occured in Lisbon. The British Ambassador arranged for Holmes and a Col. Norwood, Deputy Governor of Tangier, to be shown the King's bulls. What transpired during the visit is not recorded, but obviously something was said or done which caused offence, for Holmes and Norwood were unceremoniously bundled out of the royal bull stables. The mind boggles at what happened, and it would have been nice to have been there.

In due course a second, and much larger, expedition to Guinea was organised, and Holmes was duly nominated its leader. Officially the object of the voyage was to protect English trade, but in reality this meant taking trade away from the Dutch, and hence there was a predictable chance of falling out with them. In fact the instructions given to Holmes almost suggest the possibility of picking a quarrel with the Dutch.

Holmes sailed from Queenborough, Kent in November 1663, and started shooting before he was even clear of the Thames Estuary. Soon after sailing he ran into thick fog and had to anchor. A Dutch pink groping her way into the river passed close to him and failed to strike her sails. In the conditions obtaining at the time anyone else might have waived the salute, but this was a sore point with Holmes who fired at her and had her master brought aboard.

Ten days later he caught up with an 800 ton Dutch East Indiaman outward bound, who also failed to strike. Holmes fired but with no result. He fired again and carried away the head of her mizzentop-mast. She still declined to strike so he opened up with two guns, on which she struck both topsails, but by this time Holmes was determined that he should be obeyed and demanded that boats be put out for a boarding party. She refused, so he fired again, and this time she complied. Holmes accepted the proferred apologies, but demanded – and received – payment for the shots expended.

Having thus established a pattern, Holmes continued as he had started and actually captured some Dutch ships before he had reached the Guinea Coast. Throughout the campaign he waged a brilliantly aggresive action, so much so that in February 1664 he was able to write home to William Coventry, who had planned and organised the expedition, saying:

"You have now all the trade in your own hands from Cape

The National Maritime Museum, London

SIR ROBERT HOLMES

Two photographs of the Harbour taken from the Church Tower. The earlier one of about 1905 shows much of the Harbour drying out at low tide. Land has since been reclaimed for roads and quays and the Harbour dredged

Yarmouth Bridge has changed little since 1867, the date of the above picture. Concrete has replaced mud and stones as the boatyard expanded

The Town Hall has not altered much since the photograph taken in 1867. Note the alterations to the corner shop, enlarged and re-roofed

The Square in 1903 has an air of peace in contrast to the present day crush of motor cars. Many of the buildings remain much the same

Mr. Jack Fryer, from a photograph about 1920

The Sand House has not changed greatly in 200 years or so. It is now Hayles Boatyard

Yarmouth Mill

"Back Lane" in 1920 contrasts with modern Tennyson Road. The two photographs were taken on almost the same spot and the houses on the left and right of the pictures are unchanged

> de Verd to the Gold Coast . . . being the most considerable trade in Christendome. I hope you will take a resolution to keepe it".

He told Coventry he was sailing for Sierra Leone, and expected to make himself master of the whole coast, adding:

> " . . . if I goe beyond my instructions I hope you and the rest of the royall Company will mediate for me".

These belligerent events led inevitably to war between England and Holland, and it was therefore natural that a scapegoat should be sought. It was not necessary to look very far, and six days after Holmes arrived back in England in January 1665 he was committed to the Tower, where he lived for a few months in considerable style. He was released in March with a full pardon, and in his honour the Lieutenant-Governor gave him a lavish banquet – attended, among others, by Pepys – to mark the occasion.

It should perhaps be recorded that the treasure brought back by the expedition had been considerable, and that Holmes himself became an extremely rich man. On his way up Channel he had taken the precaution of anchoring off Portsmouth for six days, presumably to off-load that which he considered to be rightly his.

After the war with Holland was over, William Coventry wrote a report analysing its causes and summarising the lessons to be learned. In this report he describes Holmes as:

> " . . . a man of an understanding fitt to make a warre, and a courage to make it good; in the latter few goe beyond him; in the former few came short".

Whatever the officially recorded opinion of Holmes it was clear that he was a born leader and the sort of man that men will follow without question. He possessed the three qualities of leadership that ensured the devoted loyalty of his men, namely, he was brave, he was audacious and he was successful.

When war with Holland broke out again in 1665 Holmes was in command of the "Revenge", and was part of the White Squadron under his old friend Prince Rupert. In the battle of Lowestoft, in May, he distinguished himself by his conduct. The Rear-Admiral of the squadron was killed in the engagement, and Holmes felt strongly that he should be promoted to take his place. When he was passed over, in spite of Prince Rupert recommending him, he was furious, and in an interview with the Duke of York, who was Commander in Chief, resigned his commission. It may be that this dramatic move was a bluff, and that he did not expect the Duke to accept his resignation, but accept it he did, and gave Holmes' ship to another Captain. Pepys records this in his diary entry of June 16, 1665 and refers to Holmes as a "rash, proud, coxcombe".

Suddenly then Holmes found himself without a ship, though he was not without a job. He had his appointments in the Isle of Wight – Governor of Sandown Castle, Deputy Governor of the Island, and Captain of an Independant Company of Foot, so he retired to the Island, and certainly spent the rest of that year here. A few months later the King visited the Island, but refused to see him as he had not patched up his quarrel with the Duke of York. But the estrangement did not last long. Early in the new year Holmes was appointed Captain of a new 64 gun frigate building at Deptford, and in March she was launched in the presence of the King, the Duke of York and Prince Rupert. To mark the occasion his Majesty conferred the honour of Knighthood on Captain Robert Holmes. One wonders what part Prince Rupert played in effecting the reconciliation.

This new appointment, and the honour that went with it, was the start of a new chapter in the life of Robert Holmes, another opportunity to forget the past and wipe out old mistakes, and to build his career anew. Alas, although he achieved instant success initially, and did rise to flag rank, jealousy and antagonism towards his colleagues and superiors brought it all to nought in the long run.

Immediately, however, the Dutch were roaming the North Sea, and the English set out to meet them. The four-day battle that ensued was one of the bloodiest of the war, and the English Fleet took a hammering. Holmes came out of it extremely well, and in one report was said to have "done wonders". A number of Flag Officers were killed and wounded, and Homes was promoted to Rear-Admiral of the Red, but even this failed to satisfy him as two of his colleagues and rivals were given greater preferment.

In July, on St. James's Day, the two fleets met again, and this time the English were victorious. Holmes was not able to join in the chase of the defeated Dutch as his ship was crippled, and when the Dutch fleet were allowed to escape he was fiercely critical of the conduct of the action, and particularly of his rival Sir Jeremy Smith whom he openly accused of cowardice and being afraid of running aground. This accusation did nothing to endear Holmes to his superiors, but rather endorsed Pepys' opinion of him as being a "rash, proud, coxcombe".

But it was not long before Holmes was given the opportunity to show his detractors what type of man he was, and this he did in no uncertain fashion. In August he was put in charge of a "Commando" type raid on the Dutch Islands of Vlie and Schelling, which were the base for the vast Dutch East India Trade, and where there was a large harbour and many warehouses. Holmes was given a task force of 900 men, and his instructions were simple and plain:

> "You are to seize what vessels you finde in ye Harbour, which you are to make use of in bringing away ye Booty: What are not serviceable you are to sink or burn".

This task was exactly suited to Homes' temperament and he tackled it with his customary efficiency and thoroughness. When he arrived off Vlie however, he was amazed at the number of merchant ships lying in the roads – some reports say there were 170 sail – and he realised that here was an opportunity to do much more damage to Dutch trade than by just plundering a few warehouses. It was characteristic of the man that without hesitation he modified his instructions and set about the destruction of this huge fleet and the shore establishments.

This change of plan extended his stay in this rather unfriendly part of the world from a few hours to two days, but by the time he left he had destroyed upwards of 150 ships and the chief town in the island. His own losses were twelve men killed and wounded. The damage done was estimated at the time to amount to a million pounds, and the whole action subsequently became known as "Holmes's Bonfire". News of it was received in England with acclamation, churchbells were rung, and Robert Holmes was the most popular man of the day.

Strangely enough the event never achieved the sort of notice in the history books that one would expect, and one wonders whether the antagonism of Pepys and Coventry had anything to do with this. In this connection it is interesting to note that Holmes was supplied with a renegade Dutch Captain to act as pilot into Vlie Roads, but in fact declined to use him as he did not believe him to be sufficiently knowledgeable about these waters. Instead he used the skipper of a captured Danish trading vessel who knew the coast intimately, and made a bargain with him that in return for safe pilotage his ship and cargo would not be confiscated.

In Holmes' report of the action he refers to this agreement, and hints darkly at what might follow if the promise is not kept:

> " . . . by much persuasions I got him to pilot me in, finding the Dutch Captain that undertooke it before not altogether capable. I did ingage to the Master and Steerman of this

Dane in case they should bring me in safe to the place where the Dutch Fleet lay, I would give them their shipp and goods again. It made me the bolder to promise, shee haveing nothing in her but some Deale boards and firewood; I am confident that the shipp and her ladeing at the best Market cannot be worth above six hundred pounds sterl. Since my comeing into the Fleet I find that the Deale boards are disposed of, and that what I have promised will not be made good here. I shall desire that your Lordship may take care that my promise may be performed, else (lightly crossed out but still easily legible) I shall humbly desire to be excused from going to sea any more".

The promise was kept forthwith!

Holmes was now 44 years old and at the peak of his career. Sadly, his health was by no means good, and he was to get steadily worse as he grew older, but he never allowed this to interfere with the performance of his duties. Early in 1667 he was made Commander-in-Chief of a squadron based in Portsmouth and designed to patrol the waters of the Channel. It was not long before he began to harass shipping in the Channel and bring in prizes, and if the war had continued he might well have become a serious threat to the free used of the English Channel by the Dutch and the French. But following the brilliant Dutch raid on the Medway a hurried peace was concluded and his squadron was disbanded.

In January 1668 Holmes was involved in a duel as a second to the Duke of Buckingham. In this duel Buckingham mortally wounded the Earl of Shrewsbury, and Buckingham's other second was also killed. As a result of this Holmes was lucky not be be prosecuted for murder, and the affair did not enhance his reputation.

Later that year, in September, he purchased from Lord Culpeper the Governorship of the Isle of Wight and entered into his Governorship on 28th December. Immediately and energetically he set about repairing the defences of the Island, which had been allowed to deteriorate, and brought back to strength the Castles of Carisbrooke, Cowes and Yarmouth. As Governor Holmes had many opportunities to add to his already considerable wealth by exercising the traditional rights of the Office, including the profits of justice, the rights of Admiralty, wreckage, salvage and the taking of prizes. For the next three years this comparatively peaceful existence continued, though he still spent a considerable amount of his time in London. In 1669 he became M.P. for Winchester, and in 1671 had the honour of entertaining the King "in his new house in the Isle of Wight".

It has for some time been supposed that this house is what is now the older part of The George Hotel, but an eminent architect, Mr. Percy Goddard Stone, has cast doubt on this. He wrote:

> "The house is said to have been built by Admiral Sir Robert Holmes, who mostly resided at Yarmouth, as was to be expected of a seafaring man. I think, however, that this idea is an erroneous one, and that no part of the present house, now the George Hotel, dates from that period, as nothing about it is earlier than 1700. The 17th century house referred to was probably to the North, where the present Coastguard Station now is" (written in 1891).

The Coastguard Station has of course now given way to the Ferry Terminal and a Cafe, and is actually to the west of The George.

In "A Short History of The George, Yarmouth", published privately by the hotel, the writer states:

> "The original building is "L" shaped, of stone and red brick, which is still visible on the north side and consisted of two storeys and an attic".

but whatever the truth about its date of origin there are records which show that Holmes was buying property on the site in 1679 and extending it in 1680 and 1681. At the same time (1679) he bought Thorley Farm and settled this on his only child, Mary, who was to inherit his estate.

His Yarmouth house was never his principal place of residence, although as he got older he spent more and more time in the Island. His main house was a magnificent mansion in Whitehall next to the Horse Guards, and in this he used to entertain lavishly. He also had a large house in Englefield Green, near Windsor, and another in Bath. In his later days, when gout and arthritis were taking an increasing toll of his strength, he was a frequent visitor to Bath for the waters.

In 1672 Holmes was 50, and though his health was failing he was energetic and active. He was appointed senior officer in Portsmouth and was busily engaged in bringing the ships under his command up to strength in preparation for yet another tussle with the Dutch. Ever an opportunist, and with his great flair for strategy, he saw an opportunity in January to strike a major blow at Dutch readiness for the coming struggle by capturing a fleet of 22 Dutch merchantmen carrying salt and sheltering in Cowes Roads. He claimed that the Dutch were known to be short of salt, and that to prevent supplies reaching Holland would restrict them in salting down the meat needed by their fleet, and hence delay their preparedness. But alas, the Navy Board would not listen to him. The opportunity was lost, and Holmes was left feeling even more bitter and frustrated with authority.

War broke out in March, and Prince Rupert was made Commander-in-Chief. He repeatedly asked for Holmes to be appointed to a senior position in the Fleet, and wrote letter after letter to the Navy Board. To one of these, in which he had outlined alternative plans for action, he added a postscript in his own hand:

> "If his Ma'tie will have either of them well done, he must send me Sir Robert Holmes. If there were not a necessity of this, I would not, after so many denials, press it".

But all his entreaties fell on deaf ears, and as with the priests of Baal "there was no voice, nor any that answered". The authorities had had enough of the quarrelsome Holmes who, brilliant though he was, seemed quite unable to work in harmony with his colleagues and superiors.

The effect of these further rebuffs was to make Holmes increasingly bitter and even more openly critical of others. He found it impossible to keep quiet when he saw men, whom he knew to be less talented than himself, promoted to positions he had long desired. Though he was undoubtedly a master of strategy and tactics, and as courageous as a lion, he was yet far too mercurial a character for the powers that be completely to trust.

His services to the Crown were however well rewarded, and his wealth increased accordingly. There were several gifts of money and land, and substantial fee-farm rents in Southampton, Wales and the Isle of Wight. He was Governor and Vice-Admiral of the Island, Governor and Vice-Admiral of Newport, Vice-Admiral of Hampshire, one of the perks of these appointments being that he was entitled to two-thirds of the value of all ships or goods, enemy or pretended neutral, as he should seize on the high and open seas or in the ports, havens and creeks of his Vice-Admiralty. In the times in which he lived, and to a man like Holmes, this was tantamount to a license to print money.

Of his private life little is known. There is no doubt he was a ladies man with an eye for a pretty face, as Samuel Pepys had found out, but he never married. In 1678 a daughter was born to him but the indentity of her mother is obscure. In due course Mary

Holmes inherited his vast fortune, married at the age of 15 her cousin Henry, and bore him 14 children.

In 1687 Sir Robert was offered Command of an expedition to the West Indies to suppress the buccaneers, but he never went – possibly due to his increasing arthritis and gout. His last few years were spent mainly in Yarmouth or Bath, and though physically he became almost a cripple he remained mentally vigorous and active to the end. All through the troubled times of 1688, and even when James II finally abdicated, he stoutly maintained the defences of the Isle of Wight, though under no illusions about the sympathy of the inhabitants. His loyalty to James was 100%, in spite of their previous quarrels when the King had been Duke of York.

In November the Dutch invasion fleet, bearing William of Orange to England, sailed down Channel and Holmes reported to London:

> "Part of the militia is grown mutinous already . . . the island will be lost without striking one stroke for it; God knows how I shall be dealt with by this militia I have drawn into Yarmouth and Hurst".

He continued to write frequent and full reports to Pepys, giving valuable information about the movement of the Dutch Fleet. On Sunday 6th December he wrote that food was short in Yarmouth. He had sent his senior lieutenant out to forage, and while he was out the junior lieutenant, together with the greater part of the garrison, absconded. Thus Holmes was left alone with very few men to defend Yarmouth, the townspeople generally being ready to declare for the Prince of Orange. But his spirit was undimmed and he continued to be defiant, and it was not until he learned that the King had fled the Country, and the Commander in Chief – to whom he was responsible – had led the fleet over to William's side, that he agreed to follow.

Old age and ill health continued to take an increasing toll. In July 1689 he was given permission to go to Bath to seek relief, and to stay there until September.

> "I am now soe ill of my limbs that I have not been out of my chamber these twelve daies. I want the Bath as an old horse does Grass".

In January the next year the Queen of Spain paid a State visit to England, and Holmes, though far from well, sailed to Spithead to attend her. Unfortunately this short voyage was too much for him and by the time he reached her ship the gout in his feet was so painful that he was quite unable to climb aboard. This must have been one of the saddest and most humiliating moments in the life of this doughty old warrior.

He survived for two more years, but died on 18th November, 1692. Though never receiving, in his opinion, his just desserts during his own lifetime, he left £300 to be spent on "building a compleat and decent vault and monument", so that at least he would be noticed by future generations. His white marble statue in Yarmouth Church is like its original, slighty larger than life, and the legend attributed to it, that it was intended to portray Louis XIV, until Holmes captured it and had his own head substituted, is probably untrue but is typical of his flamboyant character.

The original inscription on the statue, an inscription which was subsequently replaced by his nephew with a more fulsome eulogy, described Holmes as:

"A Professional in war and in peace a convivial companion".

Not a bad description, but really doing scant justice to a man who served his King and Country well, and who, but for the flaw in his character which caused him to fall out with those around him, might have risen to the very top.

CHAPTER VIII

The 19th Century Town

"This compact little town is situated at the mouth of the river Yar, from which it takes its name, and is the only seaport for the western part of the Isle of Wight. To it all the passenger traffic to the watering places of Freshwater, Totland and Alum Bays comes. It is a corporate town and parish in the West Medina liberty. The natural harbour it possesses might, in the future, raise it to a place of very great importance".

The above was written almost exactly 100 years ago by Mr. J. E. Richardson, Yarmouth's Chemist. He goes on to say that Yarmouth was once a place of considerable importance in the island's history, and that it still retains its old character. Its streets are fairly wide, straight and clean, and there are good shops of all classes of business. The air of Yarmouth is particularly dry and bracing, and the place is very healthy – many of its living inhabitants are verging on 100 years old.

This was the opinion of a man who had lived in the town for many years, and one who took a leading part in the life of the community. His remarks are in striking contrast to those of a writer in the Whitehall Review in 1878 who visited the town, via Lymington, and wrote–:

"Neither of these towns has, it is true, much to commend it. Lymington is a dull country place with a member of Parliament and a pretence of trade, while Yarmouth, just opposite, on the other side of the water, is as dead-alive a spot as it is possible to conceive. It is not ugly, it is not pretty – in short, it is altogether mediocre".

To be fair both to Yarmouth and the writer of the above it must be said that his opinion softened a little as he approached Yarmouth on the ferry:

"We confess that the want of social attractions in Lymington and Yarmouth trouble us as little as they do the gulls

> and cormorants. The scene is, indeed, passing fair, and has a soft beauty which is in truth far lovelier than any foreign lake, for neither Como nor Lucerne can show you the fresh green tints of yonder shores save in the very early spring".

Perhaps it was the voyage across in the steamer that made him change his mind, for of this he said:

> "The little steamer that carries us over the streak of water does her work well in half an hour, and we are reminded of the end of our voyage by the attentions of an aged lady who has beguiled the time by sundry symphonies on that bygone instrument the harp, and by certain ditties sung in a voice whereof the freshness also belongs to a remote period. As we land on the narrow and altogether diminutive pier, we hear the toll-collector proudly informing a friend that "at the regatta yesterday we'd seventeen hundred people on us".

The pier was of course new in those days (1880) and popular, and the ferries from Lymington called there – complete with musical entertainment! A little earlier than this, in 1860, the Rev. Edmund Venables painted a more flattering picture:

> "Considerable improvement has taken place since 1835; new houses have been erected, the quay has been enlarged to nearly double its former size to accommodate the increased trade; the steam communication with Lymington, Cowes, Ryde, and Portsmouth has been much increased; the harbour has been defended by a breakwater; a bridge has been built across the estuary; and a general air of neatness and respectability about the place indicates that, though not a place of any considerable trade, Yarmouth is thriving".

When you see cars and lorries pouring off the ferries at Yarmouth slipway to-day, it seems difficult to believe that up to 1830 the only contact between Yarmouth and Lymington was in rowing boats or sailing boats. In these comparatively small boats the crossing could often be difficult and sometimes dangerous. Even after the advent of steamers local boatmen and wherrymen continued to run, and in 1837 the mail was still being carried by a 23 foot Yarmouth Wherry owned by Edward Webster. In that year, at the beginning of April, he capsized in a squall, and ten of the twelve occupants of the boat, including women and children, were drowned. Webster himself was saved, together with the Mail, and he made a heroic attempt to save the life of a child. Three of the passengers lost are buried in Yarmouth Churchyard, and Webster was later buried there himself on November 28th, 1844, dying at the age of 75.

The first steamship to be introduced on this passage was the S.S. Glasgow, a wooden hulled paddle steamer of 17 tons register which sailed between Lymington and Portsmouth, calling at Yarmouth, Cowes and Ryde on three days each week; and between Lymington and Southampton, calling at Yarmouth and Cowes on the other three days. On Sundays she sailed only between Lymington and Yarmouth, her time for the crossing being thirty minutes – which is the same as to-day, 150 years later.

The skipper of the Glasgow was Robert Dore, a Yarmouth man who commanded her for 18 years. When he died in 1848 aged 59 he was living in Lymington, but was buried in Yarmouth Churchyard. The Glasgow was immediately popular, and in May 1836 Tow Boats were introduced to carry horses, cattle, and carriages, thus leaving the deck of the Glasgow for its human passengers. Two boats were in operation between Lymington and Yarmouth right up to 1930.

In 1840 a new Company, known as the Solent Sea Steam Packet Co. was formed to cope with "the large influx of visitors expected with the arrival of the railway". The prospectus issued stated that the company was being formed with a Share Capital of £4,500 in £25 shares "for the purpose of securing to the Inhabitants of Lymington and its neighbourhood, and Yarmouth and the western part of the island, a full participation in the many Advantages flowing and likely to flow from the Southampton and Gosport Railways and other Improvements in progress at the former Port".

The prospectus listed a number of existing subscribers, including several Yarmouth notabilities, together with the number of shares they were taking up. Those marked with a * are designated proprietors of the Steam Packet Glasgow and Tow Boats.

Hon. W. A. a'Court Holmes, Westover	4	Shares
*Rev. Sir George Burrard, Walhampton	8	,,
*Daniel Alexander, The Towers	6	,,
Joseph Squire	4	,,
*William Squire	10	,,
John Squire	2	,,
Mr. Beere, Thorley	1	,,
*Mrs. Michell, Norton Lodge	4	,,
*R. B. Crozier, Westhill	2	,,

Rev. Robert Little	2	,,
B. Plumbly, Albion Hotel	2	,,
Miss Love	1	,,
P. Bright, George Hotel	1	,,

In May 1841 the Company launched their second boat, the Solent of 34 tons register, the naming ceremony being performed by their principal shareholder William Squire, who incidentally later became Secretary to the Company.

The Solent was a super ship of her day, being 84 feet in length, sloop rigged with a bowsprit, and one engine of 15 h.p. She had a tremendous reception from the public who greatly admired her panelled saloon, but later on, when the novelty had worn off, the public became more critical. Complaints were frequently made that the tow boats slowed the steamer down to an irritating extent, and also that sailing times were often erratic as the steamers were frequently taken out of service to tow other boats back into the harbour. The biggest complaints of all, however, came when bad weather caused the tow boats to be cancelled, for then the passengers had to share their limited, heaving deck space with sheep, horses, pigs and other livestock.

In 1840 a national survey was carried out in all parishes with a view to redeeming Tithes, and the map and schedule thus produced have proved extremely useful documents, since they record all land owners and householders, together with some details of the property involved. In Yarmouth the biggest landowners were as follows:

Mayor and Corporation	47	acres	approx.
Henry Leigh	9	,,	,,
Burrard (heirs of Sir George)	7	,,	,,
Hon. Wm. a'Court Holmes	5	,,	,,
Daniel Alexander	5	,,	,,
James Baskett	4	,,	,,
Turnpike and other roads	4	,,	,,
Churchwardens of the Parish	1	,,	,,

The land in the parish was divided up as follows:

Grassland	33	acres	approx.
Gardens	5	,,	,,
Buildings	11	,,	,,
Roads and Waste Land	42	,,	,,

The map is sufficiently detailed as to show each individual building, and is coloured with the object of differentiating between domestic and commercial buildings, cultivated land, and "yardland".

At this time a considerable export trade in sand was carried on with glassworks in England, the sand being dug in Alum Bay and brought to Yarmouth where it was stored in the "Sand House" at the top end of the harbour. This trade was conducted by the three Squire brothers, Joseph, John and William, until it dramatically collapsed in 1851. The Sand House is now a flourishing boat-yard.

For many centuries Yarmouth's water supply was obtained from Wells, and there were a great number of these. In 1852 there were four public wells, from which anyone could draw water, the first one of these being situated in the Square, near the middle of the north wall of the Churchyard. This one must have been quite close to the Stocks, which are shown in an old print belonging to the Church. It has completely disappeared now and the assumption is that it was filled in at some time. Oddly enough in recent years the Church has acquired a rather serious damp problem on the north wall, and one wonders whether there is any connection.

The second public well was in South Street, near its junction with Tennyson Road, and though not now operative the old pump which was erected over the well in 1890 is still there. The third one was in Baskett's Lane at the east corner of the High Street, and the fourth one was in Mill Road, opposite the middle of Mill Terrace. Charles Andrews in his letters claimed that there was a fifth one, but did not say where it was. Perhaps this was the one mentioned in 1859 by the Jury as being at the top of Wheatsheaf Lane. (See page 94). By the year 1873 there were only three left.

Many houses of course had their own wells, and some of these still exist. There is one in the garden opposite the Deacons, in the High Street, and one in the middle of Harwood's shop in the Square.

In October 1868 Yarmouth was stunned by the news of a tragedy at sea in which four local men lost their lives. This was the loss of the Pilot Cutter "Blonde" which was run down off the Needles by the P and O Steamer "Syria" on her way to Southampton from Gibraltar. A newspaper account described the accident.

> "At 6-40 the Syria stopped off Durstone Point, and took a pilot on board; at 7-15 she ported her helm to another pilot cutter, which was on her port bow, the cutter being on the starboard tack. When the cutter was close to the steamer on the port bow she tacked, and, seeing that a collision was inevitable the engines were stopped. The cutter struck the steamer on the port side, the port paddle-wheel going over her, and she sank immediately. A boat

was lowered, which pulled round the fragments of the wreck, but no signs of a human being could be seen; the boat returned to the Syria, and finding that any further search was useless, she proceeded on her voyage at 8-5 p.m. The Syria was at the time steering E.N.E., wind E.N.E., right ahead. The cutter was a Cowes pilot boat, No. 43, and the pilot in charge of the Syria, Jas. Andrews, is the uncle of the unfortunate pilot on board the ill-fated vessel. It is supposed there were four persons on board, all of whom have, of course, lost their lives".

The four persons on board were Charles Bright and Henry Page, Pilots, and Joseph Long and William Griffiths, Crew. The newspaper article states that the Pilot in charge of the Syria at the time of the accident was James Andrews who was the uncle of the Pilot on board the Blonde. A scrutiny of the Yarmouth Church Registers fails to confirm this, but it is interesting that William Griffiths' wife Ann was the daughter of a James Andrews, though at her baptism in 1814 her father's occupation is given as Shoe-maker.

William and Ann Griffiths were married in 1838, but not in Yarmouth, and their first child, Jane Andrews Griffiths, was born in August 1839. They lived in a house at the top of the High Street, and in the Census of 1841 were shown to have a lodger, Robert Maude the Schoolmaster. By the time of the next Census in 1851 Robert Maude had moved next door, since in the ten year's gap William and Ann had had four more children. (See page 98).

The Blonde disaster was written up in 1874 under the title of "The Pilot's Last Cruise" by W. H. G. Kingston, a popular writer of the time. This must have been written for some religious publication as it has a strong religious slant and is in fact an exhortation to young sailors to turn from their sinful ways before it is too late. W. H. G. Kingston is perhaps best remembered for having founded "The Boys Own Paper".

A Relief Fund for the dependants of those who lost their lives was started in Yarmouth, the organising committee consisting of the Rev. Canon Blackburn, Rector of Yarmouth, Vice Admiral H. O. Love, James Blake, and with J. A. Cole (father of Captain A. G. Cole) as Treasurer. An advertisement was put in The Times, and subscriptions began to pour in. A total of over £264 was collected, with expenses of £6. 12. 0d. and by the middle of November this had been disbursed. The Owners of the vessel were given 20% and the balance was distributed between the Widows and Orphans in the ration of one share to each of the Widows and half a share to each dependant Child.

A few months later, in March 1869, a decision was taken that Yarmouth Castle was now obsolete and no longer needed for the defence of the town, and consequently the large guns on the Castle platform were dismantled. The newspaper article that announced this also repeated the story of the Church bells being stolen by the French, but this at least is open to question. (See page 12).

> "**The Old Castle at Yarmouth.** For several days past, the men of the Royal Artillery have been employed in dismantling the large heavy 96-pounder guns from the top of the old castle at Yarmouth, where they were certainly neither useful nor ornamental, and would, if fired at all, have proved far more fatal to the gunners than to the enemy. There is a rumour that the castle, now absolutely useless for any purposes of defence, will shortly be sold by auction. The castle was erected at the same time as the castle on the opposite coast of Hurst, in the reign of Henry VIII as a means of defence against the French, who frequently paid the Isle of Wight a predatory visit. It is said that the stones of the three castles of Yarmouth, Hurst and Calshott, were taken from the dismantled abbey of Beaulieu. It is certain that many of the stones used in the construction of Hurst castle have marks of ecclesiastical mouldings and figures on them.
>
> The fortifications lately erected on both sides of the Solent, including the tremendous batteries of Hurst, would now render Yarmouth a difficult nut for any army to crack, even if we lose the picturesque old building that has for the last 350 years frowned defiance at invaders. It is an interesting memorial of other times, and we trust that into whosoever's hands it may fall, it may still be allowed to retain its distinctive features as a place of defence. Useless as it may be for military purposes, we should be sorry to lose it for the sake of its historical reminiscences and associations".

Another newspaper article which appeared at around the same date dealt with the names of Yarmouth residents, and was entitled "Our Odd Corner".

> "Among the oddities of our antique town we find we have persons living in the place with the following useful names:
>
> Butlers, Pages, Cooks and Fryers,

Taylors, Coopers, Smiths and Dyers,
Baggs, Cases, Long and Small,
Cammels, Does, Peacocks and Daws,
Reeds, Thorns, and Woodrows, Budden,
Pilchers, Rice, and Good Porter Brewin,
Flint, Glass, Brown, White, and Green,
Halls, Chambers, Bright, and Trim.

In addition to these we have also Paris, Blandford, Lee, Newbury, Oxford, Clydesdale, and Conway, being the names of seven towns in France, England, Scotland, and Wales".

Towards the end of the 19th century the country was swept by a wave of patriotic affection for Queen Victoria, who celebrated her Diamond Jubilee in 1897. Yarmouth was no exception, and the celebrations were elaborate and extensive. The newspaper account of these celebrations was long and detailed, but is produced here in full since it provides an excellent picture of life in Victorian England, and in particular, life in Yarmouth, Isle of Wight.

"Once again has our little town demonstrated its loyalty to its beloved Queen, and in gloriously delightful weather Her Majesty's Diamond Jubilee was on Tuesday last celebrated in right Royal fashion. On Monday the inhabitants were all fully occupied upon a transformation scene, and as a result of their labours the town was literally draped with bunting from end to end. Flags were displayed from the Pierhead, and Church tower (where floated a large St. Andrew's Cross), nearly every house had its decoration, rows and rows of bunting spanned the streets, vessels and yachts in the harbour and roadstead were gaily decorated rainbow fashion, and the Railway Station was exceedingly pretty, decked with bunting by Mr. White, the staion-master. The front of Mr. Blake's house was most tastefully decked, and presented a charming appearance, as did also the hooded villas in the Square, treated with evergreens and flags and a prettily worked motto "God Bless our Queen" in an artistic border of leaves, the work of Miss Leigh, who, to the pleasure of all, was seen out once again and who made an inspection of the decorations.

Triumphal arches were erected in St. James's Street, at the top of High Street, and at the lower part of High Street facing the Town Hall. The last named arch was an exceptionally pretty arrangement, with the Royal letters "V.R." tastefully formed of red roses, and there were miniature Union Jacks on either side. This was the work of the Misses Cole. At The Mount, the residence of the Rev. R. L. and Mrs. Dashwood, the decorations were of a most elaborate description, and at The Deacons, Retreat, Myrtle Cottage, at the business establishments of Mr. Harwood, Mr. Lee, Mr. Johnston, Mr. Reynolds, and Mr. Richardson, at the Bugle Hotel, the King's Head, as well as at other business places and private residences, too, there were effective contributions to the general display. In a window at the Police Station a large portrait of the Queen was conspicuously and loyally displayed.

At 11 o'clock a special full choral service was held at the Church, at which there was a good congregation. The Rev. E. N. Powell officiated, the National Anthem and the hymn "O King of Kings" were heartily sung, and the organist (Mr. Nicholls) at the close of the service performed the "Hallelujah Chorus". At 12-30 an excellent dinner was served at the Assembly Room of the Bugle Hotel to the aged. The interior had been prettily decorated. At the top of the room was a portrait of the Queen, with "V.R. 37-97" underneath, and a large Union Jack draped the lower end. The table was exquisitely laid out with blooms, the arrangement of the national colours, red, white, and blue in flowers, being most unique. Mr. Blake occupied the Chair, with Mr. Hall in the Vice-chair, and other members of the committee were present. A verse of "God Save the Queen" was sung, Mr. Nicholls leading on the pianoforte. The Rev. R. L. Dashwood then said grace. Host Cleary had prepared a splendid repast. Needless to say, the various viands speedily disappeared, the dinner evidently being thoroughly appreciated by all. During the dinner Mr. Cole, the hon. secretary read a telegram from Captains W. Webb and Graham Cole, his nephew and son, as follows – "Success to dinner. Sorry we cannot be with you".

At 2-30 the school children and the general public assembled at the schools, together with the Thorley children numbering 60 (accompanied by the Vicar and Mrs. Saulez and Miss Kersley and Miss Hunt, who had previously arrived in gaily decorated waggons kindly lent by Mr. Barrington.

C.C. and Mr. Harvey. A procession was then formed and marshalled by Mr. C. Edmunds and C. S. M. Gannon R.E. and headed by the pipe and drum band of the 13th Co. R.A. (by kind permission of Major Waldron R.A.) under the direction of Bandmaster Corporal Mugliston. First came the coastguards, bearing a huge Union Jack, and led by Coastguard Barnard, then the school military corps, with their Instructor Mr. Gannon, and Mr. A. Summers, pupil teacher; then the Yarmouth school children, with their teachers, Misses. Dovey, Whittington and Maund, also the excellent headmaster Mr. J. E. Furmage; and next followed the Thorley school children, with Miss Kersley and Miss Hunt, with innumerable flags and banners waving. The spectacle was a very bright and animated one.

The procession paraded through St. James's Street, Bridge Road, and Quay Street to the Pier approach at St. James's Square, where a halt took place, the children being then marched into a roped off circle, where, led by the band, they sang the National Anthem, conducted by Mr. Furmage from a raised dais, as well as a patriotic song entitled "Victoria our Queen". Mr. Blake mounted the rostrum and briefly addressed the large throng of spectators – a record gathering for Yarmouth – after which he called for cheers for the Queen, which were lustily given. The whole group having been photographed by Mr. Benjafield, the procession re-formed and went up the High Street to The Mount, turned round, and marched through Ommanney Road and South Street to a field kindly lent by Mr. J. Mills for the day's rejoicings, where some excellent racing and other competitions for prizes took place.

At 5 o'clock there was an interval for tea, not only for the children, but for the general public without exception, and very admirable were the arrangements carried out. Tea over, the sports were resumed with much zest, and at the close of the programme of competitions the prizes were gracefully presented to the successful contestants by Miss Dashwood. Our space will not admit of a detailed list of the sports and winners, but it may be specially mentioned that one of the most interesting items was a tug-of-war between Yarmouth and Thorley. The Thorley team won, and each member of it was presented with a prettily designed medal. In a tug-of-war between Yarmouth boys and Thorley boys the juvenile Yarmouthians avenged their seniors and pulled off the "tug'.

In addition to the committee there were numerous helpers at the tea, including the Misses Dashwood, Miss M. Leigh, Mrs. Harwood, Rev. J and Mrs. Dutson, Miss Johnston, and Messrs. C. Jacobs, E. C. Elderfield, and B. Mills. The band continued playing popular airs throughout the evening, and several of the old-fashioned games were indulged in by young and old.

As the shades of night gathered the scene was changed to the Square. At 9 o'clock Mr. Blake switched on the electric light, and as the 1887 Jubilee was notable for the running of the first train between Yarmouth and Freshwater, so 1897 will be remembered for the first illumination of St. James's Square by electricity (of course only for the occasion). In the front of the Town Hall was a splendid representation of a Crown, with the letters "V.R." and the figures "37-97". This was a blaze of brilliant Light. Across the Square hung incandescent lights, the front of the Bugle was all aglow with lamps of variegated colours, and a long row of Chinese lanterns hung across St. James's Street. At the Mount the front was illuminated with 300 lamps of varied colours, which, with Chinese lanterns hanging in the trees, and the windows of the residence lit up with dozens of candles, added considerably to the charm of the scene. At Myrtle Cottage, the King's Head, as well as Seaview, The Deacons, Mount Villa, and other private residences and business establishments, there were also very effective displays. Throughout the evening the streets were packed with admiring spectators.

The success which marked the celebration throughout was mainly due to the efforts of the committee, who had an indefatigable chairman in Mr. Blake, while Mr. Cole and Mr. Lee were equally zealous as Hon. Secretary and Hon. Treasurer respectively. Thanks are also due to Major Wingfield-Stratford R. E., for lending the installation necessary for the electric light; to Sergt. Major Mills R. E. who had charge of the electrical arrangements; to the several Royal Engineers who gave most valued assistance; to Mr. Barrington C.C. for the loan of his locomotive for driving the dynamo; to Mr. Stephenson and his assistants of the R.E. and the coastguards for their much appreciated services in decorating the town and to the several committees.

At midnight there was still a large concourse of people in the Square, and, to the accompaniment of the band, they jointed in singing "Auld Lang Syne", a brilliant and most successful celebration concluding with yet another rendering of "God Save the Queen".

CHAPTER IX

Proceedings of the Corporation of Yarmouth

1785 — 1862

From 1785 to 1811 we now have two books running in parallel. Firstly, there is the book recording the proceedings of the Corporation, which is in effect a continuation of the Clarke Jervoise book, and which to begin with deals mainly with elections and the taking of oaths, the only addition being that it is also used as an attendance register, so that we have signatures of the Chief Burgesses who attended. Very gradually, however, the character of the book changes as the Corporation begin to discuss more mundane matters concerning the Town, such as the state of the roads, repairs to the harbour, etc. This makes for more interesting reading.

The other book is more down to earth. Called simply "Court Leet Entries" it records the annual meetings of the ancient Court Leet, and Assize of Bread and Ale. The Court consisted of a Jury of twelve or more inhabitants whose duty was to elect annually two Constables (and later two Petty Constables), the Hayward or Haywarden, to control the payment of wharfage dues, and to keep the Town's accounts. They met always on the 18th October, unless the 18th was a Sunday, in which case they met on the 19th, under the Chairmanship of the Common Clerk and Steward, or Town Clerk. Another duty was the preservation of Law and Order in the Town and to bring to the notice of the Corporation any Nuisance which in their opinion needed attention.

The duties of the Hayward were connected mainly with the Common and the fields belonging to the Town, the rounding up of stray cattle, etc, and looking after the Pound, which was a stone built barn situated on the Marsh just to the south of the Newport Road as it passes the end of the Common. The remains of it are still there to-day, completely covered in brambles and fallen trees.

Later, in 1811, another book known as the Jury Book was started, but for many years this only recorded, again on 18th October, the names of the Jurymen and a statement that they had weighed the Bread on sale in the Town, and had checked the Weights and Measures, with a note of any deficiencies.

Both the Court Leet Book and the Jury Book came to an abrupt end in 1862 when it was decided that these ancient customs had outlived their usefulness and were obsolete.

The first entry in the Court Leet Book is fairly typical of many and I give it in full.

Borough of Yarmouth	The Court Leet and Lawday of the Borough of Yarmouth there holden the eighteenth day of October 1785 Before Richard Clarke, Gentleman, Steward there.

Names of the Jury

Mr. Charles Leigh	Jm
Mr. Richard Plumbley	,,
Mr. Samuel Udall	,,
Mr. Timothy Heath	Jm
Mr. George Heath	,,
Mr. James Heath	,,
Mr. William Rayner	,,
Mr. James Jacob	Jm
Mr. Thomas Day	,,
Mr. William Cass	,,
Mr. Robert Willis	,,
Mr. George Woolgar	Jm
Mr. Emanuel Butcher	,,

Constables	Mr. Thomas Thearle	Jm
	Mr. Thomas Lyne	Jm
Hayward	Mr. James Jacob	Jm

At this Court Mr. William Crew agreed to give Seven Guineas for the Wharfage of the Kay for the year ensuing.

	£ s d
Rec'd of Mr. William Crew One Year Wharfage	7 – 7 – 0
Rec'd of Capt. Urry one years Rent of Brambles Orchard	0 – 15 – 0

Rec'd of Mr. Squire one years Rent of the Ground called Town Lands	3 – 0 – 0
Rec'd one Years Town Rents	4 – 4 – 1
	£15 – 6 – 1

Disbursements

Town Clerk's Salary	1 – 6 – 0
Sergeant's Salary	0 – 14 – 0
One years Fee farm rent	0 – 16 – 0
One years Land Tax thereof	0 – 4 – 0
Paid William Crews Bill for repairs to the Kay	0 – 5 – 0
Paid Mrs. Wilson for Jury Dinner last year	10 – 13 – 6
	£13 – 18 – 6
Balance	£1 – 7 – 7

It is interesting to note (as Cole does in his book) that most of the money was spent on the Jury dinner. Mrs. Wilson, who provided the dinner, was the licensee of the George Inn. Her husband had died in 1780, and in 1792 she married the Skipper of a visiting Collier Brig, John Smetham.

It is also interesting to note in the above accounts the salaries of the Town Clerk and Town Sergeant, and the general level of prices.

The accounts for 1787 contain the following items:

Paid Mr. Samuel Udall's Bill for Box to hold the Corporation Records and making a shutter to the Town Hall window.	1 – 19 – 3
Paid Mr. Crew's Bill for a Rope for the Crane	0 – 10 – 6
Paid Mr. Byerley's Bill for Iron Work in repairing the Quay. (Isaac Byerley was the Blacksmith')	0 – 9 – 0
Paid William Brading's Bill for mending the Quay.	0 – 5 – 6
Paid Mr. Timothy Heath for mending the Town Hall Window.	0 – 5 – 0
Paid Mr. Squire's Bill for Paper etc for the Use of the Corporation.	0 – 1 – 8

In 1788 the Jury dinner cost even more at £16. 15. 10d. and there was a bill from Mr. Udall the Carpenter for "work about the Common Pound" of £1.18. 2d.

Around this time a new list of Burgesses was compiled to replace that lost in the box taken by Lieut. Crooke.

Name	Free Burgess Date Sworn	Chief Burgess Date Sworn
Benjamin Leigh	28–10–1748	22–4–1754
Leonard Troughear (later Leonard Troughear Holmes)	24–9–1770	24–9–1770
John Troughear	24–9–1770	24–9–1770
Jervoise Clarke Jervoise	24–9–1770	24–9–1770
Rev. Richard Walker (Dr. of Law.)	24–9–1770	24–9–1770
Thomas Dickonson	24–9–1770	24–9–1770
John Eames	21–9–1771	24–9–1771
John Blackall Jnr	21–9–1771	21–9–1771
John Tilbury	21–9–1771	21–9–1771
John Blackall Snr	21–9–1772	21–9–1772
Rev. Joseph Bayley, Clerk	21–6–1775	21–6–1775
Edward Rushworth	21–9–1782	21–9–1782

At the Assembly on 20th December, 1787 it was reported that Crooke's solicitor had paid the £500 damages awarded, plus £52 taxed costs. The Town Clerk's bill of expenses in connection with this business amounted to £144. 4. 3d, and the decision was taken to increase his salary from £1. 6. 0d to £6. 6. 0d per annum. Not a bad increase! Out of the £500 windfall a sum of £300 was lent to Leonard Troughear Holmes at 4% and when all else was paid a balance of £29. 11. 3d was left with the Town Clerk.

In 1789 it was agreed to send the following address to the King on "his late happy recovery".

To the King's Most Excellent Majesty

The Humble Address of the Mayor, Chief Burgesses and Freemen of the Borough of Yarmouth in the Isle of Wight.

Most Gracious Sovereign

Participating in the general Happiness felt by all your Majesty's faithful subjects on the most happy Recovery of your Majesty from your late Indisposition, We your Majesty's dutiful and Loyal Subjects, The Mayor Chief Burgesses and Freemen of the Borough of Yarmouth in the

Isle of Wight beg leave to approach your Royal Presence with our most sincere Congratulations, and to join in the universal Prayers of all our Fellow Subjects to the Almighty Power that your Majesty may long continue to enjoy the blessing of Health, and to reign over a free and grateful People, truly sensible of the National Benefit derived to them from your Majesty's paternal Regard to the Welfare of your Subjects. Given under our Common Seal the Eighth Day of April in the Twenty Ninth year of your Majesty's Reign.

Leon'd Troughear Holmes, Deputy Mayor
Benj. Leigh
T. Dickonson
E. Rushworth

As only four Burgesses signed, it looks as though the meetings were not very well attended, even the Major being absent. In 1792 an even more flowery Address was sent to the King congratulating him on the Proclamation for the Suppression of all Seditious Publications, and a few years later yet another upon "his late and providential Escape from the attempt upon his life". Perhaps there was something about George III which inspired these ostentatiously loyal sentiments, or could it be that the Burgesses felt subconsciously that all was not well with their little privileged world, and wished to establish a friend in the highest of high places.

Over the years the Accounts contain some interesting items, the following being a selection:

1789 Paid for coals to distribute among the Poor in the Severe Weather during the last Winter. 3. 12. 0d.

Paid for Beer given to the Populace upon the Recovery of his Majesty from his late illness. 3. 10. 0d.

(the Clerk actually wrote "his late Majesty" and then crossed out the word "late".)

Paid Mr. Squire's Bill for Candles, etc, to illuminate the Town Hall upon the King's Recovery 0. 16. 2d.

1791 Paid Timothy Heath his Bill for Locks for the Round House. 0. 6. 6d.

(The Round House was the Shelter erected on the Norton side of the river for passen-

	gers awaiting the ferry, which at this time was the only way of crossing the river).	
1795	Paid William Brading's Bill for repairing the Town Wall.	0. 15. 4d.
1799	Paid for a padlock, etc, for the Blindhouse, and repairing Lock for the Corporation Box.	0. 2. 0d.
	(The Blind House was the Town Lock-up, and stood at the bottom of what is now Tennyson Road, near the junction with St. James's Street. It was so called as it had no windows. Previous to the Blindhouse the Lock-up was a stone building in the High Street, almost opposite the modern Police Station, and now known as "Peelers".)	
	Paid a fine for the Mayor not appearing at the Assizes March 7th, 1797.	2. 0. 0d.
1800	Paid Mr. Udall's Bill for inclosing the Town Hall with rails.	11. 1. 6d.
1801	Paid Stephen Squire for Candles etc, for Illumination on the Peace.	0. 19. 6d.
	Paid for a Hogshead of Beer on account of The Peace given to the Populace.	5. 0. 0d.
	(The Peace referred to was presumably the patched up peace with Napoleon which only lasted for about a year).	
1801	Paid Mr. Jones, Schoolmaster, for teaching Eight Poor Boys of the Town for two years.	10. 10. 0d.
1802	Paid Mr. Stephens for building a necessary House near the Quay.	6. 14. 0d.
	Paid Thos. Heath for Locks for the Bridewell	0. 3. 2d.

The Bridewell is presumably the Town Lock-up, so called after the Bridewell Prison in London.

1803	Paid repairing and new Gilding the Town Mace.	5. 5. 0d.
1817	Paid John Stephens for fixing a Mark on the Wreck of the Tyger.	0. 17. 0d.

There is an entry in the Jury Book dated 22nd March, 1815, which says – "At a meeting held by the Jury this Day to present Nuisances, etc, we do hereby present as a very dangerous Nuisance to the Harbour the wreck of the Sloop Tyger belonging to Mr. Jas. Day of West Cowes".

1818	Paid Richard Wheeler, Mason, for repairs to the Quay after the Storm in March.	4. 15. 1½d.
1828	Repairs of the sea walls adjoining the Quay injured by the Storm.	44. 12. 9d.
1829	June. To Col. Burgoyne for the purchase of the Old Battery.	30. 0. 0d.

This was an old cannon staioned on the Quay as part of the defences of the Harbour entrance, and which the Corporation bought in order to be able to enlarge the Quay.

Money received from wharfage fluctuated from year to year. From the 7 guineas received in 1785 it jumped to £25 in 1799, and to £35 in 1800, but then steadied for some years at £23.

In 1795 for the first time in the Court Leet Book the Disbursements exceeded the Receipts, and the Account was balanced by an item "Received of Mr. Rushworth to Balance this Account – £3. 7. 4d." On many subsequent occasions when there was a loss Mr. Rushworth paid off the deficit, either by himself or by splitting it with Jervoise Clarke Jervoise.

Rushworth was, of course, a wealthy man. He was Mayor of Yarmouth on 12 occasions between 1784 and 1816, and was Member of Parliament three times. He is perhaps best remembered for having built Farringford, now the Hotel. He married Catherine, the only daughter of Leonard (Troughear) Lord Holmes, and there is a memorial tablet to them both, and their children, in Yarmouth Church.

It was Leonard Lord Holmes, when he was more simply Leonard Troughear Holmes, who borrowed £300 from the corporation in 1787, and each year subsequently there was an item in the accounts of £12 received in interest. These payments ceased, however, in 1804 when he died, but no explanation was given, nor was there any reference to the return of the capital sum.

In the accounts for 1830 appears another unexplained item:

October 25th. Received by Cash £264. 17. 3d.

Someone has written in pencil on the opposite page:

"In the Return of the Commission on Municipal Corporations in 1835 it is stated that this sum was presented to the Borough by the Patron, i.e. the Trustees of Holmes. But when did Lord Holmes or his Representatives repay the £300 borrowed in 1785 – interest on which was paid up to 1804 but not since?" (Actually the money was borrowed in 1787). N.B. Leonard Lord Holmes died in January 1804, the estate then went to Sir Henry Worsley. Leonard Lord Holmes left one only daughter, Catherine, wife of Edward Rushworth".

Is the inference then that this sum of £264. 17. 3d. came from Rushworth? He had already paid several small sums as mentioned above when the accounts were overdrawn.

At the meeting of the Court Leet on 18th October, 1820 the following directions were given by Thomas Sewell Esq, Town Clerk, for the guidance of the Jury when inspecting Weights and Measures.

All Bread and Butter short of weight to be seized, and disposed of agreeably to the discretion of the Jury.

All unstamped and Lead weights used in Public Shops are Illegal and may be seized.

Lead weights that have been adjusted by driving nails into them to be seized. Weights over weight to be adjusted by the Jury.

All Weights seized to be kept in the custody of the Foreman of the Jury, who is to produce them to the Court on the following Leet when the parties to whom they belong are to be summoned to answer for the same.

All Cups short of measure to be broken.

Persons using abusive or improper language to the Jury in the execution of their office, or impeding the execution of the same, to be summoned before the Magistrates.

All transactions of the Jury to be correctly inserted in the Book for that purpose, and signed by the Jury.

On the occasions when they found anything wrong they duly entered this in the Jury Book, the main interest to us now being that these entries, besides helping to build up a picture of life in Yarmouth at that time, also give us the names of some of the people involved. Typical examples are:

"Weighed the Bread, and examined the Weights and Measures, and took from Mrs. Ann Webster, Grocer, three quartern loaves short of weight, which was distributed to the Poor" (Two of these loaves were baked by James Fryer, and one by Barnabas Baggs).

"Weighed the Bread examined the Weights and Measures

and found 1 seven pound lead weight 1 oz. short at Mrs. Websters, two Quart Cups short measure at the King's Head, and four Pint Cups short of measure at the George Tap".

"Weighed Bread brought on shore from a Coal Hoy, and offered for sale in the Public Market – belonging to Thomas Mitchell and found nine Half Gallon loaves Twenty three and Half Ounces deficient in weight. Seized the same and distributed it to the Poor, per order of the Rev. George Burrard".

The Rev. George Burrard, Rector of Yarmouth for 40 years, was for a brief spell a leading member of the Corporation, serving as Mayor in 1834 and again in 1837. He might have continued to plan an increasingly important part in the affairs of the Borough had he not succeeded to the Baronetcy on the death of his brother, but this event caused him to leave the Mount to go and live at Walhampton. (see page 144).

At this time there was a very strong religious influence on the Corporation, six out of eleven Chief Burgesses being clergymen. The Town Hall was given over on Sundays to the female Sunday School, and a decision was taken in 1836 that any surplus of funds from Rents and Wharfage, after paying for the maintainance of the Quay, should be used for the benefit and support of any schools established in the Borough.

In 1837, as the result of many years squabbling among the inhabitants as to who had the right to graze animals on the Common, an enquiry was held, and the Report of the Jury in the Court Leet Book makes amusing reading.

"Stephens says that about 35 years ago he enquired of Mr. Rushworth as to the Rights of Persons to turn out on the Common. He inform him that all the Freeholders of Yarmouth had a right to tie a Cow on the Common – Recollects the Common more than 50 years ago – The Custom has been for the Householders to tie a Cow. Has tied a Cow for his Mother.

John Squire. We used to keep a Cow on the Common about seven years ago. My father was Town Sergeant and My Grandfather before him and as such used to turn out a Cow as representing the Mayor. It was the Mayor's Right. At the present time the following persons are in the habit of turning out.

John Baggs turns out one Cow. I am a leaseholder for a long term of years – I consider I have a right to turn out for the Premises – There was a Cow on the Common for the same Premises before I purchased. I have turned out about 12 years.

William Calcott turns out one Cow. Did turn out two – was ordered to turn out one only – I consider I have a right to turn out for the Premises belonging to Mr. Charles Leigh – he is a Freeholder – my Father in Law. I have turned out for nearly 15 years without intermission.

William Webb turns out one. He is a Householder. The premises belong to Mr. Henry Leigh.

George Woolgar turns out one Cow for the House and Yard belonging to me – It is my Freehold House excercised the right between forty and fifty years as a Freeholder – I consider all the Freeholders have a right. I have known Householders turn there for the last 55 years. I was a Householder before I was a Freeholder.

John Bright am just past 80 years old – Have known Yarmouth for 70 years – Have tied my Father's Cow there – I knew two tenements on the Common – Thompson and Holly lived in them – My Father had no right – never considered he had a right – other people turned out – They had a right to tie by a chain 12 yards long – If they were longer the Jury ordered them to be cut.

Henry Leigh. I heard from my Grandfather Devenish that the Freeholders of the value of 40/- per Annum were allowed to tie a Cow on the Common. And the Captain of the Castle a Horse – I understand it was by Lord Holmes permission.

Those who did turn out Cows on the Common were required to tether them on a chain no longer than 12 yards, and woe betide anyone who exceeded this, for the Hayward had strict instructions to cut and adjust any overlength chains, no matter who the owners were. He also had orders to impound stray cattle, and this was never popular, as the following extract shows:

"The Jury beg to represent an interruption to their Haywarden in the execution of his duty, viz:

On the morning of the 16th October (1826) Henry Salter, Haywarden, on going his rounds, found on the Common Three Cows belonging to George Woolgar, one tied as is the custom, and two loose. Salter proceeded to drive the two Cows that were loose to the pound, but on their way these were forcibly taken from his custody by George Woolgar, who at the same time threatened him with Violence".

In their role as watchdogs the Jury were instrumental in protecting the rights of inhabitants in many different ways. One abuse which they managed to prevent was the stopping up of the lane leading from the High Street to the sea which is now known as Love's Lane. They reported as follows:

"We the Jury of the Borough of Yarmouth, sworn on the 18th day of October 1824 to protect the rights and privileges of the said Borough

Do observe by public Notice that the street leading to the shore (about 50 yeards long and 10 feet wide) situated between the premises of Wm. Love Esq and James Basket Gent, is to be taken in, or stopped, on the 18th Day of October 1825.

Acting conscientiously and conformably to the aforesaid oath, We consider it our Duty to protest against it for the following reasons Viz

That the stopping of the same will be Dangerous and prejudicial to Seafaring Men, which we are fully prepared to prove

That it will be admitting a dangerous precedent, and That it is an improper infringement of the rights and liberties of the said Borough. Signed by the Jury Viz

Rich'd Wheeler, Foreman	Dan'l Brown
Wm. Henning	Rob't Willis
Thomas Heath	Edw'd Webster
James Cammel	Tim'y Heath
John Long Senr	George Beere
John Long Junr	Sam'l Udall

A true Copy (Signed) Wm. Henning.

It is a great pity that there was no-one to protect the interests of the inhabitants and prevent the stopping of the public way to the sea at Long's Wharf. This right of way has now been lost.

Some of the presentments of the Jury may seem to us somewhat naive, but as the years went by they became more practical and to the point. Here is one from their report in 1841:

"We present the Remains of an Old House situate in the High Street next to George Woolgar's House as a Nuisance highly dangerous to the safety of persons walking in the Street. Upon enquiry it appeared that the above mentioned Building has been for many years untenanted, and that no person is known as claiming to be owner of it – That it is in extremely dilapidated and ruinous state – And that it is essential for the safety of the public that it be taken down. It is therefore ordered that the same be taken down – and the materials sold and removed – and after payment of the expense of such removal – The Balance may be held by the Corporation to be accounted for to any persons who may hereafter claim it.

We also present the state of the Public Streets both as respects the Road and the Pavement.

That in our opinion the Roads require throughout additional Materials say a Coating of Gravel And the Pavement in being a most dilapidated and dangerous state requiring a general repair. That in our opinion it is highly necessary that two drains or bunnies should be laid down to carry off the Water which after a heavy shower now accumulates in the High Road and overflows the Houses of the Inhabitants. One Bunny or Drain being required in the Cross Street by Captain Love's House in the High Street, and another near the End of South Street by Mr. Alexander's House. Ordered that the foregoing Presentments be transmitted to the Commissioners of Highways – to be laid before the next meeting – with a request that immediate attention may be paid thereto.

We present all other things well".

This is followed by a list of Jurymen and Constables, and the next entry in the Jury Book is dated:

December 31st 1841. In conformity with the orders of Henry Sewell Esq, Town Clerk and Steward of the Manor of the Borough of Yarmouth at the annual court day on the 18th October last The ruins of a old House situated in the High Street that which has been presented by the Jury as a dangerous nuisance was this day pulled down and the Materials sold by public Competition to Mr. Charles Bright for Two Pounds and five shillings the money for which I have this day handed to Mr. William Squire to be held by the Corporation until claimed by the Lawfull owner.

Benj'n Plumbly, Foreman.

The majority of their presentments refer to matters which they feel could and should be put right for the benefit of the town and its inhabitants, and though it is obviously impossible to quote them all, a small selection will show the difference between Yarmouth then and now, and perhaps remind us of the many amenities we now enjoy, and which we take for granted.

1853 We present that an obstruction is created by a dung mixen being made in Friar's Lane and that the same ought to be at once removed.

Friar's Lane is the one running down to the sea from the High Street between the Towers and Pinings Corner, previously known as Refuge Lane, and sometimes called Fryer's Lane after Fryer the Butcher who owned the Slaughterhouse which is now "Pinings Yard".

1855 We present that the privy near the Quay has been much dilapidated by the acts of some mischievous person or persons and requires repairs.

We also present that the Breakwater requires looking to, much of the stone having sunk. 500 tons of stone should be put on it immediately.

The Breakwater had been built in 1843, and had always been a bone of contention with the local fishermen, who resented the restricted entrance to the harbour. It certainly made smuggling into the estuary much more difficult.

We also present that during the past year there have been a number of Vessels from the Eastward employed in stone dregging in and out of the Harbour. That the authority of the Harbour Master and the rules of the Harbour have been set at defiance. Vessels have been improperly berthed unnecessary space occupied in the Harbour occasioning great inconvience.

1856 We present that the pavement of the Streets is much out of repair, especially opposite Mr. Blake's house (Jireh House), and the Bugle.

We present that a Lamp upon Yarmouth Quay would be a great accommodation to the Public.

We also present the great advantage that would be derived to the Town and Shipping resorting to the Harbour if there was a good supply of water for vessels.

1857 We present that a bank near the entrance to the Harbour is inconvenient to the navigation and ought to be removed.

1858 We present that the Common is slipping away and that it is very desirable that some means should be taken to prevent it.

1859 We present that it would be advantageous if a small piece of Land could be set aside upon which the Scavenger might place the sweepings and cleanings of the Town.

We present that since the last Court a Soldier has been drowned from the Quay in consequence of the practice of leaving the moorings of Vessels attached to the gun near the shed, and the same being most dangerous to the public the practice ought to be immediately discontinued, and we request the Corporation at once to give orders to the Harbour Master that no mooring should be allowed to remain upon the above named post after dark, and the more so as there is a ring below for the purpose.

The soldier was James McCreary, aged 20, from Fort Victoria who was drowned on February 12th, 1859, the burial register that day saying "drowned at the slip in the night on coming out of a public house".

We present that the Town Drain under the new part of the Quay is a nuisance and that the same ought to be continued below low water mark.

We present that a Well has been stopped up for some years in the Square at the top of the Wheatsheaf Lane and that if the same was opened it would be a great convenience to the public and a great advantage in case of Fire.

We present that the drains ought to have stink traps at the openings as a great nuisance arises from them and the gratings have their bars so far apart that children get their feet between the bars and sustain injury and that the same ought to be altered.

1860 We also suggest that the deep pit at the South side of the Town just above the Gate going into Salters Field would be a good place for the Scavenger to place the sweepings in.

> We present that it would be a great accommodation to the Inhabitants if a Town Pump was placed in the Well in St. James' Square as the dust and dirt from the opening of the Bridge has driven down the Well and fouled the water.

This Well was somewhere near the north west corner of the Church.

> 1861 We present that a great nuisance is created by the new Bridge which cannot be opened excepting at half tides to the great detriment of the public.

> 1862 We present that a sluice should be made in the bank of the Bridge in a line with the Public Privy so as to carry away the nuisances on the Shore.

It may be thought from the above selection that the Jury were doing a good job in reporting to the Corporation matters that needed attention, but their masters obviously thought otherwise. Perhaps the Jury itself had become a Nuisance, for at the meeting of the Corporation on 21st September, 1863 the following decision was taken:

> "It appearing upon the representation of the Town Clerk that the functions of the Ancient Court Leet and more especially with reference to the assize of Bread and Beer and the inspection of weights and measures and the appointment of constables and abatement of nuisance are obsolete – he was instructed not to hold the Court until again directed by the Corporation".

So another old custom came to an end, having outlived its usefulness. In less than another 30 years the Corporation itself suffered a similar fate, its proceedings for over 100 years having been largely ineffectual.

CHAPTER X

Yarmouth Schools I

Was it St. Ignatius Loyola – who held advanced views on the education of the young – who said "Give me a boy till he is seven years old, and after that anyone can have him?" He was speaking primarily of religious education of course, but the dictum is just as true in the wider sense of general education, the first few years of schooling being of vital importance.

In this respect Yarmouth has been fortunate in having a first class village school, which over the last 125 years has consistently maintained a high standard of general education for its junior citizens, coupled with sound religious instruction.

Much of the success of this Church of England Junior School has been due to the quality of its Head Teachers, and to the fact that many of them stayed a great number of years. The record is as follows:

Frederick Charles Spray	31 years
James Furmage	30 years
John C. Pugh	2 years
George E. Stanway	10 years
Miss Vera A. Martin (later Mrs. Barton)	32 years
Mrs. Sylvia Sharp	10 years to date
Infant School Head Mistresses	
Elizabeth Lewis (later Mrs. Spray)	20 years
Emily J. Dovey	35 years
Sylvia Eugenia Pittman	4 years

Miss Pittman was actually the last Head Mistress of the Infants School. When she left in 1923 the two schools were amalgamated under the then Head Master John Pugh.

Since 1863 a Log Book has been kept in the School detailing day to day events, and the many volumes of this book make fascinating reading. I propose to quote extensively from these records, but before doing so let us take a brief look at education in Yarmouth before the Church of England School was built.

We have a record as far back as 1735 of a school for boys in the High Street. This school was in an old house on the left hand side of the street going from the Square, the site now being occupied by the Wine Bar. The Head Master was a Mr. Goodall, a member of an old Yarmouth family.

One of his pupils was John Urry, son of Captain David Urry who in 1711 bought the house known as The Refuge (now The Towers) and rebuilt it. Young John was a lively lad, full of mischief, and was responsible for playing a joke on Mr. Goodall which occasioned the latter some annoyance. Apparently Mr. Goodall, in an attempt to obtain more respect from his pupils, made it a rule that they should, on meeting him each day say "good morning" politely to him. This did not quite work according to plan however, as the boys organised a continuous and unending procession past the Head so that he was obliged to go on saying "good morning" over and over again. John Urry was reputed to be the ringleader in this prank, which resulted ultimately in the rule being relaxed.

John Urry subsequently went into the Royal Navy, and after a successful career, which included the piloting of a fleet of 200 ships into the enemy port of Havana, retired with the rank of Captain and returned to live in Yarmouth. He was apparently celebrated for his knowledge of navigation which he claimed to have learned at Mr. Goodall's school.

Charles Andrews, a boy born in 1789 and who worked for Captain Urry, himself went to school in Yarmouth, this school being up the little lane which ran from Bank Street between the Bugle and the Dolphin Inn.

In the Census of 1841 three Yarmouth school teachers are listed, all living in the High Street, but at different addresses. These are:

Robert Maude, aged 55
Hannah Udall, aged 45
Margaret Lowe, aged 65

Whether any of these were connected with Mr. Goodall's school is not known, but Robert Maude lived at the top end of the High Street, and Hannah Udall lived in the house which is now Hopkins shop, or in a cottage immediately behind it.

Ten years later, in the Census of 1851, five names of school teachers appear. Robert Maude, now aged 64, is still living up the High Street, though he seems to have moved from the house where he lodged with William and Ann Griffiths, possibly because the latter had had four additions to their family.

Hannah Udall is also still living in the High Street, presumably in the same house as before. Margaret Lowe, now aged 75 and described as a Pauper, is living in St. James' Street with her son James and his wife and seven children. And the two new names are Elizabeth Maria Tuck, aged 24, and Elizabeth Peckham, 25, both living in St. James' Street, next door to each other.

Later on, in 1883, there is a record of another private school, for "ladies", being run by a Miss Phillips in Bank House, Bank Street. A relation of hers, John Phillips is listed as running a boarding establishment at the same address.

Now let us return to the Church of England School, which opened on its present site in Mill Road in 1855. The land on which the School was built had been in the possession of the Leigh family for many years, and was conveyed, as a free gift, to the Rector and Churchwardens of Yarmouth by Miss Catharine Leigh on 25th January, 1854. Building costs amounted to £1,100, but the building provided was fairly basic, consisting of one large schoolroom and a small and fairly primitive house for the Head Master.

A Committee of Management was laid down, consisting of the Principal Officiating Minister, his licensed Curate or Curates (at the Minister's discretion), the Churchwardens, and four other persons. The original four were:

Henry Love, a Captain (later Admiral) in the Royal Navy, who lived in a house in the High Street known as The Terrace, and now called Love Shore House.

William Squire, a well known Yarmouth merchant who with his brother John ran a Timber Yard, a Coal Yard, and farmed 400 acres in Freshwater. They also owned the Alum Bay Sand workings, and a considerable amount of property in Yarmouth.

Charles Wise Hollis, Doctor of Medicine, who lived at The Deacons in the High Street.

James Blake, owner of Yarmouth and Shalfleet Mills, and also a Coal Merchants business in Yarmouth. (See page 125).

When the Log Books started in 1863 the Head Master was Frederick Charles Spray, who became affectionately known as "Skipper" Spray as his hobby was sailing. At first he meticulously entered up the book every day, giving as it were, a blow-by-blow account of the running of his school, but there were many days when there was nothing of importance to record. Gradually therefore the Log found its natural level, reporting only items worthy of record, and becoming more interesting to the reader as a result.

A perusal of the Log Books over a period of 100 years from 1863 produces some interesting and slightly surprising trends. For example, over the first 40 years the number of children on the Roll grew steadily from 64 to 148. The next 36 years, which included World War I, saw no dramatic changes but a very gradual decrease, until in November 1939 there were 113 children attending. Then in the upheaval of World War II numbers dropped sharply to under 50, and it was 10 years after peace was established before the 100 mark was reached again.

The Logs record a considerable amount of illness, particularly in the early years when there were regularly occurring epidemics of measles, whooping cough, scarlet fever, chicken pox, and "dip-theriatic croup". The only remedy for these infectious diseases seemed to be to close the school.

Attendance was affected by many things other than illness. Bad weather, for instance, could decimate the numbers in the days when many children lived at some distance from the school and there was no public transport. Hay making, harvesting, black-berrying, even the arrival of a Circus in Yarmouth, all had their effect and took toll of the attendance. There were also many half and whole holidays granted for reasons which would surely not be accepted to-day. An extract from the Log for the summer of 1863 will well illustrate this.

> **Tuesday April 14.** Rather a poor attendance in the afternoon on account of the treat given at Freshwater to the children of the Coast Guards.
>
> **Thursday April 16.** Attendance somewhat below average. Many of the boys are at work either in the fields or assisting their parents.
>
> **Wednesday April 29.** I find that even in the upper Classes it is very difficult to make the children comprehend **practical** questions in Arithmetic. These must be practised.
>
> **Thursday April 30.** The boys were to-day warned against the dangerous practice of playing with gunpowder, one having set off a (small) cannon in the playground.
>
> **Friday May 8.** Many of the boys often stop away from school on Friday afternoons.

Tuesday May 19. The stormy state of the weather caused a thin school to-day.

Thursday May 28. Some children of the place have a cutaneous disease. Particular attention must be paid to cleanliness among the scholars.

Tuesday July 21. Many children in Yarmouth have the measles. Nine are to-day absent from the school on that account.

Thursday July 23. Several boys were observed to come to school rather dirty, the school was spoken to concerning the importance and necessity of cleanliness.

Monday August 10. Small number present. 20 children are absent on account of sickness, and those who belong to the country are employed at harvesting.

Tuesday August 11. I noticed particularly to-day that many of the boys mispronounce words like 'middle', 'little', 'shoulder', etc, by leaving out the 'l' and calling them 'middo', 'litto', 'shouder', etc. It seems too rather a difficult thing to correct.

Friday August 14. I have found that there are 12 of the children away at 'gleaning', or otherwise employed at the harvest. This is more than were absent on that account last year.

Friday August 21. More than half of the children stayed away from school this afternoon in order to see a military funeral – the parents of some of the children always keep them at home if there happens to be anything going on.

Friday August 28. Fourteen children were late this morning. I have punished several that were known to have loitered on the way, but those who are kept at home by their parents are the most difficult to deal with, the parents do not certainly seem to think much of the importance of punctuality.

In September 1863 Mr. Spray refers to the problems of teaching small children the Catechism which in this Church School was compulsory.

Friday September 18. The lower division were examined in the Church Catechism, it seems most difficult to make the children 'understand' what they learn by heart, it is so difficult to make it simple to their minds.

Wednesday October 21. The larger boys were warned this

afternoon against throwing stones in the playground.

Monday November 23. A number of children are sick, most of them have glandular swellings in the throat.

Thursday November 26. The books of the School Library were changed to-day. Not so many avail themselves of the library as might be wished, but many of the books are beyond the understanding of the children.

Tuesday December 1. Lateness in attendance, especially in the morning, is still a great annoyance, in three-fourths of the cases the children are not up soon enough to get to school by nine o'clock.

Friday December 11. Some four or five children are absent this afternoon on very unsatisfactory grounds – I think a few often persuade their parents to give them a holiday on Friday afternoons.

Thursday December 17. The School has been more noisy than usual this day, the children seem to be thinking too much on the approaching holidays.

Friday December 18. The School "broke up" to-day at 12 o'clock for the Xmas holidays. We recommence on January 4th, 1864.

Monday January 4, 1864. The School was re-opened this morning with 69 present.

Tuesday January 5. The noise in the School seemed greater than usual to-day, the holidays seem to have caused the children to forget their discipline.

Thursday January 7. Writing lessons have been carried on under great difficulties during this week, owing to the extreme cold.

Friday January 8. Three boys were punished this afternoon for staying on the ice till after the time for school; they had been warned before.

Wednesday January 13. Weather very wet.

Tuesday January 19. Many children have colds, the coughing in the school is continual and causes great interruption to the lessons.

Wednesday January 20. The numbers are lower this week, the weather causes a diminution in the numbers. I never before noticed so many of the children having bad colds.

Thursday January 21. The boys were cautioned against using slings. Stones have been thrown by them in the playground rendering it dangerous to the little ones. I forbad the use of them on the school premises.

Wednesday February 10. To-day being Ash Wednesday the children attended Church in the morning and will do so every Wednesday and Friday during Lent.

Thursday March 15. The boys in the playground were much disturbed by some lads of the town. I have been obliged to interfere twice during play-hours.

Wednesday April 20. The First Class is rather small, the boys are wanted by their parents to assist in garden work at this time of the year.

Tuesday April 26. The children are more punctual now than they were in the winter, but some of the girls from Freshwater are often late in the morning.

Wednesday April 27. The boys were cautioned this morning against injuring the hedges and trees in the playground, two boys having been found cutting the gate.

Monday June 6. Several boys are away to go to hay making.

Friday August 5. The school broke up this morning for the Harvest Holidays. To meet again on 29th inst.

Friday November 4. Many boys absent in the afternoon; it seems that they are cutting furze for to-morrow's bonfire.

Wednesday November 30. The boys had half an hour at weeding the gravel round the School in the afternoon.

Friday December 16. We are unable to see to work after 4 o'clock and so we generally are out a little before the proper time.

In the spring of 1865 there was an outbreak of small-pox in Freshwater and avoiding action was consequently taken. Later in the summer attendance problems were reported, and again in the summer of the following year.

Monday April 24, 1865. As the small-pox has appeared in Freshwater it has been thought best to send home the children who come to school from that Parish.

Monday May 5. As there are still cases of small-pox at Freshwater three of the girls from Norton Green were sent home to-day.

Thursday June 8. The children attended the funeral of Annie Fryer, late assistant teacher in the Infant School. The whole of the children walked to the Church at three o'clock and returned to school to prayers at 4-15.

Wednesday July 12. Only about 20 boys were present this afternoon as there was a cricket match near the school.

Wednesday August 30. A good many of the boys stay away in the afternoons to gather blackberries.

Monday June 11, 1866. A large School in the morning; 79 present. The School was not opened in the afternoon as on account of there being a Circus in the town only three boys came.

Monday June 18. Very wet in the morning, school consequently small only 45 present.

Monday September 24. Beginning of another School quarter. Number on Register Boys 50, Girls 47. Present this morning Boys 37, Girls 31.

In November 1866 a very modest entry announced that the School would have a holiday for the whole of the next week. No reason was given, but in fact, Skipper Spray was marrying the Headmistress of the Infants School, Mrs. Elizabeth Lewis.

They continued to work together as Headmaster and Headmistress for almost another 20 years, until in 1884 Elizabeth was forced to resign due to continuing bad health. Actually their two Schools were run quite separately, not even always having the same holidays, and they kept their own separate Log Books.

The Infants School at this time contained almost 100 pupils, and hence was larger than the Mixed School. Each week all the little ones were given religious instruction, and also marching and singing lessons, and must have been quite a handful for one woman to handle with only a Pupil Teacher to help. Poor attendance due to sickness was common in the Infants School, and was a measure of the generally low standard of hygiene in the country. This low standard was not confined only to the schools, but applied throughout the land. For example, one of Elizabeth Spray's log entries obviously refers to an outbreak of Foot and Mouth Disease.

Friday March 16, 1866. The ordinary routine of the school has been set aside to-day as this has been a day appointed for humiliation and prayer in consequence of the "cattle plague".

Once a year both Mixed and Infants Schools were visited by Her Majesty's Inspectors, and in 1867 the over-crowding in the Infants School came in for strong criticism:

"The Infants Department is making satisfactory progress,

but the classroom in which the babies are taught is over-crowded.

It appears that this classroom in which H.M.I. states that from 35-40 babies are taught is a small room containing only 1050 cu. ft. My Lords cannot but express their surprise that merely regarded in a sanitary point of view the Managers should have permitted young children to be crowded together with not more than 35 cu. ft. of air for each. Should the same state of things continue next year the question will arise whether any grant whatever ought to be made to an Infants Department which involves such arrangements".

Six months later, as a result of this Report, the Infants classroom was pulled down and enlarged.

January 1867 saw a spell of very cold weather in Yarmouth with heavy falls of snow which kept many children away from school.

Friday January 4, 1867. We do less work than usual. The cold makes it difficult for the children to use their pens and pencils.

But only six weeks later Mr. Spray was recording another reason for poor attendance; and yet another in July.

Friday February 15. Not so many present. Many of the boys go out after shell fish in the afternoons as the tides arc now low.

Tuesday July 16. 70 children present to-day. In consequence of the Naval Review at Spithead to-morrow the school will not be opened.

1868 was notable mainly for an outbreak of Scarlet Fever, this being particularly severe in the Infants School. Many log entries refer to this, though there were other problems as well.

Monday June 15. School opened with 78 present. The scarletina has appeared in the place, one little girl, Annie Whittington, being now ill with it. Martha Biddlecombe was sent home there being sickness in the family.

Wednesday July 8. A great number of children away from school this afternoon in consequence of a lifeboat having been taken through the town and there being a Tea drinking at Freshwater.

Thursday July 9. (Infants). Yesterday our classroom was pulled down with a view to enlarge it.

Monday August 31. (Infants) The classroom is now finished and is again in use.

Tuesday September 1. (Infants) There are more cases of scarletina which occasioned the school to be small.

Friday September 4. Another of the scholars has died of scarletina.

Tuesday September 8. The scarletina appears to be apreading amongst the younger children.

Thursday September 10. Bessie Simmons died of scarletina after only one week's illness.

Wednesday September 16. So few children at school this afternoon that I did not mark the attendance in the register.

Thursday September 17. The scarletina still continues to spread.

Monday September 21. More cases of scarletina.

Monday September 28. Fresh cases of scarletina every day.

Monday October 5. Only 52 present in the morning. Several fresh cases of scarletina have occurred, and four children are away on account of the death of their fathers by the loss of the 'Blonde' pilot vessel.

The loss of the pilot vessel 'Blonde' here referred to was a great tragedy for Yarmouth, four local men losing their lives. A newspaper account of the accident is quoted on page 73. A. G. Cole in his book on Yarmouth says that the disaster plunged at least three-quarters of the residents into mourning.

Friday October 9. Many children were absent this afternoon there being a tea-meeting at Wellow.

Two society weddings in quick succession early in 1869 brought the children unexpected treats.

Wednesday February 17, 1869. Notice was given of a holiday to-morrow and of a feast to the children by F. Crozier Esq., on the occasion of Miss Crozier's marriage.

Thursday March 4. The children had a holiday this afternoon, and at 4 o'clock were regaled with tea and cake given by R. B. Cooper, Esq. on the occasion of his marriage.

Emma Corries Crozier married Capt. William Smith, R.A. in Yarmouth Church on Thursday 18th February.

Rowland Burrard Cooper was the brother of Mrs. Dashwood of The Mount, and grandson of the Rev. Sir George Burrard. He was well known in Yarmouth as both he and his sister had been brought up by their grandmother Emma Lady Burrard following the death of their parents.

Tuesday August 31, 1869. School very small in the morning it being the day of Yarmouth Regatta, a holiday in the afternoon.

Tuesday February 15, 1870. Mary Reed withdrawn because her parents object to her taking her turn at sweeping the school.

Thursday March 7, 1872. The children had a holiday to-day and were regaled with tea and cake in the afternoon by Mr. Blake on the occasion of his daughter's marriage.

This was a big wedding for Yarmouth. James Blake was the Mayor, serving his fourth term, and living in Jireh House. His daughter Ellen Maria married James Cartmell Ridley, an Engineer from Jarrow-on-Tyne, and for the occasion a carpet was laid across the Square from Jireh House to the North Door of the Church.

In April 1872 there is a record that military drill began for the boys under Sergeant Richardson and Sergeant Copperball of the 103rd Regiment, and there are many subsequent entries showing that this became a standard part of the curriculum. No doubt this innovation was the result of the legislation on army reform passed through Parliament at the time.

July 19, 1872. The new lessee of the Bridge tolls has refused to allow children from Norton to pass to school toll free; in consequence they have stayed away from school.

June 10, 1873. To-day there was a holiday on the occasion of the re-opening of the Church.

The Church had been closed for a month for repairs to the Chancel and other alterations. A full account of these is given on page 30.

May 1, 1874 (Infants). Many children away from school to-day carrying garlands about the town, as is the custom here.

December 1876. The first mention in the Log of James Furmage, Pupil Teacher in the 1st year. Five years later Mr. Furmage left on being appointed to a School in Abingdon, but he returned in 1894 to begin a brilliant career as Head Master, and later as Manager.

June 12, 1877. This afternoon was a holiday, Mr. Blake having treated the children to a Circus.

Friday January 21, 1881. The school has been closed since Tuesday morning. The school ground and offices are blocked with snow drifts from 3 – 6 feet deep.

1882 saw a further outbreak of scarletina, which was certainly at this time the most prevalent illness amongst the young in Yarmouth. The 1868 epidemic, for example, lasted for over a year, and a few cases occurred in the intervening years.

February 1, 1884. There have been several cases of 'ringworm' lately in the Schools. The children who come from the Forts are ordered by the Surgeon to stay away on this account.

December 1884 (Infants). I have been obliged to resign my office as head Mistress of the Infants School, in consequence of continued ill-health, and having had a promise of a Government Pension.

Elizabeth Spray.

Christmas 1884.

March 2, 1885. Took charge of this School. (Infants). Attendance Morning 82. Afternoon 86.

Emily J. Dovey.

October 16, 1885. Minnie Fryer who has been a paid Monitor for the last two years has left to-day being recommended as a Pupil Teacher to the Ryde National School.

September 5, 1887. Re-opened after summer holidays. The school room, though not quite finished, is fit for use. The cap room is not yet completed. There is a case of scarletina in the town, George Page and Fanny Page are away from this cause.

October 24, 1887. Eight of the school desks have been lengthened three feet six inches. To-day the last of them was brought back by Mr. Griffiths the contractor and the children were re-arranged in their classes. The enlargement of the Schools and the alteration of furniture are now complete. The attendance is improving. The scarlet fever cases have not increased in number.

October 31, 1887. To-day one family returned to school, but there are still members of two families absent on account of scarlet fever.

November 4, 1887. For the first time for many weeks the average has exceeded 100.

November 18, 1887. William Griffiths and Hilda Griffiths are away on account of scarletina. As far as we know the disease is in no other family.

January 3, 1888. Another case of scarlet fever has appered, – George Summers. My Monitor Teresa Summers by the doctor's orders is staying away.

January 9, 1888. This morning only 70 were present. Of the 41 absent 28 are away because either themselves or some members of their family are sick.

This evening the Medical Officer of the Isle of Wight Sanitary Board ordered the Schools to be closed for a week.

"I certify that as Scarletina is prevalent in Yarmouth it is very desirable the Parochial Schools should be at once closed.

J. Groves
Med. Offi. of Health

Carisbrooke, Jan 9, 1888"

Signed: F. C. Spray.

Actually the Schools did not re-open until February 13th, and then closed again for a short period in March when scarlet fever re-appeared. Eighteen months later saw the beginning of a further period of sickness, and in November 1889 there was a whooping cough epidemic, the following absences being noted in the Infants Log – Thomas Sleaman, Ada Kelleway, Fred Lock, Ethel Sleaman, Mahala Warder, Jessie Smith, Samuel Palmer, Rose Sebborn, and Mildred Plumbly.

The winter of 1889-90 turned out to be a bad one as regards sickness. The Infants School was closed for two weeks in January, mainly for bad colds and 'flu, the staff being affected as well, Miss Dovey having a cold on the chest, and Miss A. Whittington going down with 'flu. The following few Log entries show the effect on the senior School.

January 20, 1890. This morning only 80 are present out of 108. Colds are the chief cause of absence though I am sorry to hear that scarlet fever has appeared in the family of P. S. Matthews.

January 23, 1890. Only 57 present this afternoon.

January 24, 1890. On this day I was too ill to attend School and the School was closed.

February 14, 1890. The school was re-opened on Monday February 10th after being closed eleven school days on account of the sickness of the whole staff. Miss Long, the assistant, is still too unwell to attend.

In June 1890 the School received its worst ever report from H.M. Inspector:

"The work of the School is, I regret to say, only fair. Geography is however good. English a failure. Needlework is very poor. It is with considerable hesitation I have recommended any grant for this subject, the excersises performed in my presence were so unsatisfactory. Unless the teacher, Miss Long, improves in teaching Needlework she cannot be recognised under Article 84 . . .

February 6, 1891. Miss Long, the assistant has been ill all the week and consequently there has been no Needlework done.

July 17, 1891. Miss Long, the teacher of Needlework, has been absent since Monday, on account of the sudden death of her mother. The needlework has been taken by Miss Summers, one of the Infants Assistants.

September 18, 1891. . . . Theresa Eva Summers has taken the place of Grace Long as Assistant and Teacher of Needlework.

Poor Miss Long! They say troubles never come singly, and over the last 18 months or so nothing seems to have gone right for her. One wonders what happened to her after she left. Did she get another job! Or did she decide that teaching was not for her?

But the events of 1891 were not by any means all unhappy, and in May of that year the Head Master, Frederick Spray, celebrated his 50th birthday. On this occasion the senior pupils of the school, together with staff, parents, ex-pupils and friends, decided to give him a birthday present, and this project proved to be so successful that it was subsequently written up very fully in the Press. I make no apology for quoting this newspaper account in full, not only because it describes an outstanding and unusual event, but also because the style of the article is very typical of the time, and gives us a glimpse of what life in Yarmouth was like at the end of the 19th century.

"TESTIMONIAL – On May-day an interesting presentation was made to Mr. F. C. Spray, the respected schoolmaster of the parish schools. The idea originated among the present pupils to make their master a present on his 50th birthday on May 1st. They took the teachers into their confidence, and on the idea becoming known many past pupils expressed a wish to join in the matter. An effort had then to be made to limit the subscriptions to present and past pupils, but this limit could not be kept, and numerous friends who had known Mr. Spray, "whom to know is to respect', and who was described by one influential subscriber as 'the prince of schoolmasters and most excellent of men', also joined. A committee was formed, consisting of Mr. John Bright (chairman), the Rev. G. Quirk (hon. secretary), Mr. Joseph Long (hon. treasurer), the Misses Dovey, A. Whittington, G. Long, Magualey, Summers, and Bright, Mr. R. Riddett and Mr. B. Webb. So heartily was the response, that sufficient funds were soon to hand, and the committee resolved to let the present take the form of a new boat, fitted complete. Mr. John Bright, the chairman, undertook the selection of a suitable design, and eventually an order was placed with Mr. John Pickett, of West Quay, Southampton, for a centreboard gig 14ft. 6in. long and 4ft. 9in. beam, to be built of best pine with teak top streak and teak inside fittings. The boat was once or twice inspected by the chairman and secretary during the building, and was delivered to Mr. Bright at the Marina on Wednesday night. So well was the secret kept that Mr. Spray had no idea of it until 11 o'clock on Thursday morning, when the boat was driven into the playground during the children's playtime on a trolley, decorated with garlands, with the red ensign flying at the mizzen and a red burgee at the main, on which was the name selected for the boat, "Judy III". Accompanied by a large number of inhabitants the school trustees met in the playground. There were present the Rev. G. Quirk (chairman), Mr. James Blake, C.C. treasurer (Mayor), Captain Abbott, and Mr. H. Pickersgill, all the trustees being present except Mr. T. L. Peacock. The Mayor, as senior trustee, was asked to make the presentation, and he said he had known Mr. Spray intimately for 28 years and the longer he knew him the more he respected and appreciated him. He was under grateful obligation to him for the ready and valuable assistance he had always rendered him in the school accounts, and the hundreds, he might say thousands, of scholars he had educated. All gratefully admired and loved him, and to-day's present gathering evinced the hearty goodwill of all the inhabitants generally (cheers). He wished him every pleasure and success with his beautiful new boat, and hoped he would give him a sail in her, but not outside the breakwater (laughter). He wished him many happy returns of his birthday, and a long and prosperous life (applause). The Rev. G. Quirk endorsed the sentiments of the Mayor, and congratulated Mr. Spray on the attainment of his jubilee, especially under such auspicious circumstances. He trusted that as many more years be granted him as a good Providence saw fit to permit, would happily and peacefully pass by. He assured Mr. Spray that this beautiful boat was conceived and launched from the minds and hearts of his present elder scholars, with the unanimous approval of the school. When the numerous array of past scholars was appealed to for assistance, a gratifying response followed, letters of most grateful feeling towards their old master, to whom they owed their success in life, coming from pupils in various parts. Those letters he had preserved for Mr. Spray's perusal. The clergy who had been in the parish during Mr. Spray's time had also sent most appreciatory answers accompanied by donations to the fund. The name "Jubilee" was suggested for the boat, but it was thought too common since the Queen's Jubilee was in 1887, and as Mr. Spray had had two boats named Judy, the committee named this successor "Judy III". It was indeed a grand and thoroughly representative gathering of all classes, creeds, sexes, and ages. Mr. Jospeh Long, as the eldest of the "old boys" resident in Yarmouth, and the treasurer of the fund, also made some happy remarks, and three cheers, thrice repeated, were given for the hero of the day, who acknowledged the gift with much grateful feeling, and expressed appreciation of the handsome manner of its presentation, though he could do no more than utter a few emphatic sentences. The remainder of the day was given as a holiday to the youngsters, and at the suggestion of the charioteer, Mr. Wm. Whittington, the boat was driven through some of the streets of the town, accompanied by the children, who heartily cheered, and sang one of their school songs, "Make haste, the boat is waiting". This made quite an imposing procession, and on arrival at the Quay, the boat was taken from the trolley and launched into the harbour waters, Miss Dovey, the respected mistress of the school, performing the christening ceremony in the presence of a large gathering, who heartily cheered as the boat glided down the ways. When the craft was waterborne she was taken charge of by Mr. Spray and sailed out into the deep".

Sadly, this was the climax of Mr. Spray's 31 years as Headmaster. Two and a half year's later his health, which had not been good, finally broke down, and he wrote the following letter to the School Managers:

December 1, 1893. The following notice has this day been sent to the Committee.

To the Committee of Yarmouth School.

Gentlemen,

Feeling utterly unable to carry on the work of the School as it ought to be done, I beg to give notice of my wish and intention to give up the same at the expiration of three months from the date of this present. I am deeply sensible of the great kindness received from the Committee during many years.

And have the honour to remain

Gentlemen

Your obedient servant

Frederick Charles Spray.

Spray had seen tremendous changes during his long term of office. The school had grown rapidly, but the standard of education had risen to keep pace with this growth, and the Head Master himself had become an institution in the town, being respected and loved by all.

Reading his school Log over this period of 30 years one can sense him gradually getting older and fighting a losing battle with his health. Quite naturally towards the end he was slowing down, new ideas were becoming less frequent, and there were more references to his absence owing to illness. Having said which it must also be reported that he lived for another 33 years in retirement, dying in his house in Ommanney Road in November 1926 at the age of 86. Let us hope that in that period he was able to spend many happy hours sailing in Judy III.

CHAPTER XI

The Fryers of Yarmouth

Some people in Yarmouth still remember Little John Fryer the butcher, whose shop in the High Street is now known as Pinings, and who died in 1926. Also his brother George who lived in Victoria Road, and died in 1935. Many more know Gillian Fryer, the talented young organist and choir mistress at St. James's Parish Church, who now lives with her mother in Freshwater. But few realise that there were once many Fryers living in Yarmouth, and that the family has had quite a colourful history.

The Fryers originated in Titchfield, between Southampton and Fareham, and the first one to settle in Yarmouth was James Fryer, a baker, who with his wife Mary arrived here in about 1790. Mary's brother Isaac Butler was landlord of the Bugle Inn in Yarmouth, and this could well have been the reason why they came to live here. James and Mary had ten children in all, the last 7 of which were born in Yarmouth.

Their second son Moses was only a few years old when they came to the Island, and he lived here all his life, dying in 1862 at the age of 76. He was a plumber and glazier by trade, married twice, and had 15 children in all. His second wife Eliza Miller was the daughter of a Baker, and she bore him 6 daughters and 5 sons. They lived at the top end of the High Street, behind what is now Mount Cottage, in the little lane leading down to the Solent.

Of the eleven children of the second marriage three must have caused their father some distress. These were Jane (b. 1823), Sophia (b. 1829) and Richard (b. 1837), for early in 1853, together with Jane and Sophia's husbands, they became members of the Mormon Church, and later that year emigrated to America. But more about them later. William Aaron, the eldest of Moses Fryer's sons became a sailor, married a Swiss girl, had four children, and was lost at sea from a yacht on passage to New Zealand.

Two of Moses's younger children were twins, and were christened Albert and Victoria. They were born in February 1840, and the story is that their birth coincided to the hour with the marriage of Queen Victoria and Prince Albert. If we are to believe this story the Queen visited Eliza Fryer at her home in Yarmouth, and asked that the twins should be named after herself and the Prince. This was done, but alas Baby Victoria lived only for a month, dying before the end of March.

Another son of Moses was George Nick, who became a butcher, married, and had five children, of which one was Little John who followed his father into the butchery business. Little John Fryer was so christened as his father was an ardent member of the Ancient Order of Foresters which flourished in Yarmouth, the local Court once having 500 members. Altogether Moses had around 50 grandchildren, though 27 of these he never saw since they were born in America.

Moses also had a younger brother, William, born in 1800, who himself became the head of a Yarmouth family. In 1828 William married Hannah Tuck, a Beaulieu girl, and they settled in Yarmouth, living in a house in South Street which is now called "Halfway". William was a fisherman, and of the six children of this marriage, all four boys became sailors.

The eldest, Emmanuel, born in 1829, became a Trinity House Pilot. He married his cousin Leah, one of Moses Fryer's daughters, when she was 16, and they had 6 children, two of whom were twins. Emmanuel died in 1911 and his widow in 1921, at St. James Villa, Tennyson Road.

The second boy Henry William, born in 1837, became a master mariner and captain of a yacht. He married a Kentish girl, daughter of a coastguard, and they had 9 children. Later they moved to Cowes and their eldest daughter, Julia Harriet, married a Cowes man George Groves who later became the senior partner in Groves and Gutteridge Ltd. Their eldest son, another Henry William, married the girl next door, the daughter of a Calshot Lightship Captain. This Henry William also rose to be captain of his ship, but died of heatstroke, together with several members of his crew, when becalmed in the Red Sea. He was only 31 years old, and left his wife with 3 small children. Gillian Fryer, mentioned at the beginning of this story, is his great-grand-daughter.

The next son, James, was the father of eight children, one of whom, Kathleen Jane, died as recently as 1961 at South Lynn, Victoria Road. The fourth boy, George, also followed the sea and became a yacht steward.

William and Hannah Fryer and their family are listed in the Census of 1841 and 1851 as living in South Street, and it is interesting that the house in which they lived was also occupied in 1841 by an Ann Hiscock and her two children Charlotte and George. George became a sailor when he grew up, and of course Hiscock is a well known Yarmouth name in yachting circles. Incidentally, the 1851 census records that Elizabeth Fryer, aged 15, the eldest daughter of William and Hannah, was living next door to her parents as a Nursemaid in the house of Emma Small (whose occupation was given as Scavenger), and it is interesting that later Elizabeth married James Small, a shoemaker.

Besides the houses occupied by William Fryer and his brother Moses, the records of the time list two other houses in Yarmouth having Fryer tenants. One of these was a cottage on the corner of Quay Street and Market Square, the site now being the bakers shop of Mills & Son.

The tenant of this cottage was James Fryer. Born in 1808, the eldest son of Moses by his first wife, James was a sailor and in 1830 married Ann Hollis, a Thorley girl. They had four children, but tragically Ann died in May 1840 when the youngest child, Emily, was only a year old and the eldest, Ellen, only 9. The census of 1841 tells a pathetic story, James being away at sea, and the four children being in the care of a 20 year old servant girl, Sarah White.

In May 1843 James married again, his bride being Jane Lee of Norton, and the marriage bears some evidence of haste as their first child was born in the following August. In the census of 1851 James was apparently once again away, and his wife Jane, now 28, was caring for Emily, the youngest child from the previous marriage, also for her own three small children, and was in fact expecting her fourth.

The other Yarmouth house having a Fryer tenant was next door to the Bugle Inn, and the 1840 Tithe Award Survey describes this as a dwelling house owned by Benjamin Mew, let to Isaac Butler and sub-let to Mary Fryer. Mary was of course Isaac's sister, the widow of James Fryer the Baker, and the mother of Moses and William, mentioned above. In the 1841 census she is listed as being 75 years of age, but she may not have wished to disclose her true age, which according to her birthdate was nearer 80.

Which brings us back to Jane, Sophia and Richard, the children of Moses Fryer who subsequently became Mormons, since in 1841 Jane and Sophia, aged 15 and 12 respectively, were living just across the Square from their Grandmother Mary, as servants in the house of John Stephens the builder. Mr. Stephens, who built Westhill House, lived in one of the houses facing south on to Market Square which were demolished in 1894. Richard was aged 4 and was of course living at home with his parents Moses and Eliza.

It is interesting to trace the subsequent history of these three Yarmouth children, all of whom left their native country for a new life in America, and none of whom found happiness there.

Jane Fryer was born in 1823, and when just 18 she married Francis Jorden in Milford, and apparently settled on the mainland, her first five children being registered in Shirley Common. Sophia, born in 1829, married John Thomas Geary, a lawyer and member of parliament, in 1852. Soon after his marriage Geary became interested in the Mormon Church, and before long he and Sophia, together with her elder sister Jane and younger brother Richard, were all persuaded to become Mormons. Richard was only fifteen at the time, and perhaps not old enough to make up his own mind, but he was no doubt influenced by his elder sisters. Jane's husband Francis apparently had reservations, but when the command came that all who accepted the revelation of Joseph Smith, the Mormon founder, should emigrate to Salt Lake City in Utah, and Jane intimated that she was going whether he accompanied her or not, Francis gave in and joined them.

Moses and Eliza Fryer and their other children would have nothing to do with the Mormon Church, but accepted the fact that these three were determined to go to America. They never lost touch and in fact were still writing to them in 1862. John Thomas Geary, however, who was 30 years old, was apparently dependent on his parents, and after failing to disuade him from becoming a Mormon and emigrating, they cut him off with the proverbial shilling. There must have been many times in the future when he wished he had heeded his parents advice.

There were problems associated with the voyage across the Atlantic, which took 6-8 weeks, and they were not all able to travel together, but in the early summer of 1853 they joined forces once more in St. Louis to prepare for the long and hazardous wagon train journey across the plains to Salt Lake City. Now their trials and tribulations really began. None of them was really used to roughing it, and they were faced with a journey of nearly 2,000 miles through unknown and often unfriendly country, driving wagon and ox teams, and a herd of cattle.

In June Sophia gave birth to her first child, and her sister Jane had perforce to act as midwife. In fact, Brigham Young the Mormon leader, commanded Jane so to do, and from then on she was official mid wife to the party. Jane, who had had no experience whatsoever in medical matters wrote home in desparation to her mother in Yarmouth, and asked her to send out a copy of "Dr. Gunn's Medical Book", and this completed her training.

It was not until October 1853 that they all arrived in Salt Lake City, having survived the rigours of the journey which included attention from unfriendly Indians. Houses then had to be built and preparations made to supply themselves with food during the coming winter, which proved to be exceedingly severe.

In the Spring Frank Jorden, Jane's husband, had had enough. He had never been an ardent member of the Mormon Church, and he decided that he and his family would be better off in California, where gold had just been discovered. Plead as he would however, he could not persuade Jane to travel any further, and in the end, after many tearful farewells, he set off by himself, the plan being that he should return after two or three years.

It may be that Frank was wrong in leaving his young wife and two small children in this way. Jane was also just beginning her third pregnancy, though he may not have known this. There is evidence that he wrote her several times begging her to join him, and there is little doubt they loved each other. Whatever the rights or wrongs of the case the subsequent behaviour of Brigham Young, the Mormon leader is difficult to condone. Young was opposed to any Mormon leaving Salt Lake City unless he especially wished it, and his word had almost the power of holy writ. Less than a year after Frank Jorden had left, Brigham Young offered Jane as second wife to a Richard Harrison who was being sent to southern Utah, 300 miles away, to help start an ironworks, and Young himself married them. Frank Jorden Jnr., Jane's eledest son, later wrote in his diary "Here in the spring of 1855 you might have found us just entering upon the life of Polygamy. Oh, that I could wipe out from my memory the bitterness to which this introduced us".

Jane had seven children by Richard Harrison but did not find happiness with him. One of her grand daughters, Bessie Snow of Pine Valley, Utah, has written a most interesting and informative book about Jane, Sophia and Richard Fryers life in America, and it this book which is the main source of information. Of her grandfather Richard Harrison she writes:

"He was the sort of man who was master of his household. He was fussy, particular, and precise. Everything around him had to be just so. He expected and generally got prompt obedience from those around him. He was strict, firm, determined, irritable and domineering to the point of cruelty".

Jane's first husband Frank Jorden continued to write to her and there is evidence that Richard Harrison intercepted many of his letters and prevented Jane from ever seeing him again. Jane died in 1898 at the age of 75, and her youngest daughter said of her that she was the saddest person she ever knew, and one of the kindest. Her grand-daughter Bessie Snow said "Only grandmother herself will ever know what she went through. I do hope God had reserved a nice peaceful nook for her up in heaven where she found Frank Jorden, with out-stretched arms, waiting for her under an apple tree in full bloom".

The Mormon religion certainly brought no happiness to Jane Fryer, nor to many of her children. One of her daughters, Annie Jorden, fell in love with a James Haslam when she was 16 and they wished to marry. Haslam unfortunately was not a Mormon, so Annie was not only forbidden to marry him but was told she must marry a 60 year old man, Robert Richey, who already had two wives, or her own step father Richard Harrison. Of the two she chose Robert Richey. Her brother, Frank Jorden Jnr., tried to prevent the marriage and as a result his life was threatened. Frank was ultimately expelled from the Church, and several attempts were made on his life before he managed to get away. He left, determined to find his long lost father, and after a journey of 6,000 miles was rewarded for his steadfastness.

Thanks to Bessie Snow we know a great deal about the Fryers who went to America, far more in fact than about those who remained in Yarmouth. But a letter written in May 1862 by Albert Fryer of Yarmouth to Richard Fryer in Utah does give us a little information. Albert was 22 at the time, and was the survivor of the twins named after Queen Victoria and Prince Albert.

In his letter Albert besought Richard to leave the Mormon faith and return to the relegion he was brought up in. He said that their father, Moses, was seriously ill and had been bedridden for four months and was not likely to recover. In fact Moses died two months later, in July 1862 aged 76.

"Mother stays upstairs now almost all of the day with Father. Her leg is better than it was. It was very bad a little while ago Annie is getting along pretty well. She is still at the school. She sends her love to you both wishing you many happy returns of your birthday. William's wife was confined last Good Friday with a son. She is getting along pretty well excepting she has a cold in her leg which confines her to her bed. William is away from home in a yacht called the "Florence". The Duke of Leeds is the owner. William is the Mate of her. George and Leah are getting on pretty well. Their children likewise. Aunt Griffin is quite well, likewise Uncle and Aunt Cove. Uncle William is still living. He is pretty well. Old Mr Maud is still alive. He get out a little but is very much altered. Edward Woolgar is married and has two or more children. He is in a yacht here. Robert Butler has a very nice school in which he is Master. He has a two class man. Archibald Bannister and William Day are in the Training College at Battersea. Bannister has obtained a first class scholarship. He has a Queens Scholar likewise; he is first on the list in the college. Day has not been there long enough to pass yet. Our dear school master died last month. He was greatly beloved by all who knew him. He has left a wife but no children. Your old friend William McWhite is still alive. He very often enquires for you. He is married and has several children. Doctor Clarke has left here and we have a new doctor by the name of Dr. Meeres. I think I have told you of most of your acquaintences. I must tell you now of Yarmouth, and its neighbourhood.

"In Yarmouth we have a new Coastguard House and cottage besides a large house for the Lieutenant. We have a new Key. I mean to say that it is much enlarged. A Bridge from Yarmouth to Freshwater. Those houses where Grandfather used to live are taken down and new ones put up. A new house also where Taylor Taber lived and that land on the top of our hill where old William Law used to live is filled up with nice houses from number 16 to number 72 and one villa at a much high price. We have a new Gas House, Steam Mills, New Schools, New Malt House built against Mr. Tenkins, a new and very fine Rectory near Lady Burrards for our minister. Those gardens behind Old Blacksmith Harness are entirely filled up with new cottages by the name of Alma Place. There are a great many cottages built going down toward the mill . . ."

Another letter written about the same time by Eliza Fryer, the wife of Moses and mother of Albert, contains the following.

> "I am still with Albert and Leah and my sister Ann lives in the same house with us, but by herself. We have a great many new houses, a Bridge to Freshwater, a gas, clam Boats, and large new Forts. Yarmouth is very much altered. Old Mr. Clark is dead and they have left Yarmouth. Leah has three children, George three, William two . . . your aunt Cove is still living at Hill Top, Beaulieu. Mary has four children and not a very good husband. Captain of a Yacht. Albert has not very good health. But he fights on. Some times cuts Headstones which he does well. He is a very steady labourer and quiet and very kind to me and so is William. And they are all very good to me. I hope you are finding sufficient for the day so that you may not want. My love, deep love dwell on your hearts. May God bless you and be with you for ever hence. My blessings for your welfare in Life, and your Eternal Happiness in Heaven with all our united Love.
>
> Your affectionate Mother,
> Eliza Fryer."

Soon after receiving the above letters Richard Fryer and his wife Teresa, together with Sophia and John Thomas Geary and other Mormon families were sent down into southern Utah to found a new town at Toquerville. When the Gearys arrived they were met by the church authorities, including the local Mormon Bishop Joshua Thomas Willis. Sophia is reputed to have been a very beautiful woman, and the story is that when Bishop Willis first saw her he said "My God, that is the most beautiful woman I ever saw in my life. I'm going to have her if I have to go to hell to get her". Hardly the sort of remark one would expect to hear from a senior dignitary of any church.

He was apparently as good as his word, and the family blame him for breaking up the Geary marriage. Anyway they separated, and John Geary went back up north to Salt Lake City where in 1867 he died in a shooting accident. Some say he committed suicide. Sophia was married to Bishop Willis – divorce seemed to present no difficulties to a Mormon who had his eyes on a woman – and Bessie Snow has since written "Whether Bishop Willis went to hell for Aunt Sophia I don't know, but according to her Geary children *she* went *through* hell after she married him. They say he did little to help her support her children . . ."

Sophia had three children by Joshua Willis, and the last one killed her, on May 27th, 1872, both she and the baby being buried in the same casket.

Richard Fryer, the youngest of the three immigrants, was 25 years old when he and his wife and small daughter moved down south. From all accounts he was an ardent Mormon, and a friend of Brigham Young. He was also, according to people who knew him, artistically very talented, not only as an artist, but also as a sculptor and musician. He played for dances, trained the choir, painted curtains and scenery for local plays, and gave music lessons. He was a talented violinist.

Richard was also a very hard worker, but found life in Toquerville difficult, and the struggle to feed and clothe his family a constant battle with the elements. Whether this finally got him down, or whether the fact that he was beaten up on two occasions damaged his brain, no one knows for certain, but he began to experience periods of temporary insanity. He got it into his head that this wife was having an affair with their next door neighbour, Thomas Batty, and finally ordered her and their infant son Moses out of the house. Teresa Fryer accordingly left him and lived most of the time after that with the Batty family.

Early one morning Richard went to the Batty house and demanded to see his wife. He then produced a loaded revolver and shot first Thomas Batty, then Teresa and finally his son. He then went and barricaded himself in an unfinished house he was building and prepared for a siege. The local Sheriff formed a posse and surrounded the house, and on firing their first salvo Richard Fryer fell dead.

So all three Fryer children found nothing but hardship, bitterness and tragedy in America, and in reading of their unhappiness one cannot but come to the conclusion that the strange, dogmatic Mormon faith must carry much of the responsibility. In all charity however one must remember that these early pioneers suffered untold hardships, both in travelling to Utah and in building a life for themselves once they were there. This life was never easy for them, and there is no doubt that their religion sustained and comforted them, even though it brought many of them pain and grief. Perhaps one should not judge them too harshly but only reflect that their lives might have been very much happier had they not abandoned the faith they were brought up in. The little parish church in Yarmouth, where the Fryers used to worship, which had already been there for 200 years when they left, is still there, comforting and unchanged, and the last of the Yarmouth Fryers, Gillian and her mother, still worship there every Sunday.

CHAPTER XII

Proceedings of the Corporation of Yarmouth

1854 — 1891

In considering the conduct and management of affairs by the Mayor and Burgesses during the last phase of their life it is necessary to go back a few years. Although in the past their relationship and constitution had been almost incestuous there were district signs by the middle of the 19th century that they were beginning to take more of an interest in the town and its development. The enlargement of the Quay, and the building of the breakwater in 1843 were perhaps the first indications that a new awareness was creeping in, and although the motives for development may not always have been the right ones, yet in the second half of the century much good was done. In 1850 it can be said that Yarmouth was at the beginning of a new and unprecedented stage in its development, the results of which were far reaching, and which affect all our lives to-day.

From time to time the Corporation had discussed the matter of Education, and had agreed that Yarmouth needed a school, but it was not until the Church became a major influence in the affairs of the town that anything was done. At a meeting of the Corporation on 10th January, 1854 the Rector put forward a proposition:

> "The Rev. John Blackburn stated that as Rector of the Parish he was desirous of erecting some Parish Schools within the Parish. That Miss Catherine Leigh has given a piece of Land marked 97a on the Tithe Commutation Map for this purpose. That a small piece of Land immediately adjoining this piece of Land and which would be essential for effectually carrying out the intended plan, marked 97, is the property of the Hon. William a'Court Holmes. That the Corporation of this Borough are the owners of a piece

of Land adjoining another field belonging to Mr. a'Court Holmes marked on the Tithe Map 84, which said last piece of Land altho' larger in dimensions is equal in Value to the piece adjoining Miss Leigh's.

That it is very desirable for the purpose of the Schools to obtain the piece of Land belonging to Mr. a'Court Holmes. The Rev. Blackburn had made an application to Mr. a'Court Holmes suggesting the possibility of some arrangement for this purpose and the exchange of the two pieces of ground having been proposed such exchange had been assented to by Mr. a'Court Holmes by a letter of which the following is a copy-:

Westover.
December 3. 1853

My dear Sir,

I will with pleasure consent to the exchange of Land with the Corporation of Yarmouth as proposed by you, providing it is clearly understood that the field I give up is appropriated as a site for a School which is my sole Motive in consenting to the exchange.

Believe me, my dear sir,
Yours truly,
Wm. a'Court Holmes.

The Rev. J. Blackburn,
Yarmouth.

The Minutes of the Meeting then record the following:

"And therefore William Squire Esq, proposed and John Clarke Esq seconded the following Resolution which was carried unanimously.

That the proposal submitted to the Corporation by the Rev. John Blackburn be agreed to and that the Town Clerk be instructed to take the necessary steps for effecting the Exchange of the piece of Land numbered 84 for the piece of Land belonging to the Hon. Wm. a'Court Holmes marked 97.

That when such exchange shall be completed the Corporation appropriate it as a site for the proposed School in addition to the Land given by Miss Leigh, and that the necessary proceedings be taken for that purpose.

From this beginning sprang the Church of England School

which was opened in 1855, and which has been such a part of the life of Yarmouth for the past 125 years. (See page 98).

At this same meeting of the Corporation in 1854 another significant matter arose:

"At this Assembly the Wharfinger Henry Warder attended and stated that Mr. James Blake had refused to pay Wharfage on the goods landed by him since the time of his appointment, and desired instriuctons as to the course he should take. And therefore the Wharfinger is directed to seize and distrain upon any goods for tolls due from any person refusing to pay the same – and in case of such distress to sell in the regular course and recover the Tolls. And the Town Clerk was instructed to write to Mr. Blake to secure payment of the Tolls due and in default of payment to take legal proceedings against him for enforcing the same. The amount due is £4. 19. 5d".

A letter was accordingly written to Mr. Blake demanding the payment of the Wharfage due from him before Saturday next, or else . . . etc, etc. But Mr. Blake still declined to pay, and at the next meeting in December the Town Clerk was instructed to get tough with him (and with another man, John Baggs) and threaten legal proceedings. Presumably they then both paid up as there is no further reference to the matter in subsequent Minutes.

The significance of this incident is that it is the first time that James Blake makes an impact on the town. His head-on collision with authority is interesting since he was destined to become the Grand Old Man of Yarmouth Corporation, serving 17 times as Mayor, and actually being at the head of affairs when the Corporation was abolished in 1891.

Two years later, his difference with the Corporation obviously not settled, he is in the news again. There was a meeting of the Corporation on 20th September, 1856 (the 21st was a Sunday and so the traditional date could not be used) and The Minutes record the following:

"The committee on general purposes reported that at a Meeting held on 1st May last a Memorial from twenty of the Inhabitants of the Borough was read and Mr. Blake and Mr. Baggs attended as a deputation when the subject of the Memorial was discussed and explanations given.

Also the same Committee reported that at the meeting

aforesaid they had inspected the Quay and Wharfs and had ordered the necessary repairs to be completed.

Also at this Assembly Mr. James Blake, Mr. John Baggs, and Mr. John Findlay were unanimously elected as Free Burgesses of this Borough.

Also at this Assembly Mr. James Blake, Mr. John Baggs, and Mr. John Findlay were duly chosen and unanimously elected into the office of chief Burgesses of the Borough in the room of Sir George Burrard, Sir Wm. Symonds, and John Squire Esq who have died since the last meeting.

There is no record of the Memorial brought to the meeting by James Blake and John Baggs, but it seems that their refusal to pay their tolls was due to the deplorable state of repair of the Quay. Their action obviously had the desired effect, and marked the start of James Blake's 40 years service to the Corporation.

At the above meeting the Town Clerk reported that he was being chased by the Government to pay Stamp Duty on the election of all Free and Chief Burgesses since 1832 when for some reason they stopped paying it.

On Monday 22nd September, 1856 the Corporation met again and the new Burgesses, James Blake, John Baggs and John Findlay, were elected to the general purposes committee. A clear case of "if you can't beat them, join them".

And then things started to happen. We shall never know exactly how big a part James Blake played in the events of the next few years, but the Minutes take on a new and hopeful look, and one senses a feeling of expectency, even of excitement.

21st September, 1857 It was resolved that the consent of the Corporation should be given to the intended application to Parliament for powers to make a Bridge across the Harbour.

21st September 1859. James Blake was elected Mayor for the first time.

3rd July 1860. It was mentioned that Mr. Blake was about to erect a Gas Works for the purpose of lighting the Town and that Mr. Squire (William) was about to give to Mr. Blake for the above purpose his interest in the pieces of Land Nos: 92 and 93 on the Tithe Map, and thereupon this meeting came unanimously to the determination to join with Mr. Squire in enfranchising these pieces of Land and conveying the same in Fee to Mr. Blake. (William Squire was the Treasurer to the Corporation).

21st September 1860. James Blake re-elected Mayor. The record of this meeting covers four pages – the longest ever – there being much business to report on improvements to the Harbour and Quay.

On the 13th October, 1862 a new table of Tolls was agreed.

Table of Tolls

	s	d
Ale, Porter, Cider, or Vinegar, per Hogshead	0	3
ditto per Barrel	0	2
ditto per Kilderkin	0	1
Ale, Porter, or Aerated Waters in Hampers per dozen bottles	0	1
Bark, per ton	0	8
Bed or Bedsteads, each	0	2
Biscuits, per ton	1	4
Biscuits, per Cwt	0	1
Bottles, empty, per Gross	0	2
Boxes according to size, small	0	1
ditto large	0	2
Bricks, per 1,000	0	8
Brooms, Heath or Hair, per doz	0	1
Butter, per Cask	0	1
Cattle, Bulls, each	0	3
Other Beast, each	0	2
Yearlings, each	0	1
Calves, each	0	0½
Cattle, Horses, each	0	2
Sheep, per score	0	6
Lambs, per score	0	3
Pigs, each	0	0½
Carriages, four wheeled, each	0	8
two wheeled, each	0	6
Waggons, loaded, at per ton	1	4
Coal, per ton	0	2
Corn, Wheat or Malt, per Quarter	0	2
All other kinds, per Quarter	0	1
Dogs, sporting, each	0	2
Drapery Goods, per Barrel Bulk	0	2

Earthenware, per Crate	0	8
Brown, per load	1	0
Fish, fresh or salted, per ton	1	4
per cwt	0	1
Flour, per Jack	0	2
per Barrel	0	1½
Glass, per Barrel Bulk	0	3
Grindstones, under 2 feet diameter	0	1
above 2 feet diameter	0	2
Gun powder, per Barrel	0	3
Grocery Goods of all kinds, per ton	1	4
per cwt	0	1
Hay, per ton	0	8
Headstones or Tablets, each	0	2
Hides or Leather, per ton	1	4
per cwt	0	1
Hops, per pocket	0	3
Household Furniture, small packages	0	1
large do:	0	2
per waggon load	2	0
per cart load	1	0
Hurdles, per dozen	0	2
Iron, Lead, Copper, or other Metals, per ton	1	4
per cwt	0	1
Jars of Liquor, Oil, etc. Under 3 gallons	0	1
Over 3 gallons	0	2
Laths, per 1,000	0	3
Lemons or Oranges, per Chest	0	2
Lime, per Quarter	0	2
Manures, Artificial or otherwise, per ton	0	8
Marine Stores viz rope, canvas, yarn or oakum, per ton	1	4
per cwt	0	1
Meal, Bran or Pollard, per Sack	0	1
Meat of all kinds, per ton	1	4
per cwt	0	1
Oils of all kinds, per ton	0	8
per Barrel	0	3
Oil of Vitriol, per Carboy	0	2
Peat, per load	0	6
Potatoes, per ton	0	6

Potatoes, per Sack,	0	1
Paint, per small Cask	0	1
per large Cask	0	2
Parcels, small	0	1
large	0	2
Pipes, per Barrel	0	2
Pipe Clay, per Cask	0	1
Pianofortes, Harps or Harmoniums, each	0	6
Rape and other Cake, per ton	0	8
Salt, per ton	0	10
Sand, Chalk, Shingle, or Gravel, per ton	0	2
Seeds of all kinds, per ton	1	4
per cwt	0	1
Stones, Rough and Paving, per 100 feet	0	4
Ashlar, per ton of 16 cu. feet	0	4
Slates, Countess, per 1,000	0	6
Duchess, per 1,000	0	10
Spars, small, each	0	2
large do:	0	4
Tar, Pitch, or Varnish, per Barrel	0	2
Tea, per Chest	0	3
Tiles or Pipes, all sorts, per 1,000	0	8
Timber, per load of 50 feet	0	6
Deals in sizes per 100	2	0
Quartering per 100	1	0
Firewood per Fathom	0	6
Trees and Shrubs per Bundle, small	0	1
large	0	2
Wool, per Bag	0	4
Wine or Spirits, per Hogshead	0	8
per Quarter Cask	0	4
in bottles per dozen	0	1

Rates on Vessels entering or using the Harbour.

For every Vessel under the burden of 15 tons	4d
Or for a year paid in advance	5/-
For every Vessel under the burden of 50 tons	6d
Or for a year paid in advance	10/-
For every Vessel under the burden of 100 tons	8d

Extra for the use of Buoys, Anchors and Chains	2/-
For every Vessel under the burden of 150 tons	10d
Extra for the use of Buoys, Anchors and Chains	3/-
For every Vessel of the burden of 150 tons and upwards	1/-
Extra for the use of Buoys, Anchors and Chains	4/-

Goods remaining on the Quay for a longer time than 48 hours shall pay Three pence per ton for each day during which the Goods shall remain after the first 48 hours.

James Blake was Mayor again 1865, and it was during this year that the first discussions were held about a Railway, the original proposal being for a line connecting Yarmouth with Bembridge.

A year later Charles Wyatt Estcourt, the Town Clerk, died after sixteen years service. Announcing this the Minutes go on to say "Arthur Harbottle Estcourt of Newport, Isle of Wight., Conveyancer, was elected Common Clerk of this Borough and Steward of the Courts and View of Frankpledge, and took the oath faithfully to perform these offices". And this he certainly did, faithfully and well, for the remainder of the life of the Corporation, and for some time afterwards. He had a good start in 1867 since he worked for his first year nder Admiral Henry Ommanney Love who was serving his sixth term as Mayor, and who was very highly thought of in the town. It was Admiral Love who presented Yarmouth with the 3 ton Crane which is still in use on the Quay to-day.

And then a strange thing happened. Since his election as a Chief Burgess in 1856 James Blake had missed only one meeting of the Corporation, and that was the one at which his brother Burgesses had unanimously elected him Mayor for the first time. His excellent attendance record continued until the meeting of September 23rd, 1867 at which Sir Andrew Snape Hammond, Bart, was sworn in as Mayor for the ensuing year. Blake was missing on this occasion, and did not attend a single meeting during the next two years while Sir Andrew was Mayor. At the end of his Mayoralty Sir Andrew stopped attending, and in fact only came to one more meeting before he died in 1874. James Blake started attending again and resumed his almost 100% attendance.

Was there friction between these two men? They certainly came from very different backgrounds, Hammond – who assumed the additional surname of Graeme in 1873 – was a typical wealthy aristocrat, whereas Blake was a prosperous coal and corn merchant and a self made man. At the time in which they lived there was a vast social gulf between them. It is perhaps ironical that James Blake was again Mayor when Sir Andrew died, and there is a Minute in the book which says:

> "It was agreed that the Mayor and Corporation should attend the funeral of the late Sir Andrew Snape Hammond-Graeme, Bart, one of the Chief Burgesses of this Borough who has twice served the office of Mayor of this Borough".

While this apparent clash of personalities was working its way out of the system, various homely items were appearing in the Minutes:

1868 A new fender, fire irons and bracket for these, and a new tablecloth were bought for the Town Hall.
The Town Clerk's salary was doubled.

1869 More repairs to the breakwater were required.

This is a recurring theme at fairly frequent intervals, 100 tons of stone being used on each occasion.

A letter from Admiral Love having been read tending his resignation as Chief Burgess it was resolved unanimously that this (Meeting) wishing to mark their deep sense of the great obligation which this Borough and Town are under to Admiral Love for his services during the 29 years which he has been a Chief Burgess and during which he has served the office of Mayor 10 times and has been ever foremost in promoting both by his personal exertions and pecuniary benefactions every improvement which has taken place earnestly request him to withdraw his resignation and to allow his name to remain enrolled as a member of the Corporation so long as life shall last. (He would not change his mind).

1870 The Hayward attended and made presentations as to the threats thrown out in the event of his pounding any cattle or sheep. The following people now tie on the Common.

Mrs. Plumley of the Wheatsheaf (widow of Barnabas) 2 cows

Mr. Hillier the butcher	2 cows
The Hayward	1 donkey
Mr. Meager	1 donkey
Mr. Reed (timber merchant)	1 donkey
Mr. Daw	1 donkey
Mr. Flint	1 goat
Mr. Singer	1 donkey

The Hayward did not consider that any of the foregoing had any right, except Mrs. Plumbley. The Town Clerk had looked into the legal situation to see what rights existed, but could find no legal basis – only custom and practice over a long period of time.

James Blake attended the meeting on 25th October, 1870, his first one since 21st September, 1867, and at this meeting it was decided that enquiries should be made about building a Pier.

At this time it had not been decided on the type of Pier, and it seems the Railway Company had put forward plans for building a pier out from the Castle, and to bring their railway to it. The Corporation were against this, and instructed an engineer, Alfred Giles, to produce plans for a pier. Giles suggested a pier 560 feet long, 8 feet wide, terminating in a bridge 60 feet long and 6 feet wide to rest on a floating dummy, properly secured to Dolphins. The estimated cost of this was £1,500, or without a floating dummy about £1,100.

This was a period of great expansion and excitement for Yarmouth. The possibility of building a Pier and having the Railway was a great step forward in the expansion and development of the port. The Minutes of the negotiations with the railway company (the Yarmouth and Ventnor Railway Co.) are a bit tantalising as they give very little detail of the plans put forward. As mentioned above the original plan was to acquire the Castle and build the Pier out from there, possibly with the railway running to the pierhead, but the War Office fortunately declined to give up the Castle. Another plan was to build the Pier out from the Common, and yet another one was to go through what is now the George Hotel garden. Of course at this time there were still houses and cottages where Pier Square now is.

Negotiations with the various bodies were slow, and time passed. By September 1872 it looked as though the Railway Company had lost interest in the project, and the Corporation decided that they themselves would have to undertake the construction of the Pier. In the meantime life had to go on, and domestic matters occupied the attention of the Corporation.

A complaint was made about the state of the lane on the west of the "Lytton" (i.e. Snakes Lane, which ran from the High Street to what is now Tennyson Road along the west side of the old churchyard). The lane was inspected by the Mayor and the Rector who found that it was never used as a thoroughfare, but had become a nuisance, being used as a deposit for rubbish and offensive refuse, and they recommended that a bank should be formed across each end of the lane with turf and planted with thorns.

In February 1873 it was reported that the sea was undermining the Quay. The Mayor (James Blake) and Mr. Meager were given authority to spend up to £10 on repairs. At the same time the Lock-up house was repaired at a cost of £1, and was let to Mr. Richardson, the chemist, for £1 per annum.

September 28th 1874. James Salter, Hayward and Scavenger, having retired, the position was offered to Thomas Doe at 2/- per week. An interesting letter of appointment was sent him.

To Mr. Thomas Doe,

The Mayor and Chief Burgesses of Yarmouth are willing to engage you as Scavenger and Hayward through all the Streets Roads and Commons of the Borough of Yarmouth during their will and pleasure at the sum of two shillings per week. You are therefore to keep all the said streets and roads clean and free from filth dung and litter. You are to take care that no cattle Donkeys Horses or other animals be allowed to stray loose in the said Streets Roads and Commons and to impound any found so straying loose. If any Cattle Horse Donkeys or other animals be tethered or tied on the Common you are to see that they are tied so as not to encroach upon or cross any public road and with Chains not more than 12 yards long. You are also from time to time to report to the Mayor the names of all persons tyeing or tethering Cattle or other animals on the said Common and when ordered by the Mayor you are to imp-pound the same. You are to take to your own use all the Sweepings of the said roads and Streets and all fines and payments for impounding stray cattle and other animals but such fines and payments shall be approved by the Mayor and Chief Burgesses.

By Order,

A. Harbottle Estcourt, Town Clerk.

2nd April 1875. Twelve tenders were received for the Pier, ranging from £2,250 to £4,097. The lowest of these (from J. Denham) was accepted. The contract was signed and sealed on 6th May, 1875. Giles, who designed it, was asked to superintend construction for a fee of £50, but refused as a Clerk of the Works was being appointed.

1st July 1875. A question was raised whether the Pier was set out in the right direction, but it was inspected and found to be according to plan – "that the direction was to the east of magnetic north, thus fulfilling the condition of the grant from the Crown of the site".

8th July 1875. Objection was raised that the sides were too high, clumsily large, and that the railing was dangerously wide. The design was altered accordingly.

3rd August 1875. The Contractor, having lost 10 feet in length of the Pier, offered to drive two more piles making the last two lengths 20 feet instead of a 30 foot span. This was agreed.

14th March 1876. The heaviest storm ever known in the memory of old inhabitants took place on Sunday 12th instant, and the tide rose at least two feet over the Quay. A vessel belonging to Captain John Brown was driven against the Wall opposite Mr. Blake's yard, and broke down a large portion of the Wall. Ordered that Fryer the Mason be employed to rebuild the Wall, and to make such other repairs to the Quay as may be necessary. The sea wall at the end of the lane between Mr. Richardsons (the Chemist) and the Refuge to be repaired at the same time. (This is Friar's Lane).

But the storm mentioned above was nothing to the storm that was about to break over the Corporation of Yarmouth. Apparently with very little warning the Hon. Member for Chelsea, Sir Charles Dilke, stood up in the House of Commons and made a series of charges against the Corporation, claiming that they had failed to publish their accounts, or to have them audited, and that in fact the accounts were fictitious anyway, as they represented that large sums of money had been spent on harbour repairs, which it could be proved had not been so expended.

The Town Clerk was instructed to prepare and submit to the Home Secretary a statement refuting these charges, and also to request the Member for the Island to take an opportunity of questioning Sir Charles Dilke in the House as to his authority, and to call upon him to withdraw his charges. This was done, but without success, and as far as the House of Commons was concerned the matter was dropped. But the damage had been done, and though it was another fifteen years before the final act of this drama was played, this was really the beginning of the end.

Meanwhile, on the domestic front the minor triumphs and irritations continued to be reported.

> **26th July 1876.** Reported that the Pier was opened on the 19th!!

The Town Clerk, justifiably proud of the fact that in spite of many difficulties they had managed to build their Pier, unbent so far as to put two exclamation marks against this entry in the Minute Book.

> **24th August 1876.** A complaint from the Board of Trade that Yarmouth Harbour's lights were extinguished on 12th August, elicited the reply that the lights were never lighted during the summer months. For good measure the Town Clerk added that the Corporation proposed to continue this practice.

A few days before this Meeting was held the new Pier suffered extensive damage from the steamer "Prince Leopold" as she came alongside. This resulted in a most extraordinary letter being written to her owners, the Southampton and Isle of Wight Steam Packet Company. Instead of claiming damage or reprimanding the Skipper of the boat for carelessness the Corporation wrote an apologetic letter, and even congratulated Captain Beazley for not doing more damage than he had done. One can only assume that they were terrified that the Steamship Company might remove their patronage and go elsewhere.

The landward approach to the Pier through Bank Street was very narrow, and it was decided that the Street ought to be widened. To this end a letter was written to Martin & Co., of 68 Lombard Street, asking them if they would give a up strip of land in Bank Street so that the necessary alterations could be made. But this request fell on stony ground, the following reply being received:

> "Sir,
>
> We are favoured with your letter of the 4th inst, and much regret that the Corporation of Yarmouth did not arrange terms with us before building their Pier. We are not disposed to entertain any application for a strip of land except on the basis of an exchange of land. If the Corporation can

possess themselves of the little Public house or some other bit that would be an equivalent we might entertain the subject.

We are, Sir, your Obedient Servants,

Martin & Co.

Further trouble occurred with the Pier when it was decided to erect gates at the entrance close to Bank Street and demand tolls of all persons passing on to the Pier. These gates apparently restricted access to the beach, and this was the start of the trouble.

At the next meeting on 17th July (James Blake, Mayor, in the Chair) the Town Clerk read out "a Memorial to the Mayor and Corporation of Yarmouth signed by 37 inhabitants demanding the removal of the obstruction between the Toll House and the Kerb Stone of Bank Street" and threatening removal in seven days if their request was not complied with. It was resolved to apply for an injunction to restrain any such attempt. Mr. Frederick Blake was retained as solicitor to the Corporation to act in this matter. But the residents were as good as their word – they broke down the gates one night and took them away.

In August 1877 the Clerk reported that an action had been commenced "against several of the ringleaders in the late violent proceedings at the Pier, and an injunction had been obtained against them to restrain any further act until the hearing of the case".

Troubles never come singly, and the next complaint was in the shape of a long, rambling letter from William Webb, a respected senior member of the community. His letter contained various charges of mis-management, all connected with items in the accounts which he either did not approve of, or did not understand, his thinly veiled implication being that certain members of the Corporation were making money dishonestly out of the Town.

He was invited to attend the next meeting of the Corporation to discuss his complaints, and duly turned up on 17th June, 1878. He was given answers to all his charges, but it must be said that none of these sounds very convincing.

For example, he claimed that the price of gas (from James Blake's Gas Works) was double that charged in Southampton or London. The answer given was – "the price is double, but it is the same as is paid throughout the town". Another example – £16 was paid for the Lamp on the Quay, and he reckoned this was about twice as much as it should have been. The answer was – "This was ordered by the Corporation, and ordered to be paid at a Meeting of the

Corporation at which Mr. Webb was present". Which is no answer at all.

One phrase in Webb's letter sums it all up very well – " . . . it's all very much of a piece and I presume so much of a ring that one party cannot find fault with the other". After the explanations given, Webb decided he was fighting a losing battle against the entrenched might of the Establishment, and stated that although he was not satisfied that all the payments were judicious he withdrew any expressions in his letter of a personal character.

The Pier certainly upset the economy of the town, many of its inhabitants feeling that it was depriving them of their livelihood. The dispute over right of access to the beach at the end of Bank Street went to Court, and Mr. Justice Fry's summing up – all eight and a half pages of it – is given in the Corporation Proceedings Book. This a masterly piece of sitting on the fence, though he finally found for the Corporation on the basis that even if a right of way from Bank Street to the beach had once existed the Pier was now clearly in the way, so that it was a waste of time investigating the question further.

In the end of course a compromise was reached, and a gap left in the fence so that people could get on to the beach.

Another argument arose with the Solent Steam Packet Co. with whom the Corporation had an agreement that their boats would call at the Pierhead, and then come into the Harbour. But after a time they tended to omit the Pierhead stop, thus inconveniencing passengers waiting there.

Also the tow boats from Lymington were dropped at the Pier by the steamer, and had to be warped into the Harbour. It was suggested (by William Webb) that a rope should be strained from the Pierhead to the north-west corner of the Castle with a running block, but there were snags in this plan, mainly due to the tow boats sometimes being left on the Eastward of the Pier.

Then there was trouble with the drains. Waste disposal in Yarmouth had always been fairly primitive, as previous extracts from these records will have shown, but a Rural Sanitary Authority had been set up, and had designed and installed new town drains. Originally they planned to put the effluent into the river, but the Corporation objected strongly to this. Ultimately, however, it was agreed to have the outlet of the main sewer 20 feet from the north west corner of the Castle, subject to terms for removing the same in six months time if it was found to be a nuisance.

When all was ready to go the Sanitary Authority wrote to the Corporation saying that the new drains would require flushing, and that the penstock would have to be lifted at the right time of tide. They suggested the Harbour Master might be the right man for this job. The Corporation did not comment on the last suggestion, but did agree to take responsibility for flushing the drains, providing that the Authority would bear all the expense.

Just over a year later another letter was received from the Sanitary Authority asking the opinion of the Corporation as to the cause of the offensive water in the cellars of the George Inn. The Town Clerk was instructed to reply that in the opinion of the Corporation the evil arose from the defective manner in which the drains were laid. Complaints were also received of offensive smells coming up through the floors of many houses in the High Street, and the man hole on the Quay was said to be unsound and leaky.

It was ultimately realised that the drains needed constant flushing, and the Sanitary Authority wrote asking if the Corporation would take over complete superintendence. The reply was very much to the point. The Corporation said:

> "We disapproved of the system of sewerage from the start, the drains have proved to be a very great nuisance and great expense will be thrown on the town by the need for constant flushing, great dissatisfaction will necessarily follow, and we cannot undertake the responsibility of interfering further in the matter, and request the Rural Sanitary Authority to make fresh arrangements for the superintendence in future".

Other domestic matters were also occupying the attention of the Corporation.

27th September 1880. Sundry goats tethered on the Common illegally to be removed. Those belonging to James Trim, Baker, High Street, and Robin Hood Salter, Shoemaker, High Street, amongst them.

3rd January 1881. The Town Crier to submit all Notices to be Cried to the Mayor or Treasurer, or in their absence to some member of the Corporation.

24th February 1881. Reported that the sanbdank on the north west side of the Harbour from the Breakwater to Norton was much washed away and the groynes which formerly existed there had been neglected. Also that parties were now in the habit of landing goods on the hard near the Shelter House. (This of course avoiding paying wharfage dues) Resolved to acquaint Lord Heytesbury about this.

26th September 1881. Thomas Love Peacock elected a Burgess. Two years later he served for two years as Mayor.

On 11th July, 1882 it was reported that a Bill had just passed the House of Lords by which the Corporation of Yarmouth would be entirely abolished. It was resolved to get up a petition to her Majesty Queen Victoria for a new Charter. This was duly presented and the Privy Council arranged a local enquiry, but alas, the Enquiry was not in sympathy and turned down the request for a Charter.

News of this further blow was received with gloom, as it was virtually the death knell of the Corporation, but meetings went on as usual as they waited for the axe to fall. Complaints continued to come in too, one from W. S. Nicholson of Eastmore who wrote to the Board of Trade complaining that money received from harbour dues was not being spent on the harbour, but on the town. He suggested that a Harbour Board should be formed to run the Harbour which he claimed was at present in a poor state – "break-water rapidly falling to ruin, and the harbour and bar much require dredging".

February 28th 1885. S. E. R. Nicholls, Organist at the Parish Church was appointed Pier Master at a salary of 18/- per week.

In September 1885 James Blake was unanimously elected Mayor "for the ensuing year or until the dissolution of the Corporation in case it shall be dissolved before the expiration of the year". But the time was not yet. In September 1887 an illuminated address signed by 81 inhabitants of the Borough, with a Gold Medal, was presented to James Blake in acknowledgement of his services to the Borough during many years. Actually the Gold Medal was struck on the occasion of the Golden Jubilee of Queen Victoria, and had the Arms of the Borough on the obverse, and the name of James Blake, Mayor, on the reverse.

A year later meetings of the Corporation were still going on, and the Town Clerk reported on the composition of the Town Trust, the body which was to replace the Corporation when it was abolished. The Clerk had been asked to put forward suggestions as to the composition of this body, and he had suggested, inter alia, that Trustees should be elected by the Vestry of Yarmouth, and that all co-optative Trustees should live in Yarmouth. He also suggested that the Railway Company should not have a Representative, since he claimed the Company had no interest in the town, pier, or harbour, except as Carriers, in fact their interests in some respects conflicted.

In February 1889 the (late) Town Clerk wrote a strong letter protesting against the Railway Company's plan to build another Pier for Railway use, projecting into the sea at the top end of the Common. The Board of Trade decided it was safer to stay neutral, and declined to help. The Clerk wrote to the Charity Commissioners, who did lend their support, and in May he was able to report some – but only partial – success.

He reported that the Promoters of the Bill were willing to abandon that part of their scheme if the Corporation would consent to a substituted line from the Quay, over the end of the Yar Bridge and the mudland to the present Station near the Mill. This was discussed at a meeting on 2nd May, and the following Minute was recorded:

> "Resolved that the Bill should be opposed unless the Promoters unconditionally withdrew their Railway crossing the Common and running into the sea. If they would do this then the Corporation are willing to assent to the construction of the Railway from the present Station across Mill Road over the Mudland as far as the Yar Bridge Road, but not to any scheme with any powers by deviation or otherwise of crossing the bridge or running on to the Quay".
>
> **14th May, 1889.** Mr. Bayliffe and Mr. Fox (Railway Company) attended and explained the proposed railway extension of a Pier and three lines of railway 600 feet in length from the Bridge Road northwards into the sea.

On 3rd April, 1890 – almost a year later – the Clerk was able to report that the Bill had been opposed with the sanction of the Charity Commissioners, and had in fact been withdrawn. So, thanks to the energy and zeal of the Town Clerk, whose job was on the verge of being abolished, supported by a defunct Corporation, Yarmouth was spared the desecration of railway lines across the Common, or across the Harbour.

After the excitement and relief of this announcement in the Minute Book, the next one is something of an anti-climax. It says:

> "Three pumps have been fitted to three public wells, i.e. Mill Terrace, South Street, and Basket's Lane, at an expense of £7. Two lamps have been put up, one opposite the School and the other facing South Street".

The pump in South Street is of course still there to this day, outside the bungalow "Little End" – which, incidentally, used to be the town's fish and chip shop.

Finally the day arrived when the ancient Borough of Yarmouth, which received its first Charter in the year 1135, was due to be wound up. The last meeting of the Corporation was held on 27th February, 1891, only five Burgesses attending, and the Town Clerk wrote the following Minutes.

Present: James Blake, Mayor.
P. Thomas Love Peacock
Walter Thomas Grigg
William Webb
George S. Meager
P. Charles G. Butler
P. J. E. Richardson
P. James Phillips (P signifies Present)

Proposed and seconded that the thanks of the Corporation are due to the Town Clerk for his services during the many years which he has held that office.

Proposed by Mr. Richardson and seconded by Mr. Peacock as the last entry in the Minutes and the last Resolution of the Corporation that the Special Thanks of the Corporation be given to the late Mayor James Blake Esq for his valuable Services during the time he has been a member of the Corporation for the benefits which the Town has received from him, for the kindness and courtesy with which he has presided over the meetings of the Corporation, and the hospitality and kindness which he has invariably displayed.

Signed by all present. (Including James Blake).

So an era came to an end, on a rather sad note. One might say that it was something less than fair to abolish the Corporation when they were doing so well, working hard for the development and prosperity of Yarmouth. In the last 50 years the Corporation had done much – the Breakwater, the Bridge, Extensions to the Quay, the Pier, the Railway – and even after they were officially dead they refused to lie down, but still went on fighting for Yarmouth, trying to get a better sewage disposal scheme, fighting the Railway Company's plans for another Pier.

In the 18th and early 19th centuries the Borough was certainly "Rotten", and all its members did was elect friends in to the office of

Burgesses, and themselves or their friends as Members of Parliament. But latterly they had worked hard, and the Minutes are full of business being carried out to improve and develop the town. No doubt the members of the Corporation feathered their own nests at the same time, but are things so very different to-day in similar situations? It would seem that their main crime was to be a self-elected body, and this ultimately led to a "we" and "they" situation in the town.

The Corporation did towards the end suggest that a more democratic method of election should be adopted, but by this time it was too late, too much damage had been done. One wonders what motivated Sir Charles Dilke, Member of Parliament for Chelsea, in his slashing attack on Yarmouth, because it was he who turned the spotlight on the administration of the town. Did something happen to him down here? Perhaps somebody belittled him, or even worse, ignored him. Perhaps he wished to become a Burgess and was not accepted. Whatever it was it had far-reaching effects.

The "heroes" turned up by these stirring events are perhaps Estcourt the Town Clerk who fought so hard and untiringly for the town, particularly at the end; William Squire, who was Treasurer for many years and several times Mayor; and of course James Blake who joined the Corporation as a result of refusing to pay his harbour dues, and who, after being Mayor on 17 occasions, had the melancholy task of winding matters up and declaring the Corporation defunct.

These three were not the only ones to work hard and conscientiously for Yarmouth, but they stand out. In the Church there is a stained glass window to the memory of William Squire, on which window is his epitaph. It is a simple message that many could do well to study – "Go Thou and Do Likewise".

CHAPTER XIII

The Mount

The Mount was the largest house ever built in Yarmouth. As its name applies it was situated on the high ground to the east of the town, its north front having magnificent views over the Solent to the mainland, the south side facing across the marsh to Thorley Copse and the Downs.

The house was built in 1809 by a local builder named Udall for the Rector of Yarmouth, the Rev. George Burrard, and in its comparatively short life span it housed two of Yarmouth's most wealthy and influential families, the Burrards and The Dashwoods. It was not the most beautiful building in the world, but it was an imposing sight from the sea; and what it lacked in architectural elegance was more than counterbalanced by the influence which its owners excercised on the life of the town.

The Burrards were an old and wealthy Lymington family, records showing that they were important landowners there in Queen Elizabeth's reign, and a George Burrard was Mayor of Lymington in 1584. Their wealth, and it was considerable, came mainly from Salt and judicious marriages. In 1668 the family purchased the Walhampton Estate and in 1711 Paul Burrard pulled down the old Walhampton House, and erected the central part of the present mansion. The eastern part of the house was built by Sir Harry Burrard Neale in 1815.

This Sir Harry was a distinguished naval officer, sometime Commander-in-Chief of the Mediterranean Fleet, and friend of George III, who had assumed the surname of Neale in 1795. In 1797 he was credited with helping to quell the Mutiny at the Nore. When he died in 1840 his younger brother, the Rev. George Burrard, Rector of Yarmouth, succeeded to the Baronetcy and estate.

The Rev. George was quite a character. Educated at Christchurch and Winchester College he went up to New College, Oxford, and after graduating spent twelve years as a Fellow of Merton College.

During this time he frequently stayed with his brother Harry at Weymouth, when the latter was in attendance on the King. He then took Holy Orders, and was honoured by being appointed a Chaplain-in-Ordinary to George III. This office he subsequently retained in the reigns of George IV, William IV, and Queen Victoria.

He became Rector of Yarmouth in 1801, and was also Vicar of Shalfleet, Vicar of Middleton Tyas in Yorkshire, and Vicar of Burton Coggles in Lincolnshire. He was Mayor of Lymington five times, and Mayor of Yarmouth on two occasions.

During his early years as Rector of Yarmouth, and until the Mount was built, he lived at Shandon (then called the Terrace) in the High Street. In 1804 he married Elizabeth Anne, daughter and heir of a rich Jamaican landowner, but she died in 1815 leaving only one child, a son George.

In 1816 he married again, his bride being Emma, daughter of Admiral Joseph Bingham. Emma had had a fairly unconventional childhood, having spent a considerable time before the age of seven sailing with her father in various parts of the world. George and Emma had a family of six, all born in Yarmouth, two sons and four daughters.

When the Rev. George became the Rev., Sir George Burrard in 1840, and found himself the possessor of estates and much wealth, he left The Mount and went to live at Walhampton. For a time he retained his position as Rector of Yarmouth, but Sunday services became somewhat erratic, the parishioners never knowing for certain until the last minute whether there was to be a service or not. A watch had to be kept on the Solent for the Rector's boat, and when and if this was seen the flag was hoisted on the Church tower and the bell was rung.

This arrangement obviously had its drawbacks, as did also the fact that the Rev. Sir George was somwehat partial to the good things in life, and believed in enjoying "those things which are requisite and necessary, as well for the body as the soul", and in 1841 he decided there was really no more need for him to continue working, and so he retired to Walhampton to a life of opulence and ease. No one can begrudge him this, he had been Rector here for 40 years and was entitled to a rest.

He died in 1856 and was succeeded by his eldest son George. On his death his widow, Emma Lady Burrard returned to The Mount to live, and remained there for the rest of her life, playing her part in the life of the town, graciously visiting the sick, succouring the poor, and carrying out all those functions expected of the aristocracy in the pre-Welfare State era. Of her children by her marriage to the Rev. Sir George, the elder boy Harry unexpectedly came into the title when his step brother George was drowned in 1870 in a bathing accident, but he only lived to enjoy it for another six months. The younger boy, Sidney, went into the Army, achieved the rank of Lieut-Colonel, and died in 1893 at the age of 66.

The eldest girl, Harriet, married Frank H. Crozier of West Hill in 1845, and the youngest daughter, Theresa, married in the same year Rowland Edward Cooper of Pains Hill in Surrey.

In passing, one little story about Theresa as a child. When she was 10 years old her mother took her on the grand tour of Europe, and on this holiday she gathered a number of wild flowers and pressed them in a book. This book has survived and is now the property of Mr. Raymond Doe who, with his sister Ena, has done so much to preserve the memory of the Dashwood family. One entry in this flower book indicates that Theresa Burrard was not always charmed with what she found in Italy.

> "Bobli Gardens, Cascina, March 27th, 1835, at that horrible, dirty, tiresome, dismal, uncomfortable, noisy, unwholesome, muddy, windy, rainy, snowey, haily, cold, ugly town of Florence".

Her mother also kept a flower book, and one entry (the flower has disappeared) reads:

> "Between Sestri and Genoa, April 6th, 1835, the day on which we had green peas in abundance".

Rowland and Theresa Cooper had two children, Rowland Burrard Cooper and Edith Theresa Cooper, but both parents died when the children were very young. Thus it came about that Rowland and Edith Cooper were brought up by their grandmother Lady Emma Burrard, and lived for a time with her at Walhampton. In 1866, when she was 24 and had been living at The Mount for 10 years, Edith married the Rev. Robert Lewes Dashwood, who was Curate at Shalfleet, and for a time also Curate at Yarmouth. On the death of Lady Burrard in 1897 The Mount passed to her granddaughter Edith Dashwood, and remained in the Dashwood family until it was demolished in 1967.

But before considering the Dashwoods further, and the part they played in the life of Yarmouth, let us have another look at Emma Lady Burrard, and also at another of her grandchildren.

Lady Burrard was 60 years old when she returned to live at The

Mount on the death of the Rev. Sir George, and she was still caring for her two grandchildren. Rowland was aged nine, and Edith eight at this time. One might consider that bringing up two young children was, at her age, quite a task, but then she was perhaps tougher than she appeared to be. Four years later she suffered a rather alarming accident, in Yarmouth High Street, and although she was badly injured and shaken she very soon recovered completely. The current newspaper account is dated 26th October, 1860.

> "An accident of a very serious and alarming character happened in the High Street about half past 8 p.m. on Friday, the 26th inst, when a horse in a chaise, belonging to Messrs. Long and Son, grocers and provision merchants, etc, of this town, which they had let out on hire, ran away, and most furiously went down the High Street from the Mount, the residence of Lady Burrard, and on the horse entering the road opposite Mr. Long's shop, leading to the coal stores, he ran against some iron railing, and precipitated a young gentleman named Richardson, who held the reins, and Lady Burrard, to the ground in a very violent and alarming manner. The horse, consequently, dragged her ladyship several yards on the road by her dress, which unfortunately hung on to the iron work of the chaise on her falling out. The news of the casualty soon spread over the town, and caused a sincere feeling of regret for her ladyship's said misfortune, as she is an estimable and kind lady to the poor of the place at all times when help is required by them in the time of need and distress. People innumerable were soon to her assistance, to extricate her from her perilous position, when it was discovered that she was very much injured externally about her arms, face, and body. She was shaken, also, to a fearful extent. Her dress likewise was literally torn to atoms by the severe accident. Her ladyship was conveyed as speedily as possible to the residence of Mr. Long, in a very weak and exhausted state from the fright and the serious injuries she had received. Dr. Hollis was unremitting in his attentions to her ladyship in dressing her wounds and relieving her of the pain she so greatly felt. After she became a little composed, she was removed in a close carriage to her residence, where she has been since, quite unable to remove from her room, although very favourably recovering under the medical treatment of Dr.

Helsham. We had almost omitted to mention that Mr. Richardson, who was likewise thrown from the vehicle, escaped apparently uninjured from the effects of the accident".

When Lady Burrard finally died at the age of 83 several newspapers published short obituaries, one of which will suffice to show the respect and affection in which she was held in the town.

"It is with the greatest regret we announce the death on Monday, after an illness of only three days' duration, of Lady Burrard, of the Mount. This venerable and much esteemed lady, the widow of the late Rev. Sir George Burrard, Bart, of Walhampton, and rector of this parish, has been for many years widely known and highly esteemed in this district, and from her genial and kindly manners will be deeply regretted by all classes of society. Spared to a good old age and happy in the affection of her children and children's children she was mercifully preserved from a long or painful illness, and has passed away leaving a gap which it will be hard indeed to fill up".

But let us finish this account of the Burrards on a more cheerful note. Another of Lady Emma's grandchildren was May Burrard, the youngest child of her son Sidney, and by all accounts a bit of a beauty. May married Captain Harry Pakenham Mahon, an Irish landowner, and the following description of her tends to suggest that she did indeed possess many attractive attributes.

"Mrs. Pakenham Mahon is one of the most interesting of the beauties of the day. She is tall and slender, with blue-grey eyes, dark hair that has never been profaned by 'wash' or dye, and an ivory skin. She is a good shot, and enjoys the reputation of walking well. She is an excellent conversationalist, knows when to say clever things, and when to stop – and above all, how to listen. Socially, she is in great request, for she takes an intelligent interest in things interesting, and never wearies her fellow creatures with long-winded stories about some other woman's delinquencies".

The Dashwoods were also a very old and wealthy family, originating in Dorset, thence moving to Somerset towards the latter part of the reign of Elizabeth. The Isle of Wight branch of the family sprang from the Dashwoods of Stanford Hall, Nottinghamshire, whose Pedigree claims that they were the direct descendants and sole representatives of the ancient Welsh family of Lewes of Stanford-on-Soar, Notts.

Robert Lewes Dashwood was the youngest son of the Rev. Samuel Vere Dashwood of Stanford Hall, and being the youngest son it was logical that he should follow his father's example and take holy orders. He obtained a curacy at Shalfleet in 1863, and also for a short time filled a similar position in Yarmouth, and it was during this time that he became acquainted with Edith Theresa Cooper who was living at the Mount.

Their wedding on the 15th August, 1866 was a big occasion in Yarmouth, and was reported at very great length in several local papers. These reports give us an interesting insight into the life of the town in the middle of the 19th century, and in particular show the special relationship which existed at this time between the townsfolk and the so-called high society who lived at the "big house".

> "For some few weeks past preparation on a very grand scale has been going on at the Mount, Yarmouth, the residence of the Dowager Lady Burrard, in anticipation of the approaching nuptials of Miss Edith Theresa Cooper (grand-daughter of the above named lady) with the Rev. Robert Lewes Dashwood, son of the Rev. S. V. Dashwood, of Stanford Hall, Loughborough, Leicestershire, rector, and lord of the manor. The young lady, who has since the death of her parents resided with her grandmother, has endeared herself to those with whom she has come in contact by her kind and affable manners to all, hence the excitement that prevailed here on Wednesday last, the day appointed for the wedding. At early morn busy hands were at work in all parts of the town putting up evergreens, and bunting in the shape of flags streamed from every conceivable point. The staff on the church tower was decorated by a Union Jack presented by the bride herself. Long ere the time appointed for the ceremony to take place numbers of people here moving about attired in their holiday best, all Yarmouth having evidently determined on having a day out. The neighbouring parishes had also a large number of representatives of the fair sex, who on occasions of this sort generally muster pretty strong. As eleven o'clock approached the bridal party began to arrive at the church, and a few minutes after the bride-elect, accompanied by her brother,

Two pictures, 1890 and 1980, taken from the Church Tower. The modern camera had a wider angled lens but it is clear how much more open the Square is after the buildings were removed from in front of the Pier entrance

The Mount in about 1866 with, from the left, Lady Emma Burrard, Rev. R. L. Dashwood and Mrs. Dashwood

The North Front of The Mount in 1920

Since 1905 the pier entrance has been rebuilt and the road asphalted. A fine steam yacht is at anchor off the Pier

Mr. W. Griffiths, who was the Pier Master, standing at the Pier entrance about 1905

This photograph, taken about 1870, shows much of the modern Harbour silted up. The brig in the picture is the collier that regularly shipped coal from the north-east coast

The ticket office stands where the slipway used to be and the Harbour entrance has been narrowed to accommodate the present day car ferries

The top picture, taken about 1905, shows a skyline very much as it is today. The Harbour has been dredged and the Quay extended

Rowland Burrard Cooper, Esq, on whom devolved the duty of giving her away, was driven to the doors in a carriage drawn by four greys. On alighting they at once proceeded up the middle aisle of the church to the altar rails, where the bridegroom, with his best man, (Captain Richard Lewes Dashwood), was awaiting their arrival. The central aisle, in, which was the bride with her fourteen attendant maids, now became the centre of attraction to all. Sure never was such a scene in Yarmouth church before, the place being literally crammed, all the 'elite' of the town and neighbourhood being present. While the parties generally were getting into their places the choir sang the marriage hymn, after which the aged rector, the Rev. J. Blackburn, who was to officiate, having taken his place commenced the marriage service, which he read in a very impressive manner, after which the contracting parties, together with some of their friends, adjourned to the vestry, where the usual records were signed and attested. On the bridal party leaving the church, which they did by the north door (from whence a carpet had previously been laid to the corner of the High Street, where a triumphal arch had been erected), a number of young girls, members of the bride's Sunday-school class, strewed flowers in the path of the now happy couple, who, upon being driven off in the carriage, were heartily cheered by the assembled spectators. The invited guests subsequently met at the 'Mount', where a magnificent breakfast had been prepared by Mr. Hookey, of Lymington, in a tent erected for the special occasion. Among the company present were the Hon. Mr. and Mrs. Craven Berkeley, Sir George Burrard, Bart, and Lady Burrard, Mr. and Mrs. Burrard, Mr. Harry Paul Burrard, Colonel and Mrs. Sydney Burrard, Mrs. Leonard and three Miss Rookes, Mr., Mrs. and Miss Peers Williams Freeman, Mr., Mrs. and Miss Rookes, Mr. and Mrs. L. Shedden, Mr. and Mrs. Peacocke, Mrs. and two Misses Price, Dr., Mrs. and Miss Brown, Sir John Rivett and Lady Carnac, Miss Rivett Carnac, Rev. John and Miss Blackburn, Rev. John and Miss Cottle, Mr., Mrs. and four Misses Crozier, Dowager Lady Burrard, Mr. Burrard, Mr. Pearson Crozier, Rev. W. and Mrs. Marriner, three Misses Paris, Admiral R. and Mrs. Crozier, Mrs. Martin, Rev. F. Rowden, Mrs. Pretyman, two Misses

Farnall, Mr. Herbert Farnall, Miss Surtees, Rev. S. Vere Dashwood, Misses Edith and A. Dashwood, Mr. and Mrs. Heaton, Miss Campbell, Mr. Darwin, Rev. and Mrs. Pellew Gaze, Rev. John S. Orton, Mr. Rowland Burrard Cooper, Mrs. Richardson, Miss Hollis, Mr., Mrs. and Miss Banks Wright, Mr. and Mrs. Chaworth Masters, Mr. G. Masters, Dr. and Mrs. Mayo, Mr. and Mrs. F. St. Barbe, Dr. and Misses Harding, Rev. R. Dunn, Mrs. and Misses Cooke, Dr. and Mrs. Herbert Taylor, Mr. Graham Eden Hamond, Dr. and Mrs. Meeres, Mrs. Peers, Rev. Birch, Captain Jervoise, Colonel Graham, Mr. Desmond Richardson, Mr. Montgomery, Mr. Gubbins, Mr. Kelsall, Mr. Watkin, Mr. and Miss Pennethorne, Mr. Harry Rooke, Capt. R. V. Dashwood, Mr. and Mrs, Horace Packe, etc, etc. During the progress of the breakfast the Rev. J. Blackburn proposed the bride's health in a very touching speech, which was ably responded to by the bridegroom. Several other toasts were given, and everything went "merry as a marriage bell". The band of the 1st Hants Engineers was present, and performed a selection of music. In the afternoon the children of the various schools in the town, to the number of 220, headed by the Lymington drum and fife band, marched on the lawn, where they were plentifully supplied with tea and cake *'ad libitum'*. Between four and five o'clock the happy pair left for Ryde, *en route* for the continent, where they intend spending their honeymoon. On their deparature from the grounds a number of slippers were thrown after them for luck, some of them too energetically, having been pitched into the carriage. Just at this part of the proceedings two young fellows, evidently tourists by their knapsacks, happened to be passing, and picked up a shoe each (white satin ones by-the-bye), which seemed to tickle the fancy of one of them, for he said he should take it home for his lady as a keepsake. In the evening a large number of people assembled on the common to witness a display of fireworks, which took place from a small yacht belonging to H. P. Burrard Esq., which was moored just off the shore. The rockets fired on the occasion were certainly the finest we ever saw. The front gate of the 'Mount' was illuminated with gas, and there was also a star erected on the common facing the houses. For the information of our lady readers

> we must not omit to state that the bridal dress consisted of a rich white silk trimmed with pearls, a pearl necklace, with a head dress ensuite, trimmed with orange blossoms, and a wreath and white tulle veil. The bridesmaids, fourteen in number, were Miss Edith Dashwood, Miss Alice Dashwood, Miss Harriet Frances Crozier, Miss Emma Crozier, Miss Gertrude Crozier, Miss Mary Alice Crozier, Miss Mary Anne Rooke, Miss Emily Rooke, Miss Surtees, Miss Farnall, Miss Helen Farnall, Miss Price, Miss E. Price, and Miss May Burrard. They were all dressed alike, viz, white grenadine, trimmed with blue, and blue sashes. Their wreaths were composed of lilies of the valley and forget-me-nots, and the *'tout ensemble'* of the scene at the altar was very charming and effective".

The following year, in 1867, the Rev. R. L. Dashwood put this advertisement in the Church Times:

> "Wanted – a country sole charge, or curacy, on the South Western Line, Hampshire or Dorsetshire preferred. By a Graduate of Cambridge, in full Orders. Views Moderate. A good house (furnished or unfurnished) either to form part of stipend, or to be rented. Address R. L. D., The Mount, Yarmouth, Isle of Wight".

In September that year the Guardian announced his appointment as Curate (Sole Charge) of Sherfield English, Hampshire, a position he held until he retired in 1892. It is reasonable to assume that the Rectory at Sherfield English went with the job, and that he and his wife Edith lived there at least some of the time, though newspaper records show that they were often in Yarmouth. All their seven children were christened in Yarmouth, and it would seem that Edith Dashwood returned to her grandmother's house for the birth of each of her children.

There is certainly some confusion about what positions he did occupy. The Dashwood Pedigree – for which I am indebted to Mr. R. H. Adams – states that he was not only Rector of Sherfield English, but also Rector of Stanford-on-Soar from 1876 to 1884, but the Yarmouth records give the Stanford dates as 1877 – 1881, adding that leave of non-residence was granted him by Bishop Wordsworth in Lincoln. In a newspaper account of the Harvest Festival in Yarmouth in 1880 Mrs. Dashwood is credited with arranging the flowers, and the Rev. R. L. Dashwood with reading the lessons, which seems a little odd if he was at the time Rector of a

Parish in Nottinghamshire. Plural livings were however quite common – we have already seen that the Rev. Sir George Burrard actually held four at the same time.

Mr. Hugh Farmar, who is related to the Dashwoods, and who has contributed some interesting information about the family, has written:

> "It is not clear whether the Rev. Robert ever held a living. He was a rich man and collected porcelain. Occasionally some of the "Dashwood Collection" comes on the market. He also had inherited a good collection of pictures, furniture and books.
>
> My mother remembered going to The Mount before the first World War when her father took a house in the Island for Cowes Week. It was then a centre of hospitality presided over by old Mr. Dashwood, a typical Victorian pater-familias who, alas, did not consider any possible suitors good enough for his daughters".

Robert and Edith Dashwood's seven children were:

Theresa	born March 1868
Robert Vere	born September 1869
Edith Caroline	born March 1871
Claude Burrard	born October 1872
Cuthbert	born January 1874
Constance	born May 1877
Sidney	born November 1882

Of the four sons, the eldest, Robert Vere Lewes Dashwood followed in his father's footsteps, took holy order, married a local girl, Agnes the daughter of Mr. W. S. Nicholson of Eastmore, and spent 28 years as Rector of North Perrott in Somerset, dying in 1949. Claude Burrard Lewes Dashwood married a South African girl, entered the army and was killed in 1916 as a major in the Northumberland Fusiliers. Cuthbert William Lewes Dashwood never married and spent most of his life at The Mount, dying in 1960 at the age of 86. Sidney Lewes Dashwood, the seventh child, married a cousin, Joan Burrard, and died soon after his 84th Birthday, on Christmas Day 1966.

The three girls, Theresa, Caroline and Constance, all remained unmarried, all lived at The Mount, and died in their late eighties. Their father died in 1912, their mother in 1920, but these three girls, together with their brother Cuthbert, lived on and on, living graciously, doing good, becoming an important and integral part of the Yarmouth scene. They saw their family fortunes decline, and the world about them dramatically change. When they died it was the end of an era, and in a very short space of time The Mount itself was pulled down to make way for a new road. Hugh Farmar says:

> "I did not know these distant cousins until my parents retired to live in Yarmouth. By then the three unmarried Miss Dashwoods and their brother Cuthbert (quite a talented water colourist) were all still alive. But The Mount was rather a sad place, with copies of e.g. a pair of Romneys which had been sold, empty china cabinets and bookshelves. Eventually the surviving sisters and brother migrated to what had been the nursery upstairs, and the principal rooms were unused".

In our modern society of so-called equal opportunities, in which wealth has been redistributed in a somewhat meretricious way, there is obviously no room for such a family of non-workers, but nevertheless it is immensely sad to see the passing of a system which was not wholly bad, and which brought a considerable stability to the social structure. A stability which seems to be sadly lacking to-day.

Fortunately for us, there are many people living in Yarmouth who still remember the Dashwoods and their life at The Mount, and I am particularly indebted to Mrs. Ena Morton, who worked at The Mount for 40 years, for much information about the routine of life in this typically Victorian household. Another invaluable source of information is a scrapbook of newspaper cuttings which must have been started by Edith Dashwood in 1866 as a young bride of 18, and which was continued by her daughters. This book has kindly been lent to me by Mrs. Diana Foster of Mudeford, who is a descendant of Claude Dashwood.

All the Dashwood children were artistic and talented. Cuthbert played the piano, organ, and violin, besides being a skilled painter. On many occasions he visited Cornwall during the winter to paint the rough seas. Theresa played the violin, Caroline the 'cello, and Constance the violin and viola. The girls also painted and put their talents to good use by selling their pictures for charity. These talents were inherited from their mother, and there are several accounts extant of the concerts in which they appeared.

> "**September 22nd, 1898.** An excellent concert, arranged by the Rev. R. L. and Mrs. Dashwood, of The Mount, on behalf of the church organ fund, was given in the Foresters'

> Hall on Thursday evening before a most appreciative audience, including the elite of the neighbourhood. Among those taking part were Mrs. Horton, Miss Clement Smith, Mrs. and the Misses Dashwood (3), Mr. C. Dashwood, the Rev. R. V. L. Dashwood, Mr. Sidney Dashwood, Mr. and Mrs. Mann (Ningwood), Mr. Snook (Lymington), Mr. Argyle (Freshwater), Mr. Hyde, and Mr. T. A. Cleary, with Mr. S. E. R. Nicholls as accompanist. Conspicuous among the many and varied items were the splendidly sung songs by Mr. Snook, the possessor of a rich baritone voice, who delighted all with his perfect vocalisation. Miss Clement Smith, too, with her charming voice and style, scored a decided success with her songs, receiving an encore for each. The efforts of the other performers were equally appreciated, a special word being due to the instrumental selections by the talented family of the Rev. R. L. Dashwood, which were greatly admired. The concert was an eminent musical success".

In another account of a concert given at the Foresters' Hall in 1907 in aid of the Yarmouth, Thorley, Wellow and Ningwood Nursing Association the writer says:

> "An instrumental quintette – Mozart's allegro from 'Serenade' – was splendidly rendered by the three Misses Dashwood (violin, 'cello, and viola), Mr. Cuthbert Dashwood (violin), and Mrs. Dashwood (pianoforte). They were deservedly recalled, and the same talented party of musicians afterwards played another quintette, Mozart's Rondo, which was another grand piece of instrumentation".

The Dashwoods were also a most generous family, especially where the church was concerned, and their names invariably appeared on any list when an appeal was being made for charity. Typically, they provided the prizes annually for the Sunday School Treat, contributed to the organist's salary, to the provision of coal for the poor, to the school cricket club, the R.S.P.C.A., to the Girls Friendly Society. Theresa started the Parish Magazine, and for many years produced a nicely bound edition every twelve months. She also learned Braille and wrote to blind people. Caroline adopted an African family and wrote to them regularly, and sent money. She also supported an orphan boys home in Birmingham. Constance contributed to the Church of England Training College at Kelham, and to the similar establishment at Mirfield. Her last cheque was a donation of £100 to the Deaf in response to a radio appeal by the Bishop of Southampton. They all supported the Church Army. At Christmas they saw to it that every poor person in Yarmouth received a suitable present. Who can say that their lives were not useful?

They were all quiet, shy, and reserved people, living orderly and decent lives, shunning publicity, and quietly doing good up to the limit of their ability. Photographs show a strong family likeness, the men being handsome, and the girls very attractive. The daily routine in the house was settled, serene and unchanging; discipline was firm and unhurried, and as a result the staff were happy. They too lived a quiet, orderly life, knowing exactly where they stood, appreciating that their employers were honest, sincere, and generous, and this being so they gave the family their unswerving loyalty.

The house staff, in the early years of this century consisted of a butler, footman, hall-boy, two housemaids, a parlour maid, a cook, kitchen maid, scullery maid, and a daily help to assist with the scrubbing. All the staff had their own bedrooms, and had the same food as the dining room. No meat was eaten on Wednesdays and Fridays, only cheese or fish. Each Saturday a 20 lb. round of beef was cooked and was put on the sideboard for Sunday breakfast. With boiled eggs.

Work started at 7 a.m. sharp, the first job for the housemaids being to clean the hall linoleum, sweep up and mop, shake the door-mat and sweep the steps. Then the library, which was a large room with a carpet and red felt surround, had to be swept and dusted. The sweeping had, of course, to be done by hand with a dustpan and brush, wet tea leaves being scattered over the carpet to lay and collect the dust. After the library, the study and two smaller rooms had to be done. The head housemaid was responsible for the drawing room, and the parlour maid for dining room. The latter also cleaned the silver.

The servants had their breakfast at 8 o'clock, so that this meal was out of the way in time for prayers at 8-55 a.m. and the family breakfast, which was served at exactly 9 a.m. Punctuality was a fetish with the Dashwoods, and when they said breakfast was to be served at 9 o'clock, they meant that it must be taken in as the clock was actually striking.

The flagged passages had to be scrubbed and whitened, and this was not a popular chore as the whitening used to tread into the red felt in the library, and the green felt in the lower drawing room.

This lower drawing room was reserved for the reception of visitors; there was an upper drawing room for daily use. They were both large rooms, the upper one containing 50 pieces of furniture, and 50 pictures. In dusting, the standard required was high, some of the mouldings having to be cleaned with a tooth brush. Charlie Jacobs, the plumber and blacksmith who came up from the town to do odd jobs, used to say "There ain't enough dust in this house to choke a gnat".

The dining room seated 20, and there were rarely less than 20 for meals, so that together with feeding the staff cooking was quite a major operation. Mrs. Dashwood visited the kitchen every morning at 10 a.m. – precisely – to give orders for the day, but she would never enter the room if the servants were talking, as she regarded this as an intrusion on their privacy.

The family sat down to lunch as the clock was striking one, and the servants began theirs at 1-20, when the family sweet went in. After lunch the maids washed and changed, and from 2 o'clock until tea time occupied themselves with sewing. At 6 p.m. the under housemaid took the mail down into the town. After tea there was more sewing, much of it for bazaars held to raise money for the Society for the Propagation of the Gospel.

Dinner for the family was at 7-30 p.m., hot water being taken up to the bedrooms at 7 o'clock. A three course meal was served each evening, the staff sitting down to theirs as the family were finishing. After dinner the wash basins had to be emptied, beds turned down, and hot water bottles put in. The maids were in bed by 9 p.m. This daily routine was never varied. Servants had one half day off per week, and every other Sunday afternoon, and received two weeks holiday a year, this being taken either in May, June or September. In the spring each year the family went abroad, usually to the South of France, and during this period a three months spring cleaning was carried out. There is an old saying that cleanliness is next to godliness, and there is no doubt that this was a clean, as well as a godly, house.

In the mornings the maids wore blue cotton dresses, which in those days cost 6/- each from the Yarmouth dressmaker, Miss Baker, and a black dress in the afternoon (12/6). They each had to have two morning caps and one for afternoons with a black velvet ribbon.

And so life went on from day to day, and from year to year. Mrs. Dashwood ran the house efficiently and calmly, letting nothing upset her. After her death in 1920 Theresa as the eldest daughter naturally took over, and the routine was barely disturbed. Theresa was small and dainty; took a 2½ shoe. After her mother's death she did all the housekeeping, and paid the wages, every penny was meticulously accounted for, and all expenses were divided by four, so that they all paid their share.

Theresa died in 1953 aged 85. Caroline followed her in 1958 when she was 86. Cuthbert was also 86 when he went in 1960. So Constance was left alone in this huge house, surrounded by her memories and her servants. She died on 22nd June, 1966, the last of the Dashwoods of The Mount.

Her death sealed the fate of the house. It was in a poor state of repair, and there had been a considerable amount of subsidence. Traffic congestion in Yarmouth High Street was an urgent problem and the County Council had plans for a so-called by-pass, which necessitated the removal of The Mount. The following short paragraph appeared in a local paper.

> 'The fate of The Mount was discussed at length at Monday's meeting of the Parish Council when Mr. G. Kelsey (chairman) presided. Members stated that demolition appeared inevitable as the new link road was planned to cross the site. Mr. Budden hoped that as many trees and shrubs as could be spared would be left, as the area was virtually a bird sanctuary. It was also felt that any houses erected should be within the scope of purchase by the ordinary townspeople and not expensive property which might be left empty for long periods of the year. There were plans for a limited open space for public use. Two-thirds of the meeting was carried out by candlelight owing to the failure of the electricity supply".

Somehow it seems fitting that the meeting had to be conducted by candlelight; after all, it was in the nature of a Requiem.

CHAPTER XIV

The Last 80 Years

The first national event to cause any excitement in Yarmouth in the present century was the Coronation of Edward VII in 1902. After the gloom caused by the death of Queen Victoria this was a welcome occasion for rejoicing, and Yarmouth was not slow to seize on it, the celebrations being on the same scale as the Diamond Jubilee in 1897.

An oak tree was planted in Pier Square by Mr. Hall, Chairman of the Town Trust, in the presence of a large crowd. This was to be known as King Edward's Oak, but in fact throughout its comparatively short life it was invariably called the Coronation Oak. The usual sports were held, with events for all ages and sections of the community, and it is good to be able to report that this time Yarmouth's Tug-of-War team won easily, thus somewhat atoning for their poor display at the Diamond Jubilee, when they were soundly beaten by Thorley.

The festivities went on until late in the evening with a torchlight procession and a tableau, in which the central figures were "Peace" (Mr. F. C. Cleary), the "King" (Mr. B. Reynolds) and the "Queen" (Miss H. Budden). The tableaux was enacted in the Square outside the Bugle Hotel; the coastguards let off rockets; and "Coloured lights of various hues were lighted, adding to the already brilliant spectacle. The band continued discoursing gay music, and dancing was largely indulged in until 10.30, when the National Anthem concluded a memorable day's proceedings. The organiser was Mr. J. E. Furmage, headmaster of the National Schools".

That was in 1902, when it must have seemed that the sun was going to shine on the British Empire for ever. But throughout Edward VII's reign the political climate was gradually deteriorating, though few could have guessed at the extent of the cataclysm that was to break over the western world in 1914. There was still no hint of disaster in 1907 when the following piece of "society" news appeared in a local paper.

"Royal Visitors. On Saturday afternoon Yarmouth was honoured by a Royal visit, which very few of the inhabitants were aware of until the distinguished party had taken their departure. The Royal visitors were Princess Henry of Battenberg, Princess Christian, and Princess Victoria, with Miss Minnie Cochrane in attendance. They had motored over from Osborne, and on arriving at Yarmouth visited the "Charles" rooms adjoining the Pier Hotel and also the Castle, afterwards inspecting the Parish Church, evincing much interest in the historic edifice. The Royal party then went on to the Solent Yacht Club, where the race for 'seabirds" had just finished, and partook of tea on the terrace, being received by Mr. W. S. Nicholson, J.P., and the acting Hon. Secretary of the Club (Capt. Ramsay Saunders). Both gentlemen had the honour of being presented to the Royal visitors, who during their short stay also visited several of the principal shops".

The Great War of 1914 – 1918 brought its own brand of sadness to Yarmouth. Many local men went into the armed forces, and several failed to return. The names "Burrard" and "Dashwood" frequently appeared in despatches, and several medals were won. In 1916 Captain Claude Dashwood, second son of the Rev. R. L. Dashwood, died of wounds received in battle, after having been in the trenches continuously for nine months.

Through the war years Yarmouth was the Headquarters of the Western Patrol, and with several naval vessels based on the port the town was unexpectedly lively, and was never able to forget the war. The town also at least once, saw a Zeppelin on its way to drop its diminutive bombs on the mainland. The Western Patrol was disbanded early in 1919 and many Yarmouth girls were sad, and their parents glad, to see the sailors go.

"The Deserted Roadstead. Yarmouth roads present a very deserted appearance now that the vessels of the Western Patrol have left, prior to the demobilisation of the R.N.R. men who mainly comprised their crews. From the outbreak of the war until a week or so ago the roads have been the headquarters of H.M.S. Magpie and her attendant fleet of mine-sweeping and anti-submarine trawlers, and naturally the crews, numbering several hundred, have made Yarmouth quite a lively little town during the war. The town misses their presence, and the numerous social functions connected with their stay. Over the actual war work in the Channel accomplished by the Western Patrol the censor has drawn the veil, but if rumour is correct many thrilling and interesting details of their four and a half years vigil off the western shores of the Wight may one day come to light. The inhabitants have been on excellent terms with the gallant sailors during their stay, their conduct, generally speaking, having been exemplary, and they regret their departure. H.M.S. Magpie, with a skeleton crew aboard, is the only vessel of the patrol remaining in the roads. It is un-understood that she has been sold out of the Service and will be leaving this week-end".

Later in 1919 the Yarmouth War Memorial was erected in the Churchyard outside the North Door of the Church, and was dedicated by the Bishop of Southampton. Actually, his lordship very nearly did not turn up for the service, as he missed the ferry in Lymington. However, the military authorities at Fort Victoria offered to fetch him, but only from the mouth of the Lymington river, so the Bishop persuaded a local boatman to row him down the river where he was picked up by the soldiery, and he arrived in Yarmouth just in time.

In August 1921 Yarmouth had two visits from H.M. Queen Mary, who was staying at Osborne House. The first was on August 4th.

"On Thursday afternoon Her Majesty, continuing her motor trips to various places in the Island, visited Yarmouth. The Royal car arrived quite unexpectedly at about 4 p.m., and Her Majesty drove to "The Olde Spinning Wheel", Mr. B. Reynolds' antique shop in Quay Street, where she remained nearly an hour, and made numerous purchases. Her Majesty and the Countess of Shaftesbury both autographed Mr. Reynolds' ledger as a memento of their visit. A large crowd assembled outside the shop, and as Her Majesty left they raised hearty cheers which the Queen graciously acknowledged.

Yesterday (Friday) afternoon the Queen paid a second visit to Yarmouth, where Her Majesty spent about an hour looking over the Church and the ancient Castle attached to the Royal Pier Hotel. She did some shopping at Mr. Lee's antique stores".

Over the last 80 years or so the Isle of Wight has become increasingly popular as a holiday island, and as one of the three ports of entry Yarmouth has seen a dramatic increase in the number of visitors, cars, and lorries arriving on the ferry from Lymington. Up to the year 1938 this annual increase was fairly steady, but at that time there was a sudden and staggering increase in traffic due to the introduction of the "roll-on, roll-off" type of ferry. Traffic statistics have been produced at intervals of 10 years, and these tell their own story:

	Passengers	Cars	Lorries
1937	219,000	2,400	200
1948	441,000	20,000	6,200

One might think that an increase from 2,400 cars a year to 20,000 is enormous, but this was only the beginning, and the figures are now over 250,000 per annum. Foot passengers have increased in numbers three times, from 441,000 to over 1¼ million, and lorries nearly four times. (See page 204). These figures are quoted in order to demonstrate the extent of the revolution in Yarmouth's way of life which took place with the introduction of the new type of ferry in 1938.

Other changes have taken place during the last 80 years too, not all of them for the good. Many people from the mainland have bought holiday homes in the town, and though this has certainly brought money into Yarmouth, it has also meant that for a large part of the year many houses are empty. This is obviously a bad thing for the community life of the town, and has led to a certain amount of antagonism between the "Overners" and the "Islanders". This is fortunately diminishing, but it definitely exists.

Many of the Islanders have fascinating memories of Yarmouth as it used to be, some of them being able to go back up to 80 years. Among the older ones who have come forward with information are Mrs. Blanche Smith, Archie Cooke, and Ted Levey, and in Chapter 15 I have included Archie Cooke's account of his schooldays in Yarmouth, which started in 1902. It is fascinating to compare this with the following account of the same period by Mrs. Blanche Smith.

> **"Schooldays**
>
> Started at the age of three years – not five as it is to-day. One feels for the patience and endurance of the teacher Miss H. Griffiths, with the title of the Infants Teacher. One big problem being that the toilets then were a separate block across the playground, on the other side by the wall, and all too often a good old sou'wester and driving rain would add to her trials!

Nevertheless, the children were well looked after and many good scholars emerged eventually. Quite a few boys coached by their Headmaster, affectionately known as "Skipper" Spray became Yacht Captains, which was, of course, in the balmy days of steam yachts and large sailing ships.

Swimming lessons started quite early at school and took place at Sandhard. We children had to walk from the School, across the Bridge, which was then a one penny toll bridge, and the undressing and dressing took place in a stone-built small round shelter, which was called the Round House, though it was not really a house as such. It was a structure, divided into four sections, North, South, East and West, and was used in the very old days for people waiting to be ferried across to the town. They could wait in the section which was away from the prevailing wind. The swimming lessons were given by the Rector of St. James's Church, the Rev. H. F. Speed, who would be waiting offshore in his rowing boat, the oars of which must have been of a very strong type as the children, who were nervous, were suspended by a large towel round their middle to the oar, held firmly by the Rector in the boat. Yells of protest were of no avail, as the Rector was stone deaf. The Round House on Sandhard came to grief during the second World War – more's the pity.

Annual 'treats' or celebrations looked forward to by children were the Sunday School outings, when they were taken by train to Stone Steps at Calbourne where a good tea was provided and sports held in the Grounds. This was for children of the Methodist Chapel Sunday School. Those from St. James's Church usually were entertained with tea and sports at The Mount, a residence occupied by the Dashwood family, which stood on the Common overlooking the Solent. This beautiful old house with lovely grounds and gardens, eventually had to go to make way for a so-called new road to serve the needs of modern traffic through the town.

Summer holidays from school were eagerly looked forward to as most of the time could be spent on the beach, paddling or crabbing, and watching the liners pass through the Solent. These were much more numerous in the old days and a lovely sight.

The Annual Regatta was another joy of the past. This was held on the Common Green, where crowds would gather to watch the water sports and to patronise the ice-cream vendors and balloon sellers. At one end of the Green Roundabouts would be in full swing, churning out the latest hits and giving good value in quite a long ride for one penny (Adults 2d). Dancing in the Square followed in the evening.

The end of the year Prizegiving at the School was attended by the School Governors, and the prizes were given by local people and some of the teachers. A great day for the few. At 12 years old, pupils could sit for a Grammar School scholarship exam, and successful entrants then went on to the Secondary Grammar School at Newport, and travelled daily by train.

Shops in the Town

These were 'Supermarkets' in some respects, for instance, one small shop was at the cottages opposite St. James's Church and was owned by a little old lady named Nina Brown. The front tiny department contained toys including wooden hoops, china dolls (which started in price at one penny each), china cups, saucers, plates, ornaments, etc, – then at the end of a long passage, through the house, a store of fish was always to be had. She would come trotting up the passage with a lovely smoked haddock held by the tail – well clear of her black dress and apron! Yes indeed a 'Fish and Toy and China Shop'.

Another 'Fish and Cycle Shop' combine, was in South Street, where Mr. Attrill now lives (Grove Place). One could hire a bicycle for 6d an hour, or secure a real bargain, a second hand one, overhauled and in good condition! It was the only way growing boys and girls could own their bicycle, as money was not plentiful in those days – and no such things as Family Allowances!

Another little 'Front Window' shop was in a cottage at the end of Mill Road, where the Car Showrooms now stand, The little cottage window was full of sweets – a joy to children who passed on their way to school. The shop-keeper, Russell by name, also sold fish, which arrived daily from the Mainland and was always quite fresh. The husband would sell it from a barrow, which he toured the streets with and called at his regular customers' homes. So this was one more shop combining fish with something quite different.

The shops in the High Street were normal ones and all but one, the butchers, belonged to one owner, Mr. Harry Lee, who also owned many house properties in the town. His High Street shops ran as follows – on the left-hand side, looking up from the Square – first was antiques, next was soft furnishings, then boots and shoes, followed by gents outfitters, and then drapery and millinery – quite a Monoply! Mr. Harry Lee also carried on household removals – with a lage black van with gilt lettering – Removals – Harry Lee by Road, Rail or Sea – Estimates Free – which rolled off the tongue!

One other shop, where 'Pinings' now occupies was a butchers owned by Mr. L. J. Fryer, who sold only English beef and lamb. He would never stoop on any account to sell foreign produced meat. A nice 2 lb piece of Topside then cost about 3/6d (sounds like a dream to-day!) The end shop on the corner (now Pinings Corner) was Richardsons the Chemist. After which the lane leading down to the seashore was known as Fryer's Lane. The Towers on the opposite corner was the residence of Major Dean and family, and later of Mrs. Reynolds. On the opposite corner, now the Chemists, was a grocers shop, who also owned and ran a bakery across the street, on the corner where the Milk Depot now operates. Lovely homemade bread, cakes, and best of all, doughnuts – great favourites! A very appetising smell was always present in that area. The baker, a Mr. Odell, could be seen crossing the road in his white hat and overall, carrying trays of 'goodies' across to the shop. A 1 lb loaf was then 2d and a 2 lb 4d. Cakes (small) were 1d each, doughnuts 1d each, and smaller ones even ½d each.

The two other shops in the town were Mills and Harwoods, still going strong, in their old position, except that the corner part of Harwoods was then a sweet shop run by the Vincent family. A very popular Tea Rooms was in the corner, next to the Church (north entrance). It is now a private residence (Dolphin Cottage) but in the old days the Tea Rooms run by the Denhams were noted for their home cooked ham and ice-cream. The ice-cream always came by train at mid-day from Newport, in a large milk churn, and old Mr. Denham used to meet the train with a pole over his shoulder, which he carried the churn on, and he could be seen walking with it down the road to the shop, quite a way, but the children knew the ice-cream had arrived and a nice cornet was to be had for 1d.

All supplies from the Mainland for this end of the Island had to be brought from Lymington by Paddle Steamer and Towboat. The Towboat drawn by the Tug 'Jumsey' often contained livestock, cattle and sheep, which would be driven through the town to the railway station, en route for the weekly market at Newport. (A firmly closed front gate was a must when this happened!)

One other small business further up the High Street on the right-hand side was a Leather and Saddlers workshop. This was carried on by a Mr. Stanley Flint, a wonderful craftsman. Leather goods and harnesses could be seen hanging in the front window of No. 2 East End Terrace, next to 'Ailsa' (cottage). Mr. Flint lived with his father, who after reaching his 100th birthday was visited by the late Queen Mary. The Queen visited Yarmouth during her stay at Cowes, in Cowes Week.

A memory of Cowes Week was seeing lovely black shiny carriages and equally black shiny horses travelling from Norton, through the town to the railway station, to meet distinguished guests of Mrs. F. Crozier who held a banquet at her residence (Westhill House) on one evening during every Cowes Week.

Industries

At the end of Heytesbury Road, a turning off Station Road, a business concern employing quite a good number of staff was a first class Steam Laundry – The Isle of Wight and Lymington Steam Laundry Co. Ltd., established in 1895. They served the whole Island, and customers from Lymington. Combined with this they generated their own Electricity, which they introduced to the town. A company was formed known as the Yarmouth Electricity Supply Co., and gradually the town was lit by it. St. James's was the first Church on the Island to change its candles for electric lighting. The firm's buildings still stand, but are now occupied by an Engineering firm.

One other little memory. We could always have the services of a local Town Crier to Concerts, or a 'Jumbo' Sale, as he always put it, though I never saw any elephants on the stalls except white ones! I've often wondered what became of his bell, etc, – no doubt tucked up with someone else's souvenirs".

Both of these grand old "senior citizens" Blanche Smith and Archie Cooke were 86 years old when they wrote down their recollections of their childhood – and Ted Levey is not far off that age – and it can only be regarded as a great privilege to have heard their first hand account of what Yarmouth was like in the early days of this century.

Archie's father used to work at The Mount at one time, and told a lovely story about a casual employee there named 'Bung' Salter, who when engaged on trimming one of the trees actually sawed off the branch on which he was sitting. As he made his rapid and undignified descent his wig – about which he was very sensitive – caught up on one of the other branches.

In the general election of 1910, Winston Churchill visited the Island to address a big liberal Meeting in Newport. Archie Cooke has written about this – "Late that night a boat waited at the Pier to take him to a special train waiting in Lymington. Also waiting in the Square was a huge crowd threatening to push Winston into the sea. A gang of Liberals also waited to see their hero on to the boat. When the great man arrived there was a sharp tussle, but we got him safely aboard".

Another "citizen" who is not quite so senior as the above, but who has lived in Yarmouth all his life, and still works in the town – for which reason he shall be nameless – has come up with a number of amusing stories about local characters. Speaking of the early 1930's, when he had left Yarmouth School and was attending Newport Grammar School, they had school on Saturday mornings, which was a trial in the summer to anyone with a boat. And on Saturday afternoons he and a few of his cronies used to help an old man in Yarmouth. This was "Sailor" Mann, who had spent all his life in the Navy, and now in his retirement was earning a few bob by delivering luggage from Yarmouth Ferry and Railway Station to the big houses and hotels in the West Wight. Totland was at the height of its popularity at this time, with many large houses and hotels, and there was considerable holiday traffic at the weekends.

In the playground at the old Grammar School was a single small apple tree, which was the pride and joy of the headmaster. One might say that of all the unfortunate things to have in the playground at a boys' school a lone apple tree must rank high. Inevitably each year the apples disappeared, and equally inevitably there was an enquiry, in fact it ultimately became almost an obsession with the headmaster to preserve his apples.

One year he was so incensed at the disappearance of apples that he kept the whole school in one Saturday afternoon until the culprits confessed, and of course on this particular afternoon the Yarmouth boys were not able to help Sailor Mann hump his usual Saturday quota of heavy cabin trunks, many of which had to be carried from the van and up several flights of stairs. When he finally got home from school my friend went to see Sailor Mann to apologise, and told him the reason why they had been missing. And that was that.

The next day Sailor contacted him and asked him whether he could rake up one or two friends to help with a little job he had to do that evening, and my friend was only too happy to oblige, as working with Sailor was always interesting, and profitable.

Sailor's 'van' was an old, solid tyred, Model T Ford with a plain platform back, and in the evening they all piled into this and set off in the direction of Newport. In those days Newport was not the busy town it is to-day, and on Sunday evening there was no-one at all about. By the time they got there it was quite dark, and Sailor parked his van outside the wall of the Grammar School and climbed over. They all followed him and with fascination watched as he quickly and skilfully attacked the apple tree with a saw and cut it off about a foot from the ground.

It was not a very large tree, and between them they managed to carry it across the playground and roll it over the wall and on to the van. Off they set then for Yarmouth, only diverting slightly at Bouldnor to ditch the tree where it was not likely to be found.

On Monday morning the balloon went up. The headmaster was frantic, the police were called in, and for some days the young culprits lived in fear and trembling. But the perpetrators of the crime were never discovered.

Another character was Yarmouth's last Town Crier, 'Ern' Chambers, known to his friends as 'Newbury'. He was an ex-heavyweight champion of the Navy, and big with it. He was also a star turn in the King's Head on a Saturday night with the 'yachties'.

His party piece was to drink 9 pints in 4 minutes. On one occasion when asked to perform he declined and shortly after left the bar. He was back again in half an hour and asked if they still wanted him to do it. He was told they did, but someone asked him where he had been, and he said "Well, sir, my insides have been a bit poorly to-day and I wasn't sure whether I could do it, so I've been round to the Wheatsheaf to practice".

A favourite trick of his when asked to have a drink was to request a pint of bitter. As the last drops were being poured he would say, "If it's all the same with you sir, I'd rather have an ounce of baccy".

As Town Crier he had an enormous voice, but it was fatal to pay him before he completed the round as he would stop at the first pub, and that would be the end of the announcements.

Methodism, like Liberalism, has always been strong in the Island, and John Wesley himself is said to have preached in Yarmouth Parish Church once when he was storm-bound in the town. The original United Methodist Church was in South Street, and is now a builders's workshop. Fifty years ago here the singing of hymns was loud and strong, led by the organist, Mrs. Minnie Flint, who was noted more for the power of her voice than for the accuracy thereof. One small boy who had to attend Chapel twice every Sunday particularly remembers her singing "Jesu, lover of my soul, let me to thy bosom fly", and wondering idly whether a bosom fly was anything like a horse fly. On a week day Mrs. Flint was a butcher, and ran Fryers the butchers in the high Street.

In those days a man used to cycle in from Brighstone to preach. He was a "thumper", and used to beat the pulpit when he preached, and also sang loudly. Once in his sermon, and to the delight of the children, he stumbled over Jonah "in the welly of the bale", and though he had several shots at correcting this, he just could not get it right.

At the other end of South Street was Yarmouth's Fish and Chip Restaurant, built by a couple who lived next door in Tennyson Road. One small boy after school used to earn a few coppers by peeling and chipping the potatoes. The work was very hard, and not frightfully well paid. But there were compensations and remunerative opportunities. The lady of the house was large and extremely well endowed, and while the potato peeling was in progress would strip to the waist in the scullery, soap herself well, and have a vigorous wash, which to a schoolboy was something of an entertaining educational eye-opener. So though the pay was not good, he found it possible, and indeed easy, to sub-contract the work to his friends for a very satisfactory figure.

Many of the stories told concern the harbour, where there has always been plenty of activity. One such concerns a man, a very large man of 18 stone, whose job was connected with boat maintenance, and who was somewhat accident prone. On one occasion he went out to a boat which was leaking badly, to pump her out. This he did, and pumped it all into his dinghy which promptly sank. When he came to go ashore he was stuck, as he could not reach the dinghy due to the yacht's high topsides. His cries for help were not heard, and he was only rescued at Midnight when his wife phoned to say her husband had not been home, which was unusual, but – and this was much more sinister – he had not been seen in the Wheatsheaf all evening.

It was the same man who was working on the engine of a boat one day and dropped a spanner in the bilge. Owing to his girth he found it difficult to reach, so in order to get the maximum length of his arm he lay down on his back and reached down. While in this position the half belt on the back of his boiler suit got hooked round the starting handle, and he was caught. Wriggle as he would he could not get free, and in fact this only seemed to make matters worse. He struggled to get out of his overalls but this was no good either, and it was quite by chance that someone rowing across the harbour several hours later heard him shouting.

A final "harbour" story concerns another respected engineer and his mate who went out to a boat to attend to the engine. Unfortunately their dinghy painter got caught round the propellor, and as the shaft turned this gradually wound the dinghy down until the bow was hard up against the A-bracket, and only the transom was showing above water. Nothing they could do would shift it, and ultimately too they had to be rescued.

But no mention of the harbour, or of Yarmouth characters, would be complete without at least a passing reference to Billy Doe, its most famous Harbour Master. Billy ran Yarmouth Harbour for very many years, and during this time he endeared himself to all the countless yachtsmen who came in and out. He was a great and lovable character, and though he died in 1961 he is still remembered today, 18 years later, by residents and yachtsmen alike. He would be very proud to know of the way the harbour is growing and developing, and of his son Raich, who is Clerk to the Harbour Commissioners.

And so the 20th century rolls on. In 1965 Yarmouth was honoured by a visit from H.M. the Queen, who was in the Island to install her Uncle, Lord Louis Mountbatten, as Governor of the Isle of Wight. In 1977 Yarmouth rejoiced at Her Majesty's Silver Jubilee, and once again the streets of this old town were gay with flags and bunting. Later in the same year another Royal visitor, The Duke of Kent, visited us to name our proud new lifeboat, the Joy and John Wade.

Let us hope it will not be long before we are able to welcome our next Royal visitor.

CHAPTER XV

Yarmouth Schools II

1894 — 1923

"Skipper" Spray's successor, James Furmage, took over on January 18th, 1894, and proceeded to liven things up. He was no stranger to Yarmouth School, having worked under Mr. Spray as an Assistant Master as far back as 1875, later being promoted to a school on the mainland. During his first year as Head the Log contains many references to the problems he was meeting in trying to improve the standard of work.

> **March 9, 1894.** I examined the 2nd Standard and they are very backward in all subjects. Six of them know little more than their letters, viz, T. Logan, H. Logan, W. Wood, G. Bentley, W. Pallett, and A. Doe. The two Logans have been in the Standard 6 years.
>
> **March 12, 1894.** I am keeping in a few of the very backward ones in Standard 2 to try and get them on myself.
>
> **April 13, 1894.** I heard the poetry in the 2nd Standard. It was said much too fast and with very little intelligence. I took the class for 15 minutes myself before the Teacher in the hope of improving it.

Later in that year the School Inspector was able to say "The general condition of the School gives promise of further progress", and the report for 1895 says "Discipline, Drill, and Instruction show remarkable and praiseworthy improvement".

> **January 8, 1896.** I punished Fred Cleary, at the request of his parents, for throwing stones in the street and breaking a window.
>
> **April 26, 1896.** We started a Cricket Club today for the School boys. Mr. James Blake one of the Managers has kindly allowed us the use of a field for practice.

May 4, 1896. I have kept Elsie Wadham (delicate), Rosa Wilkins (deformed), Elizabeth Steel (delicate), and William Prince (scarlet fever) back in the 2nd Standard. I hope they will now keep pace with the newcomers.

May 11, 1896. I punished George and John Bulford for taking toys from the Infants School. These boys a few weeks ago came from Plymouth. It is the first time I have heard of anything missing. I spoke to the children and tried to impress upon them all the absolute necessity of being strictly honest in all things.

At the end of 1896 H.M. Inspector wrote:

"The School is well managed and the Head Master takes great interest in methods for developing the intelligence of the Scholars . . ."

And in 1897:

"It is impossible in a short report to do justice to the carefulness of the instruction and the variety of interests which are awakened in the scholars. The intelligence and good sense of the instruction are shown in the choice of Readers, of passages for Recitation, and of songs. The Master stamps each choice with a refreshing individuality. Great pains are taken to secure good illustrations for all the lessons, and in Arithmetic practical Mensuration and Book-keeping are not neglected. The voluntary help of professional instructors is secured for Drill and Ambulance work. Swimming is taught, and Gardening for boys and Cookery for girls are about to be introduced".

In this year too the Infants School received a very good report from the Diocesan Inspector. "The children are being beautifully trained in habits of reverence and religious earnestness. The elder ones have received clear and definite teaching, of a most valuable kind, which has been admirably grasped by some, but not by all in the class . . . A happy spirit pervades this School".

In August 1900 James Furmage married Annie Whittington, Assistant Mistress in the Infants School, though there is no reference to this in either Log. Annie continued to be an invaluable help in the school, standing in on many occasions when staff were ill.

The almost ecstatic reports from the Inspectors continued to come in, reports of which any Head Master could be justly proud, but in 1903 a vast and fundamental change in organisation came over the school. This change was brought about by the Education

Act of 1902 which drastically altered the whole organisational structure of schools in this country. One result of this Act was that secular education in the Yarmouth Church of England Schools came under the control of the Isle of Wight County Council Education Authority.

A new board of management, known as the Foundation Managers, was set up under the chairmanship of the Rector, the Rev. H. Fiennes Speed, the Hon. Secretary being Mr. J. E. Richardson (Yarmouth's Chemist), and with Dr. E. T. Carlyon as the Hon. Treasurer.

The first meeting of the Foundation Managers was held on 8th October, 1903 to discuss various letters received from the Education Authority. These were all couched in very bleak official language, and one can sense the antagonism which they must have generated.

The first was dated 29th September and informed the Managers that September 30th was the "Appointed Day" on which control of Secular Instruction was to be taken over by the Education Committee. The letter also referred to a report by the Surveyor employed by the Local Education Authority, and asked the Managers to give it their immediate attention. The letter closed with a threat that if the recommendations made by the Surveyor were not complied with within three months the results would be dire. " . . . they will consider the desirability, or otherwise, in accordance with section 7 of the Education Act, 1902 of continuing the use of such buildings for the purpose of a Public Elementary School".

The second letter, dated 1st October, referred to Teachers salaries and stated that accommodation was not to be provided as part of the salary.

The third letter said the Education Committee had appointed Mr. C. Flint as their Representative Manager of the Yarmouth I.W. Public Elementary School.

At this first Managers' Meeting the Report of the Surveyor was considered, and the amount of work ordered to be done was obviously considered to be unreasonable, and beyond the Managers' financial capability. The Minutes of this Meeting contain an instruction to the Secretary to write the Board of Education in Whitehall, asking them to mediate between the Local Education Authority and the Foundation Managers, but there is no trace of this letter having been sent.

In the meantime the Chairman (the Rev. H. Fiennes Speed) received a charming letter from Mr. Charles Flint of the High Street, Yarmouth.

"Sir,

I beg to inform you, although appointed for the School Management, I shall not hold myself responsible for any debt you or the committee may contract.

I am

Dear Sir

Yours truly

C. Flint".

The next salvo from the Education Committee came in a letter dated 5th November, and the correspondence that ensued is worth quoting.

Education Offices,
Newport, I.W.
5th November, 1903

To the Correspondent,
National Schools, Yarmouth

Dear Sir,

I am directed by the Education Committee to ask you to bring before the notice of the Managers of Yarmouth Schools the serious question of the inadequate accommodation for the children attending such School.

In my visit yesterday I found 148 children present. This is no unusual thing as I find on reference as many as 151 have been present, and will no doubt be severely dealt with by H.M. Inspector on his visit to the School.

Will you kindly lay this matter before the Managers without delay, and favour me with a reply thereto.

Yours faithfully,

F. G. Flux,

Secretary.

Yarmouth,
Isle of Wight.
November 9th, 1903

To the Education Committee,
For the County of the Isle of Wight.

Gentlemen,

In reply to your letter of November 5th I am directed by the Foundation Managers of the Yarmouth Schools to state that these Schools have lately been accepting scholars from neighbouring Parishes for special reasons.

These children will now receive notice to withdraw from these schools and attend those situated in their own Parishes. The Yarmouth Managers then calculate that the accommodation will prove sufficient.

I am, Gentlemen
Yours faithfully,
J. E. Richardson.
Hon. Secretary.

The following letter was then sent to the parents of children attending the Yarmouth Schools from other Parishes – i.e. Thorley, Wellow and Freshwater.

Yarmouth.
Isle of Wight.
9th November, 1903.

The Managers of the Yarmouth Schools finding that under the New Education Act the accommodation of these Schools does not permit them to take children outside their own Parish regret that it will be compulsory for you to withdraw your children and make arrangements for them to attend your own Parish Schools after Saturday November 14th 1903.

Signed: H. Fiennes Speed, Rector and Correspondent.
E. T. Carlyon
J. E. Richardson
Charles Flint
R. W. Scott Rogers

Education Office,
Newport, I.W.
19th November, 1903

Dear Sir,

I am directed by the above named Local Education Authority to draw your attention to the serious matter of dismissal of children from the Yarmouth School this week, and to refer you to the Code 1903 under the heading "Extra District Children" viz – "If a school is more than full, the Board of Education do not consider that the school authority are justified in dismissing from their school children already in attendance on the ground that they belong to an adjoining Parish", and to ask that you will inform your committee and let my Committee know what steps, "if any", you propose to take to re-instate the scholars so dismissed in your school.

I am to respectfully point our that if scholars are to be summarily dismissed (in contravention to the Code) as in this instance, my Committee will have to consider the desirability of reorganising and maintaining your schools as a Public Elementary School.

Thanking you in anticipation of an early reply.

Yours faithfully,

F. G. Flux,

Secretary.

Yarmouth
Isle of Wight.
November 21st 1903

To the Education Committee,
for the County of the Isle of Wight.
Gentlemen,

In reply to your letter of November 19th I am directed by the Foundation Managers to inform you that they have re-cinded their notice to the Parents of Children from other Parishes hitherto attending these schools and have notified them as follows.

"The Managers of the Yarmouth Schools withdraw their letter of November 9th, and your children will be again received as scholars in these schools from this date".

Yours truly

J. E. Richardson.

Hon. Secretary.

This round can fairly be said to have been won by the Education Committee, who swiftly followed up their victory by switching the attack to that most sensitive of areas – finance.

County Education Office,
Newport, I.W.
27th November 1903.

To the Correspondent,
Yarmouth Non-Provided Schools.
Dear Sir,

I am directed by the above named Local Education Authority to inform you that by a return received it is shown that an endowment exists in connection with your school and to ask that you will kindly favour me with the particulars of same and also with the recommendations of your managers as to its future division.

In forwarding this information may I ask that the source and amount of income, whether a permanent fixed sum or otherwise, and the reasons for the division as recommended by the managers may be given.

As it is desirable to arrive at an agreement at an early date, may I ask you to kindly give me an answer at your earliest convenience.

I am, Dear Sir,
Yours faithfully,
F. G. Flux
Secretary

This was an extremely shrewd blow. They did not specify the endowment of which they had heard, and hence the Managers had little option but to disclose information on all the six small endowments that the school possessed.

Yarmouth, I.W.
December 7th, 1903

Dear Sir,

In conformation with your request as per letter of November 27th/03 I herewith forward complete list of endowments of these Schools showing all information asked for. The Managers would like to point out to the Education Committee of the Isle of Wight County Council that these endowments constitute the chief source of income besides the rent of the Masters house from which they can draw any revenue to carry out their obligations, and the Yarmouth Parish being under 1,000 inhabitants any other way of obtaining money would be extremely difficult. They hope that the Education Committee of the Isle of Wight County Council will bear these facts in mind if any division is to be made.

I am Sir,

Yours faithfully, etc.

While this exchange was taking place the Education Committee produced a superficially disarming letter announcing the Christmas holiday, and awarding half holidays for good attendance – but even this had a sting in its tail.

County Education Office,
Newport, I.W.
5th December 1903

To the Correspondent,
Yarmouth Schools.

Dear Sir,

I am directed by the Local Education Committee to inform you that they have decided that the schools maintained by them should close for their Christmas holiday on Wednesday, 23rd December at noon, and reassemble on Monday the 11th day of January 1904.

Will you kindly cause this information to be conveyed to the head Teachers in all departments under your management, so that this arrangement may be carried out.

My Committee also decided that in the Boys' department where the average attendances for any month reaches 95%, Girls department 93% and Infants 90% such departments should receive a half holiday on some convenient day in the following month. Will you also convey this information to the Teachers.

I am also to call your attention to a letter addressed to you on the 30th September last and to express the hope of my Committee that advantage will be taken by the Managers of this Vacation to place in hand the alterations and recommendations made in Mr. Blizzard's report which accompanied my letter.

I am Sir,

Your obedient Servant,

F. G. Flux

Secretary.

The reply of the Managers to the above was terse and to the point, and was contained in a letter dated 15th December which was taken up mainly with other matters.

" . . . I have also to inform you that during the holiday we are undertaking as much of the work recommended to be done to these Schools as is possible in the time".

Early in 1904 the Managers moved on to the attack, and wrote further about the endowments.

Yarmouth
Isle of Wight
February 3rd, 1904

To the Education Committee
for the County of the Isle of Wight.

Gentlemen,

Adverting to your letter re the endowments of Yarmouth Schools, at a meeting of the Foundation Managers held on Monday February 1st 1904, I was instructed to ask your favourable consideration regarding the managers retaining these endowments. The managers in endeavouring to carry out the wishes of your committee and to meet in every way possible the requirements of the board of education find that the income at their disposal will fall far short of the amount required. They have now in hand considerable work which was required to be done (although not yet quite complete) and find that the funds at their disposal are exhausted; and this parish being so small the committee have but little prospect before them of raising a building fund from voluntary subscriptions. Under these circumstances if your committee could grant to the foundation managers the whole use of the annual income from the endowments this committee hopes to see its way clear to carry out all necessary requirements enumerated in Mr. Blizzard's report.

I am, Gentlemen,
Yours truly,
J. E. Richardson
Hon. Secretary

Later that month they had occasion to write again, though on an entirely different subject. This was to request a half holiday for the children to assist in the welcome to Lord Tennyson of Farringford

House, Freshwater on the occasion of his arrival in the Isle of Wight after his term of Office as Governor General of the Australian Commonwealth. The half holiday was willingly granted by the County Education Committee, and on March 1st, 1904 the children assembled at the Pier under their teachers' care "and assisted materially in welcoming Lord and Lady Tennyson on their arrival. This act of assembling the children gave much pleasure to Lord and Lady Tennyson".

From then on, and all through the summer, peace reigned, but on October 20th the Education Committee launched an all out attack.

County Education Office,
Newport, I.W.
20th October 1904

Dear Sir,

I am directed by the County Education Committee to call your attention to the several applications made to your Managers for certain alterations and improvements necessary to make your School efficient as set out in the report of Mr. J. H. Blizzard, and to inform you, that from the returns submitted to the Committee it would appear that the recommendations have not received the attention of your mangers.

As a meeting of my committee will be held on Wednesday next the 26th Instant, when this matter will receive their attention, I am to ask you to be kind enough to favour them before that date with a reply as to whether it is the intention of your managers to comply with the request of my committee by causing the reasonable requirements, contained in Mr. Blizzard's Report, being carried out, and if so, at what date it is anticipated such will be completed.

The items to which your special attention is called are:
Provision of a system for Heating, Ventilation, and Lighting.
System of surface drainage for playground.
Boys and Girls Playgrounds divided.
Lavatory basins with water to be supplied to lavatories.

Yours faithfully,
F. G. Flux,
Secretary

Yarmouth
Isle of Wight
October 23rd 1904

To the Isle of Wight County
Education Committee
Gentlemen,

Adverting to your letter of October 20th I have to inform your committee that the heating and ventilation of these schools is at the present time under the consideration of the Foundation Managers, and that plans are being prepared for the system which the Managers hope to carry out during the Christmas holidays. The extra lighting has already been completed and H.M. Inspector signified his approval of the same. The Committee will as early as possible carry out the dividing of the Boys and Girls Playgrounds. The surface of the playground naturally slopes towards the River Yar and drains into it, we intend to provide a new covering of shingle to the worn parts. Lavatory Basins shall be supplied to the Lavatories. I beg to lay the subject of extra accommodation before your committee in an extra letter.

I am, gentlemen,
Yours faithfully,
J. E. Richardson
Hon. Secretary.

Yarmouth
Isle of Wight.
October 23rd 1904

To the Isle of Wight County
Education Committee
Gentlemen,

With regard to providing extra accommodation by the enlargement of these schools I have to say that it would be an impossibility to raise the amount of money required by voluntary contributions as the parishioners consider the school rate they have to pay sufficient for them to pay. I am desired by the school Managers to ask if you will favourably consider their request and grant them the use of all the endowments of these schools for say 4 or 5 years, and if this is granted the school managers will at once have plans prepared to enlarge the school say 20 to 25 feet and put the required partitions in the room. Trusting you will favourably consider this.

I am, yours faithfully,

J. E. Richardson

Hon. Secretary

County Education Office,
Newport, I.W.
27 October 1904

Dear Sir,

In reply to your letter of the 23rd inst I am directed to inform you that my committee are unable to sanction such part of the endowments as may be due to the Ratepayers of the District being appropriated for any other purpose than that laid down by the Education Act 1902. I am to suggest that the proper course would be for a parish meeting to be called so that the Ratepayers may have an opportunity of expressing their opinion on the proposal for the use of the endowments for the purpose mentioned.

Yours faithfully,

F. G. Flux

Secretary.

Yarmouth
Isle of Wight
October 28th 1904

To the Isle of Wight Education Committee
Gentlemen,

I have to lay before your committee the following resolution passed at a meeting of the Foundation Managers of the Yarmouth Schools on the proposition of Dr. Carlyon seconded by Mr. Preedy. "The Foundation Managers find it impossible to reply definitely as to providing extra accommodation at these schools until they hear from the County Education Committee as to the appropriation of the endowments, which information will be necessary to lay before any future meeting of the ratepayers of this parish".

I am, gentlemen,

Yours truly,

J. E. Richardson.

Hon. Secretary.

County Education Office,
Newport, I.W.
October 31st 1904

Dear Sir,

In reply to your query, my committee agree to an arrangement for the division of Endowments on your School by allocating one half to the Managers for the purpose of meeting expenses to be incurred by them, and one half to be paid to the county Fund to be credited to the Poor Rate for the Parish of Yarmouth.

Yours faithfully,
F. G. Flux
Secretary.

Was this a victory for the Foundation Managers? It certainly looks like it, though perhaps it had best be described as a grand old British compromise.

While this battle between the Managers and the Education Committee was raging, life (and death) at the school continued much as usual. 1904 was in fact a bad year for fatalities in Yarmouth' and the Head Master's Log records two such sad events.

May 30, 1904. On Whit Monday Blanch Robertson, Standard I, was accidentally burned to death at Fort Victoria.

October 2, 1904. Owing to the death of their father, Fred'k, Victor, Dorothy, and Alfred Henderson will not attend school this week. A very wet day.

October 6, 1904. A half holiday was granted this afternoon by the Education Authority. It was the occasion of the funeral with full naval honours of the late Mr. Jas. Henderson, Chief Officer of Coastguards.

One scholar who attended Yarmouth School at that time is still very much alive (in 1979) and remembers these events well. Archie Cooke lived in Wellow and was at Yarmouth School from 1902 – 1906, travelling daily either by train or by bicycle. Fortunately for us Archie is a writer, and is possessed of a phenomenal memory, and he has written a fascinating account of his schooldays in Yarmouth, which he has kindly agreed should be included in this current account.

BOYHOOD AT YARMOUTH SCHOOL

by ARCHIE B. COOKE

When I was about 9 years old, my Father bought me a small bicycle and sent me to Yarmouth School. I was placed in a class taught by Fred Cleary, a member of the Bugle family, and I remember being rather shocked when my new mates addressed him as Fred. This was not from lack of respect for he was a wonderful teacher and I regretted leaving his class after a year to join the next stage taught by the Headmaster Jim Furmage. Jim was one of my Father's cricket cronies, and was popular. Certain subjects were neglected, but in arithmetic we worked on sums far in advance of our years. As to English he was content to get us to read, and our lessons in this subject usually consisted of reading Scott and Dickens obtained from the small School Library. Of grammar, English composition, nature study, we knew nothing, but he taught us how to write business letters and quite a lot of elementary gardening.

Yarmouth was a wonderful place for small boys. In those days the River Yar washed the playground wall, which was only about eighteen inches high. At Spring tides river water came through the sluices into the playground and our tennis balls frequently got kicked overboard, which we retrieved by long sticks and a garden rake. I do not remember anybody falling over this low wall, and I suppose we must have realised the danger.

There were no school meals, and I carried my dinner packed in a small satchel. As soon as our food was eaten, there was a long hour or more to wander round the old mill or down to the Quay. The Mill was full of mystery to a small boy. It had in its working life been driven by steam, and the old machinery, still in position, was a source of interest to us. Besides, it was all boarded up, and out of bounds, which gave it an added thrill. We had discovered a way in, where one of the boards could be moved.

It was on the Quay where we spent most of our time. There was a large coal yard, where now cars line up for embarkation, and there were regular visits by a large Brigantine (called the "Rapid") owned by one, Captain Digby, whose sons were also at school with us. She brought a regular cargo of about 200 tons of coal from Hartlepool, which was unloaded in baskets carried ashore by workmen. The arrival and departure of the Rapid was a special event to which we looked forward. Then another Yarmouth boat was a large barge owned by Gus Warder, which traded between Southampton and the Island. Freight from Lymington was brought across in "tow boats", large flat bottomed vessels dragged along by the passenger steamers to the Pier Head, and then pulled into the Quay by the ships' crews. All sorts of merchandise used to arrive, including furniture conveyors, which had to be hoisted up by a large crane operated manually. We boys watched it all, jumping in and out of the tow boats, and although there were no protecting rails along the quayside, nobody fell overboard.

In addition there was, as now, a regular service of steamers from Lymington, paddlers in those days, and the shipping using the Solent was much more numerous then than now. On Wednesdays, just before afternoon school, one of the big four funnelled German boats came through, en route from Hamburg to New York, having made a brief call at Southampton. These were lovely ships and I remember the "Kaiser Wilhelm der Grosse" and the Kaiser Wilhelm the Second" and one other whose name is forgotten. The first named was sunk in World War I when she was equipped as an armed cruiser. The Union Castle boats sailed through on Fridays, and the St. Paul and her sister ship on Saturdays. Every day the Jersey boat was expected at 4 p.m. and was always up to time. Frequently a man'o'war anchored off the Common for a day or two, sometimes one from a foreign power. Our own battleships, cruisers and torpedo boats were another source of interest, and if possible identified with the aid of a friendly porter on the pier.

Many of my contemporaries went to sea, and the names of most of them are inscribed on the War Memorial on the Town Hall. My particular pal, Jack Eldridge, began life at a very early age as a Cabin Boy in the City Line, and after many adventures, including two years in sail, became Captain of a large tanker bringing oil from the Gulf.

There were occasional excitements for us. I remember a small ship laden with barrels of oil on fire, abandoned and drifting down the Solent on the tide. She was eventually sunk by gunfire (when she became a danger to shipping) from one of the forts on the Western entrance to the Solent.

One morning we found a Channel Island boat high and dry on the ledge inside Black Rock. She had got too close to the Island shore during the night, but eventually floated off on the rising tide. Then there was the tragedy of H.M.S. Gladiator, a three funnelled cruiser, sunk when entering the Solent after collision in a snow squall with the St. Paul. An attempt was made to beach her but she sank in shallow water between Fort Victoria and Black Rock, with the loss of thirty two of her crew.

In those days some Government boats were based up at the West End of the Harbour. Their job was to service forts and tow targets for the Gunners, and I remember the largest of these was called the Burgoyne.

However, all this, which probably stimulated an interest in geography, ended for me in 1906, when I managed to pass the examination for admission to the new secondary school then forming at Newport.

Archie returned to Yarmouth briefly in 1911 as a Student Teacher, but later decided that the teaching profession was not for him. In 1915 he joined the army, was commissioned, and subsequently became a regular soldier.

One of his stories concerns James Furmage, his Head Master, at Yarmouth. In his time Archie has been a keen and accomplished cricketer, inheriting a love of the game from his father who was locally celebrated as a fast bowler. Jim Furmage was also a cricketer, and had much to do in encouraging the young Cooke in his early years. Archie's story concerns a match at Afton in which his father and Furmage were both playing, and in which his father opened the bowling to a renowned batsman called Tankard. His first ball was a longhop, which Tankard drove to the off with considerable power. Furmage was fielding at silly point and received the ball fair and square in his stomach, and was promptly knocked over and out. Like a true cricketer, however, he did not panic, and when they picked him up and revived him he was found to be still clutching the ball.

As a Head Master James Furmage went on from strength to strength. For nearly 20 more years, and all through the first World War, he ran the school efficiently, coped with all the day to day problems, received good reports from the Inspectors, and generally played his part in the life of the town. A few random Log entries are of interest.

> **March 1, 1905.** School closed for two months due to an outbreak of measles.
>
> **April 27, 1906.** With permission of the Education Committee I attended the funeral this afternoon of Mr. J. E. Richardson, Hon. Secretary to the Foundation Managers.

(According to the Burial Register Mr. Richardson died in a fire caused by upsetting a lamp. He was 63 years old and had been a Churchwarden of the Parish Church for many years).

November 8, 1906. Mr. A. Jolliffe addressed the children on the "Physiological Effects of Alcohol" from 3 to 4.

August 30, 1907. A circus being in the town the School was not opened to-day. Average for the week 108.

December 7, 1909. During the dinner hour Percy Spink, Standard II, had the misfortune to break his leg. It was purely an accident, only about 6 boys being in the playground. I happened to be in the School and rendered "First Aid". The doctor soon arrived and set the leg when two of our ambulance boys (L. Townsend and Harold Hawkes) conveyed him to his home on our School Stretcher – the doctor complimenting them upon their work.

January 11, 1911. A very windy day. The rough seas prevented the children from Norton from attending School.

June 15, 1911. (Infants) Miss E. J. Dovey, Head Mistress of the Infants School wrote – Children dismissed at 11-45 to enable them to see H.M. Ships passing the Pier.

October 27, 1911. (Infants) Attendance suffering greatly through Whooping Cough.

February 16, 1912. (Infants). The Diocesan Report said – "The School has suffered a great deal during the past year from illness and consequent irregular attendance. The teaching is evidently very thorough and kindly . . . Number on books 66.

July 5, 1912. (Infants). School closed for Chicken Pox – and remained closed until September 2nd, after the Summer Holidays.

September 23, 1915. Mr. A. Jolliffe, by permission of the Education Authority, gave the children a lesson on "Alcohol and Muscular Power" this afternoon.

November, 1915. (Infants). The start of another period of sickness. Very heavy colds, actual sickness, one child had a fit, several with measles, one fainted in school.

May 5, 1916. The Managers sent a letter of condolence to Mrs. Dashwood on the death from wounds in action of Captain C. B. L. Dashwood. A complaint was received from Captain Cole that boys were not baring their heads during the National Anthem.

November 28, 1916. (Infants). Ena Doe met with an accident in the cloakroom, hurting her chin on one of the pegs. Dr. Bickerstaff came and put a stitch in it.

February 27, 1917. (Infants). The Diocesan Inspector wrote "These children are receiving a very good religious training, and are responding well to the admirable teaching which is being given to them . . . It is a very good Infants School.

In January 1918 Miss Fanny Riddet, who had been an Assistant Mistress at Yarmouth for 25 years, suddenly died from heart failure and her position was taken by Miss May Phillips of Sunderland. This lady commenced her duties in March but it was not long before she disagreed with Mr. Furmage on the way he was running the School, and on 15th April she thought fit to write the following letter of complaint to the Managers.

St. Kilda,
Yarmouth, I.W.
15th April, 1918.

The Chairman of the Managers,
Dear Sir,

I have received to-day the Forms of Agreement of my appointment to the School, but before signing the same I should like to bring certain facts before your notice. I understand that the time for assembly is 8 50 a.m. and as Teachers should be there in readiness, the Schools should be open. This has not been the case on any morning. I have always strictly followed the Time Table, but here I am unable to do so. It needs alteration owing to various changes which have occurred in the Staff. I also feel it my duty to point out the amount of time which the children waste in the playground. I earnestly wish to do my very best for my children, especially now when education is of such vital importance; but under existing circumstances, and with such lack of discipline, I feel it is practically impossible.

I ask you to kindly consider the position from my point of view, as it is a most difficult one my being an Assistant Mistress.

Thanking you for your kind support.
I am, your faithfully,
E. M. Phillips.

From an Engraving by G. Brannon dated 1838 and before the Bridge was built

Quay Street in 1867, the buildings on the right have been rebuilt as part of the George Hotel

Quay Street today

The School, from a photograph dated 1867

Yarmouth School as it is today

The Managers considered this letter and sent it to Mr. Furmage for his comments. His reply was lengthy, but glorious.

The Schools,
Yarmouth, I.W.
May 4th, 1918.

To the Local Managers, Yarmouth, I.W.
C. E. Schools.

Gentlemen,

I have received your letter per the Chairman in connection with a communication which you received from Miss Phillips who has been one of my colleagues during the last few weeks.

You have summarised the allegations against me thus:

1. The Schools have not been open at 8-50 a.m. according to regulations.
2. She has been unable to follow the Time Table which she states needs alteration.
3. The children have been allowed to waste time in the playground.
4. Lack of discipline.

I am indeed grateful to you for giving me an opportunity to reply. I will proceed to do so seriatim:

1. The schools have not commenced work at 8.50 a.m. but have been open. There is seldom a morning, neither has there been for the last three years, but what I am in school soon after 7 a.m. preparing B.B. for the day's work. There have been very good reasons why the schools have not commenced at 8.50 a.m. but these need not now be enumerated as I will see that the bell always starts ringing at 8.50 a.m.
2. When Miss Phillips came I asked her, together with Mrs. Ablitt, to look at the Time Table to see if they could suggest any improvements or alterations. I went through the Time Table with them and to make their work correlate I made suggested alterations. Miss Phillips could have followed the Time Table with, owing to the structure of the School, the minimum

amount of difficulty. (I am sure both the Teachers will bear me out in this).

3. The children have certainly had prolonged playtime during fine weather, but owing to our having no covered playground or shelter of any kind to protect the children from wind and weather – and we feel it here – and the playground being often in a dreadfully wet state, days and days often pass when we can have no play at all. In the agregate the play time has not been exceeded. (I am certain that the Teachers who are qualified to know will corrobrate this).

   In the future I will see that the play time is never exceeded.

4. I fail to understand this. I do not know whether the Teacher refers to her own class of 28, to Mrs. Ablitt's class of 45, or to my own division of 62. I can only say I have taught in 7 different schools, I have been Headmaster here for 25 years, I have been examined and inspected by dozens of inspectors, and I can produce reports second to none. It is 43 years ago since I started teaching in these schools under Mr. Spray (and a better teacher never lived), and this is the first time I have ever had a "lack of discipline" charge brought against me. Perhaps you will forgive my saying that "discipline" is rather a dangerous subject to criticise as there are many different opinions as to what constitutes really good and effective discipline.

I understood most emphatically from Miss Phillips that her letter had been unreservedly withdrawn and that it would never be used at a Meeting of Managers – so you can quite understand your letter came as a sort of Thunderclap.

As you say, Gentlemen, these are serious charges, even if they do not deserve a harsher title.

My actions have always been open, and above board, and whatever I have done, rightly or wrongly, has been honestly done in what I believed to be the best interests of the children. Teaching children, who have souls as well as bodies, is a great and glorious work, but it is most exhausting, and responsible Teachers need no distractions but full sympathy if their work is to be of the best.

With apologies for using both sides of the paper but in these most serious times and in the likelihood of a still more acute paper shortage one must be careful.

I am, gentlemen,

Yours v. sincerely,

James Furmage.

September 17, 1918. This afternoon 20 of the upper boys went gathering blackberries in charge of Mr. J. B. Doe, one of the local Managers. According to instructions from the Education Committee the Registers were not marked. 90 lbs were gathered.

September 24, 1918. This afternoon 20 of the upper girls went gathering blackberries. 95 lbs were gathered.

November 11, 1918. This morning we heard that the armistice had been signed.

March 17, 1919. Principally owing to the disbanding of the Western Patrol vessels our number on the books has decreased to 93. (The average had been up to 115).

June 5, 1919. Mr. Jolliffe, by permission of the Education Committee, gave the children a lesson on "Alcohol and the Blood".

November 29, 1922. I have to-day sent in my resignation to the proper authorities as Master of these Schools – to take effect February 28th, 1923.

February 28, 1923. My resignation should have taken effect this afternoon but Mr. John Pugh from the Denmark Road, Cowes, School, the newly appointed Master being unable to come at once I am at the request of the Education Authority and local Managers still remaining in charge.

March 28, 1923. This afternoon my duties as Head Master of this School ceased after having had charge for the last 30 years.

James Furmage.

And so a long and illustrious spell as Head Master came to an end for Jim Furmage. Towards the end there were signs that he was tiring, but as he said proudly in his letter to the Managers in 1918 he had been examined by dozens of Inspectors, and could produce reports second to none.

But this was not the end of James by any means. In December 1930 he was elected a School Manager and served for many years. In 1938, at the age of 75, he was taking the chair at Managers' meetings, and his hand writing in the Log Book was as firm and clear as it had been 40 years previously. He died in 1942 at his house 'Plevna' in South Street, full of years and honour. His career as a teacher had indeed been a "great and glorious work".

CHAPTER XVI

Yarmouth Schools III

1923 — 1955

The man who succeeded James Furmage as Headmaster can perhaps best be described as a ball of fire. John Pugh was selected from an original list of 37 applicants by a process of elimination, and once having got on to a short list of three he was interviewed by the Managers. Their Minute of the interview says:

> "He (Mr. Pugh) said that he was anxious to come, and if selected would do his utmost for the welfare of the School, the Church, and the place. He was asked to see Mr. Furmage, in order that he might learn everything he might desire to know about the work – and also see the house. He then retired, and the Managers unanimously decided to offer him the post; which was accordingly done. He accepted it with much pleasure and gratification".

How right the Managers were in their choice!

John Pugh electrified not only the School, but the Managers as well. He set about changing things he did not like, and stamped his authority and personality on the place in double quick time. His first two Log entries were short and to the point.

> **April 9, 1923.** This morning I took charge of this School as Head Master.
>
> Jno. C. Pugh. T.C.
>
> **April 10, 1923.** Percy Mussell having illegally left school and gone to work, I interviewed his employer and had the lad returned to school immediately.

He instituted a series of Progress Reports to the Managers, the first one being written at the end of April. The Managers' Minute Book comments on this.

> **May 1, 1923.** A Report from Mr. Pugh was read, stating the progress of the school; that he had visited the parents of most of the scholars, and that they were not averse to

home-work, that he was satisfied with the Staff. He asked that the long desks might be stored as they were not needed in the school (this Mr. Mills kindly undertook to do, if the L.E.C. did not need them) also that hooks might be put up in the boy's lobby, and a few in girls' (it was resolved that Mr. May be told to do this) also that 2 sheds might be erected in the playground (it was proposed by Dr. Carlyon, seconded by Mr. Doe, that Mr. Pugh be asked to give a more detailed proposition with regard to this: carried) also that he had requisitioned the L.E.A. for a piano.

The Chairman was asked to let Mr. Pugh know that his Report was appreciated, and to ask that it might be repeated at intervals.

His second report came a few weeks later.

May 25, 1923. A second Report from the Head Master was read, in which he proposed that the outside drill sheds should be 25 x 12 feet, and suggested the locations of them. He stated that leave had been created by the U.S. Steamship Line for the senior chilren and staff to look over the "Leviathan" at Southampton on July 14th, and he hoped that the Managers would be able to accompany them. He asked the Managers to pay individual visits to the Schools, which would be appreciated. The Town Trust had created permission for the children to be shown over the Town Hall. There had been 14 cases of measles in the school. There was a ceremony in the playground on Empire Day, when the children listened to the messages from H.M. the King and H.M. the Queen from a Gramophone; and saluted the Flag. He thanked the Managers for permission to erect a garage, which would not be unsightly. He had started a Sports Fund for Boys and Girls.

In June he took the top class to the Town Hall from 3 o'clock to 4 for a Lecture on the History of Yarmouth given by the Town Clerk, and in July he recorded a further number of innovations.

July 4, 1923. Having heard that 3 elephants were landing here at 10 o'clock I took the whole school down to the Quay to see them. Absent 30 minutes.

July 9, 1923. Piano arrived at the School, lent by Mr. Geo. Cleary of the Bugle Hotel: lent for an indefinite period, the only condition being that it shall be looked after by me.

July 10, 1923. Having collected various sums of money from Yarmouth people, the School has been supplied with a full set of Cricket Gear and two sets of Rounders.

July 16, 1923. On Saturday last (14th inst) I took 40 children to Southampton to see the Leviathan: all the staff of both departments attended.

The above short entries speak volumes about Pugh's energy and initiative. The bald statement "having collected various sums of money from Yarmouth people", and the loan of a piano from the Bugle, show that he was active in the town as well as in the School, as did his remark a few weeks after taking over that he had visited the parents of most of the scholars.

His obvious capacity for work may have influenced the Managers and Education Committee in the decision later in the year to amalgamate the Infants Department with the Senior School under one Head. Rising costs had been worrying the Managers for some time, and when Miss Pittman, Head Mistress of the Infants School, was promoted to Carisbrooke in September 1923 she was not replaced.

Pugh's report to the Managers in July spoke "amongst other things, of colours and a Badge having been chosen for the School – which had done much to give the children a feeling of esprit de corps. It also mentioned several jobs which needed to be done. Also that Boxing takes place every day at 10.45 and 3.50".

And so it went on. On May 2nd, 1924 he recorded that Mr. Forbes Robertson the actor (an old boy of the school) called to pay his compliments. On May 14th he received his first report from H.M. Inspector.

"During the year which has elapsed since the present Head Master took charge there has been a great improvement in the work of this school, especially in arithmetic. All four classes are working energetically. The children in the lower part of the school should do well when they are promoted. There are many reasons for anticipating a successful future for the School.

At the end of June 1924 Mr. Pugh took 28 children to the British Empire Exhibition at Wembley for three days. Twice in July parties of over 50 children went by train to Freshwater to start a geographical and educational expedition in the West Wight. In September the School held an Open Day, and the Head Master reported in his Log "Very wet indeed, but a good number present".

Perhaps it was no coincidence that running parallel with all this activity and newly generated interest the percentage attendance at school began to rise. There were at this time 132 children on the register, and on several occasions Pugh was able to record the fact that they were all present.

It was all much too good to last, and on June 18th 1925 Pugh recorded the following:

> "Chairman of County Education Committee (Alderman Fellows, O.B.E., J.P.), presented Banner to School for highest attendance in the Island for year to 31-3-25. He also congratulated the school on their success in Football, Swimming, and Scholarships: and the Head Master on his promotion to a larger school. Mr. J. Dufton, the County Council Clerk, accompanied Mr. Fellows".

In retrospect it is plain that his promotion was inevitable, and that Yarmouth could not hope to hold a man who was so full of initiative and drive. Pugh himself was sorry to leave. In his letter of resignation he wrote;

> "During my two years here I have been exceedingly happy with Managers, Parents, Children and Education Committee, and I shall leave this dear little town with many regrets".

John Pugh moved from Yarmouth to be Head Master of a school on the mainland, and one wonders what happened to him later. He was clearly a brilliant man, and in the short time he was here he turned out a number of exceptional children. One instance of this concerned carpentry, which Pugh encouraged, as a result of which several first class carpenters were produced. Cecil Doe was one of these. Just at this time F. O. Russell was building up his business as a builder and contractor in Yarmouth, and he took on several boys from the School as apprentices, it being a happy coincidence that as good boys were being turned out by the school, good opportunities existed for them in a growing and flourishing business.

Later, Cecil Doe turned to boat building, and acquired a reputation for the quality of his "Hornets". There are still some of these about, and when being advertised for sale their proud owners invariably claim that they were "Doe boats".

It is perhaps natural that one should feel sorry for Pugh's successor, but sympathy is not really required for George E. Stanway, who soon proved that he was quite capable of living up to the high standard set by his predecessor.

Stanway was a tall and upright man with a military bearing and a toothbrush moustache. He took over the school at the end of August 1925, and continued the good work begun by Pugh. From his entries in the Log, and the Managers' Minute Book it is to his credit that there is no detectable drop in the standard of work. In sport too, the School continued to thrive.

> **December 5, 1926.** News that the School is top in the Island for percentage of swimming learners. Cup presented by the Managers of Shanklin C.E. School was won by the girls of this school. The boys were placed third in the Island. The senior girls having won the Senior Trophy at Cowes in September makes the success highly gratifying.

The Inspector's Report for 1927 included the following:

> "A great deal of good work is done in this school. Both Arithmetic and English are well taught. The children in the lower standards write well and read fluently aloud. There is apparently no lack of industry on the part of teachers or pupils".

One of the Pugh innovations continued by Stanway was the educational excursion, not only to places on the Island, but also to London. In 1928 he took 23 children up to town for a whole week, in 1930 21 scholars spent a week in Stratford-on-Avon, and another London trip took place in 1933.

Raich Doe remembers one of the London trips well. They stayed at the Abbey Hotel in Southwark near the river and had a strenuous week. Every morning at 6.30 they went to Southwark Baths, which was a great thrill as none of them had ever been in a swimming bath before, nor of course had they seen a springboard or high diving platform. Many of them were in fact accomplished divers, but their experience had been confined to diving off the bridge into the river, or – for the more daring – off Yarmouth Castle.

They walked everywhere and covered many miles, visiting the Science Museum, the Natural History Museum, the Tower of London, and many other similar sights. They were given a ride on the Underground as part of their education, but apart from that they walked. Each night they had baths and a foot inspection, followed by a cup of cocoa as they went to bed.

Mr. Stanway's Log entries reflect the life and development of the School, and mention some of the problems.

March 1928. The Log has the first mention of "Wireless Lessons" a three-valve Wireless Receiving Set having been built by Mr. C. R. Becke and given to the School.

July 23, 1928. Classes 1 and 2 visited H.M.S. Centaur now lying off Yarmouth Pier.

November 3, 1928. Rev. C. W. Hamilton Weekes, Diocesan Inspector, wrote "I much appreciated the keenness and efficiency of the Staff which are reflected in the children. There seems to be a purposefulness about the School which points to a desire to achieve the building of character and not merely the acquisition of knowledge. This is seen all through the School. Altogether very satisfactory".

July 25, 1929. At 11 a.m. Capt. A. G. Cole, R.N.R. gave the scholars in Standards 3 – 7 a lecture on "The History of Yarmouth and ancient local customs".

May 22, 1930. Dr. Wallace visited the School. I drew his attention to the wretched condition of the Town Refuse Dump (adjoining the School) concerning which I have made persistent complaints for the past nine months.

September 26, 1930. During the past week the work of the School has been very adversely affected by the influx of large numbers of flies.

May 26, 1933. Top Class (33 scholars) to Freshwater Parish Hall to see a production of "As You Like It".

July 14, 1933. 19 scholars to London for a week.

July 27, 1933. 11 scholars swam the mile test to-day.

Stanway left Yarmouth in October 1935 having been promoted to be Head of Ryde C.E. School, his letter of resignation saying "my pleasure in moving to a higher post is very much tempered by my reluctance to leave Yarmouth".

He had been Head during a critical period in the School's history, when all the West Wight Schools were being re-grouped and reorganised. For a time under this reorganisation scheme it looked as though Yarmouth might be upgraded into a "Central" School, which would have involved a major rebuilding programme, and the loss of the smaller children. In the event this plan came to nothing, and the Senior School was built in Freshwater.

Stanway was only a comparatively young man when he died of a heart attack, but his widow is still alive to-day, now in her eighties, and living in Freshwater. He is remembered by his pupils as having been slightly aloof, but a good head master.

His replacement was a woman, Miss E. B. Chambers, and it is interesting to note that the Managers' Meeting at which the appointment was made was chaired by Mr. Furmage, and was held at his home, Plevna House in South Street.

One of the senior school Managers at this time was Mr. J. B. Doe, who was a leading figure in Yarmouth, and who had first been appointed a Manager in 1913. He was for several years Chairman of the Harbour Commissioners, and in his capacity as a Manager regularly visited the School. He also for some time supervised the swimming tests, and as his great hobby was gardening we find a Log entry in February 1936 saying he was appointed gardening instructor. Unfortunately his efforts in this direction were not appreciated by the School Examiners, who wrote as follows:

> **May 27, 1937.** Instruction in gardening is in the hands of an outside teacher who was not present on the day of inspection. The garden itself was in fairly good order, but discussion with the boys and inspection of their note books indicated several weaknesses, e.g.
>
> 1. There appears to be little if any experimental work.
> 2. There are no fruit bushes or trees. The boys have drawn a pruning knife in their note books, but seem never to have been taught to prune.
> 3. The boys have little theoretical knowledge. No boy for instance knew that nitrogen, phosphates, and potash were the main sources of plant food, or could mention the name of any fertilizer supplying any of these.
>
> **June 23, 1937.** Mr. J. B. Doe, who has been gardening instructor for the School for the past year, tendered his resignation to-day. Until other arrangements are made instruction will be given by the Head Teacher.

This arrangement did not last long, and J. B. Doe is again giving gardening instruction in February 1938. In January 1939 the "Horticultural Instructor" from the Education Authority called to discuss the gardening instruction. There is no record of what he said, but on February 15th it is recorded that J. B. Doe intimated that he could no longer continue, and that gardening instruction in future would be given by Miss Hayles.

The next six months passed peacefully. In June the school opened late one afternoon to enable the children to see the "Empress of Britain" pass through bearing the King and Queen, but in August an ominous entry in the Log foretold several years of disruption to the normal routine.

August 31, 1939. Gas Mask Drill taken this morning. Telegram from Director of Education at 2.00 p.m. ordering immediate closure of the School for evacuation purposes. Teachers to be ready to receive evacuees. (Evacuees did not arrive).

September 11, 1939. School re-opened after Closure. School Attendance Officer called. Swimming instruction given. (In other words life returned to normal – temporarily).

September 14, 1939. Information received that 110 evacuees are to be received here to-morrow.

September 15, 1930. School closed all day to enable Teachers to deal with the billeting of evacuees. (Evacuees did not arrive).

September 18, 1939. School re-opened. School Attendance Officer called.

September 19, 1939. Visit by Head Master of the evacuated school this afternoon.

September 20, 1939. School swimming contests were held this afternoon.

September 21, 1939. The Rector took prayers.

September 22, 1939. School closed all day to receive evacuees from Shanklin re-distributed to Yarmouth.

September 25, 1939. School assembled as usual. 55 scholars and 15 members of the teaching staff of the Milton Road School, Portsmouth, now accommodated in the School. (15 teachers!) To work as a separate unit. School Attendance Officer called. Miss McFarlane commenced as a Student Teacher in Infants Dept.

September 29, 1939. Miss McFarlane terminated her position to-day.

November 1, 1939. To-day the merging of Yarmouth and Milton Schools has been carried out. All Infants under supervision of Miss Andrews (Portsmouth Head Teacher). Junior Boys with Milton School masters, and Junior Girls the Milton School mistresses. The School to be run by the committee of 3 Head Teachers.

14 Teachers, 3 Head Teachers. Total number on roll 113.

One can imagine the fun of trying to run a School by a committee of 3 Head Teachers, but gradually things were sorted out, and the

Portsmouth teachers were either transferred to other schools or sent back to Portsmouth. By April 1940 there were 51 Yarmouth and 15 evacuee children on the roll, and only one Portsmouth teacher.

July 3, 1940. Air Raid warning at 9.05 a.m. All children living within 2 minutes of the School sent home, to return at the All Clear.

July 4, 1940. Air Raid warning at 9 a.m. Children sent home till All Clear at 9.35 a.m.

Air Raid warning at 1.15 p.m. All Clear 1.40 p.m.

July 8, 1940. Portsmouth evacuees returned home. Swimming instruction to be discontinued, under Defence Regulations.

July 10, 1940. Scripture lesson from the Rector in morning. Practice in use of fire fighting apparatus after school.

From this date onwards Air Raid warnings became more frequent, until in October they were happening almost every day, and several time a day. The School Air Raid Shelter was completed at the beginning of September, so there was no more sending home.

November 18, 1940. Attendance poor owing to a night raid in this area.

Life went on and gradually returned to normal, though there were frequent Air Raid warnings, which by 1943 were averaging about 2 – 3 per week. Gas Mask Drill and Shelter Drill were conducted regularly, and Gas Masks were inspected by Mr. J. B. Doe, who was now an A.R.P. Warden. In July 1943 the Diocesan Scripture Examiner expressed his satisfaction with the religious instruction being given.

"I was very pleased with the whole atmosphere of the School as well as with the standard of knowledge shown by the children. Not only were the facts well known, but there was also a ready perception of the meaning behind the facts.

I was particularly impressed by the way in which the story of the Prodigal Son had been taught, the crux of the matter being that, for a Jew, feeding the **swine** belonging to a **Gentile,** represented the lowest form of degradation. Such realism and power of imagination is not always so obvious".

The war duly came to an end, and gradually the School settled down to a peaceful existence again.

July 10, 1947. Report of Inspection by Director of Religious Education began with the phrase "This is a very happy and progressive School".

July 23, 1947. Annual School Prize Distribution. The children gave an entertainment of plays, songs, singing games, and marching. The Rector took the Chair, and the Managers were represented. Mr. G. F. Mew C.C. represented the Education Committee. A large number of parents, friends and old scholars were present.

A parting gift from the scholars and staff was presented to Miss E. B. Chambers who retires this term after 26 years service in this school.

Ella Chambers went on to live for 32 years in retirement in Yarmouth, and when she died in April 1979 at the age of 91 it was said of her "a devoted teacher at Yarmouth School, affectionately remembered by her pupils, their children, and sometimes their grandchildren.

In 1955 a particular milestone was reached – the Centenary – and this seems a convenient date with which to conclude this review of Yarmouth School. During its hundred years of life on the Mill Road site the School had had only five Heads, but had seen many changes, and had been steered through many upsetting periods including two world wars. The high quality of its teachers resulted in a high standard of education being achieved, and this inevitably contributed in no small way to the character of Yarmouth people, and hence of the town itself.

In the School Log the Head Mistress (Mrs. V. A. Barton) describes the modest Centenary Celebrations as follows:

July 23, 1955. School Centenary Celebrations.

Morning: Thanksgiving Service in the Parish Church.

Afternoon: Entertainment and Prize Distribution in the Conservative Hall, at which the Rector was in the Chair. The Archdeacon of the Island, Miss M. O'Conor (Chairman, Education Committee) and Mr. G. Moody were the guests of honour and presented the awards. This was followed by a display of maypole and country dancing in the school playground, by the children. A tea was provided in the School by members of the P.T.A. for the past and present pupils (5-15 years).

Many people visited the School to view an Exhibition of school work and old school relics.

Evening: A Film Show, Entertainment, Buffet Supper and Dance in the Conservative Hall, Many past pupils and members of Staff, together with parents and friends, joined in the day's celebrations which were a great success.

The phrase "a great success" could also be applied to the whole hundred year existence of the School, though I would like to give the last word to the Inspector who wrote "There is an excellent atmosphere of trust and friendship for their teachers and among the children themselves". No school could wish for a better testimonial.

CHAPTER XVII

Yarmouth Today

Yarmouth to-day is a bustling, active, tourist town – in the short summer season. Each year the ferries from Lymington disgorge a million and a quarter passengers, 250,000 cars, and 25,000 lorries, most of these in the summer months. In addition, each summer day a pleasure steamer from Bournemouth arrives at the Pier, and hundreds of day trippers invade the town. The streets are thronged, shops are frantically busy, people wander aimlessly about sucking their ice creams, dropping their litter as they pass, and demanding to know where to find Woolworths or Marks and Spencers. In the evening, when the trippers are gone and the ferries have stopped running, the town looks like a bombed site, and were it not for John Budden, our most efficient road sweeper, it would soon be in an impossible state. Fortunately for us John does his job well, and by the following morning the place is spotless again – ready for the next onslaught.

In the winter it is a different story. When the visitors have finally disappeared, and the town is left once more to its 1100 inhabitants, it is possible of an evening to walk from one end to the other without meeting more than one or two people. The town is quiet and peaceful, and it is a blissful place in which to live. But the town is by no means dead; there are many local organisations which emerge and flourish in the winter months, and the deserted streets are deceptive.

The social structure of Yarmouth is complex and consists of three tiers. The base of the structure comprises the "Islanders", people who have been born and bred in Yarmouth, or in the Island, who rightly consider that they have a prior right to the town, and who somewhat naturally resent the influx of the "Overners" – or those who come from England, over the water. The Overners are divided into two types, those who reside permanently in the town, and those who own holiday homes, and only appear at weekends and other odd times. The Islanders refer to the first class as "Recent Immigrants", but have no title bad enough for the second type, whom they claim come down from London on a Friday, hold a meeting on Saturday to reorganise some part of the life of the town, and on Sunday retire back to the mainland having created more than sufficient mayhem.

The social structure of the town is further complicated by another three part division, which is superimposed on the above. This consists of a basis of Islanders, who do not wish to mix with anyone and who enjoy – from choice – very little social life; the Tradespeople, some of whom are Islanders and some Recent Immigrants, who wish for obvious reasons to be at peace with everyone; and a third strata, unkindly designated "The Crust", who frequent the Yacht Club, and lead a well developed and sophisticated social existence.

All this complex organism is contained in a small area of under 100 acres, where everyone knows everyone else, and where no, or very few secrets are hid. Living in Yarmouth has been compared to life in a goldfish bowl, and the resulting scene is a rich and human mixture, throbbing and pulsating with life, a mixture which is sometimes difficult to believe, and is always completely and absorbingly fascinating.

An interesting theory has been advanced to explain the somewhat autocratic attitude of the Islander, it being said that you must never order an Islander to do anything, but only request him politely and with due deference. The theory is that during Queen Victoria's long sojourn in the Island she was visited by numerous members of foreign royal families, who found time hang heavily on their hands, and consequently dallied with the local maidenry. The result was a strange invigoration of the island blood stream by this foreign royal blood, which in the course of several generations has now permeated over a wide area and produced a superior and independent race.

There is of course no foundation whatsoever for this theory, but the independent attitude of the Islander is readily discernible. When requiring an Islander to carry out some task it is necessary to couch one's request in the most careful and diplomatic terms, and to impress upon him a slight, but not extreme, degree of urgency. To say to him that the job is either extremely urgent, or is not urgent at all, is fatal, and can only result in the task never being carried out.

The problems facing Yarmouth to-day are also complex, and have changed somewhat over the last few hundred years. We have no more stray cattle wandering the streets, and the drains work better than once they did. The water supply is better, and the streets are well lit. The Church tower is floodlit at night, and is a fine sight greeting the eyes of passengers on the ferry coming in. There are also certain similarities; though we have no "Assize of Bread and Ale", the weights and measures inspector still goes round weighing the loaves in the local bakery and occasionally finding some wanting. The Quay, though not requiring such frequent repair, carries an enormous amount of trafficc and is not getting any younger. The bridge over the river Yar, which was designed for horse drawn vehicles only, and now has to cope with double decker buses, is also a cause for concern.

The Yar Bridge, and its possible replacement, has probably caused more controversy in the town in recent years than anything else. The bridge is now nearly 120 years old, and was never designed for either the weight or volume of traffic it now has to bear, and it is logical to assume that at sometime in the future it will reach the end of its useful life. The knotty problem is how, when, and where it is to be replaced, and opinion is fairly sharply divided between those who say a new bridge must be built alongside the existing one, those who maintain that it should be sited higher up the river, and a third body who believe that Yarmouth would be better served by having no bridge at all, so that much of the through traffic that now thunders through the town would have to be diverted elsewhere. The arguments in favour of these alternatives are nicely balanced, and it is a matter for conjecture as to who will ultimately win. The only thing that can be said with any certainly is that in the present economic climate it is extremely unlikely that any practical steps will be taken to solve the problem unless and until the present structure breaks down completely.

A perhaps even greater problem, and one that is likely to raise local passions to fever pitch in the near future, is the constant growth in ferry traffic. As one of the three ports of entry into the Island Yarmouth has to carry an ever increasing volume of cars and lorries, and in the opinion of some residents this volume has already passed saturation point. But tourism is now the life-blood of the Island, and hence of Yarmouth too, and the reality of a situation which each year produces a greater demand on ferry capacity has to be faced.

The ferry operating company, Sealink (UK) Ltd., whose function is to meet this demand claims with some justification that it needs more space, and greater efficiency in loading and unloading its ships.

The Yarmouth Harbour Commissioners, whose function is to provide these facilities, also have the responsibility for maintaining and improving one of the best little yachting harbours on the South Coast, a harbour which contains many boats belonging to residents, and is used by upwards of 10,000 visiting yachts each year. This dual requirement, together with the need to preserve Yarmouth as the sleepy, old fashioned town that its residents desire and demand, makes the Harbour Commissioners' task an unenviable one.

Against a background of these and other similar problems life in Yarmouth goes on – and a very full, satisfying and rewarding life it is. The school continues to flourish, and though the opportunities for our young people when they leave school seem to get fewer and fewer, they get a good groundwork and an excellent start in their struggle to make their way in life. Nor is their education confined to the three R's. Under an enlightened Head Mistress, each year for the last few years the School has produced a Pantomime at Christmas, written and produced by a local writer and featuring its scholars, a Pantomime full of topical and local allusions that has played to packed houses, and has evoked such spontaneous and enthusiastic applause as to leave one in no doubt of the sincerity and affection of the audience.

Our young people are also well served by the Boy Scout and Girl Guide organisations. In January 1979 a new and splendid Headquarters for the Scouts and Guides was opened, marking the culmination of over two years of effort by many friends of the Movement in acquiring and converting some old garages. At the opening ceremony a large audience of Yarmouth folk was present, and the various speeches made were full of warmth and sincerity. There cannot, surely, be much wrong with a town in which such community effort on behalf of the young is so readily forthcoming.

Yarmouth to-day is a thriving, lively and friendly community, the product of very nearly 1,000 years of social development. Those of us who are fortunate enough to live here look upon it with affection, and wish to hand it on, when the time comes, in an even more prosperous condition. To do this we cannot do better than observe the precepts laid down in 1799 by the United Society of Cordwainers when that Guild was formed in the City of London. These precepts were quoted by the Mayor of Yarmouth in a message issued on the occasion of the Silver Jubilee of Her Majesty Queen Elizabeth II.

> "Let us conduct ourselves in all matters of importance with judgement, coolness and deliberation.

Let everyone lay aside his own private interest and study the good of the whole.

And lastly, let us study friendship and unanimity with one another; this will cement our structure and render it permanent. Make us the joy of the present and the praise of ages to come".